GUEST of an ALLY

TURNER PUBLISHING COMPANY

TURNER PUBLISHING COMPANY

Copyright © 1994 Anthony J. Leone
Publishing rights Turner Publishing Company
All rights reserved.

Author: Anthony J. Leone

Turner Publishing Company's Staff:
Assistant Editor: Erik Parrent
Cover Design: Luke Henry

Library of Congress
Catalog Card No. 93-060252
ISBN: 978-1-68162-126-5

Limited Edition

Cover photo: Painting by Colonel Albert Milliken.

TABLE OF CONTENTS

GUEST OF AN ALLY

ANTHONY J. LEONE

DEDICATION

To Colonel Joseph A. Moller for his undying devotion and being a cornerstone in the building of comradeship within the 390th Bomb Group during war and peace. Also to his wife, Dorothy, for her forever living generosity and Moller's Hangar Party.

To Colonel Albert Milliken whose painting adorns the dust-jacket of "Guest of an Ally"

And to my family and all the families whose prayers instilled faith in the living and blessed repose for the dead.

INTRODUCTION

The feasibility of non politically aligned nations co-existing is or seems to be a matter of conjecture of politically minded men. The situation which is most prevalent, and most advantageous to the politician, dictates his policy. Past experiences of fact, not fiction appear to have absolutely no bearing on his thinking, or presentation of such to the people. Broken promises, insulting and degrading press releases are to be ignored by the people, and we are to believe that they are not the thinking of our leaders.

It is apparent that all discussions are between the high echelon of diplomats, and the matters discussed are presented in a tongue-in-cheek atmosphere of congeniality. This is expected and accepted, for even the devil smiles as he peddles his wares. Therefore we are obliged to accept facts that were obtained under prepared conditions, ideal to the situation, and rose colored to the receiver.

The facts presented in the ensuing story were not prepared or rehearsed, but were obtained under what should have been the most compatible conditions, allies in a mutual cause, not diplomats fencing for political ambitions.

This is a story of non appointed, or elected diplomats, who found themselves representing, and presenting our way of life, as guests of an ally.

CHAPTER 1 — THE END

I felt silly sitting there in my sad sack fitting uniform, without one insignia of rank of assignment. The clothes I wore represented my entire military wardrobe, allotted to me on my return from Russia. It seemed that the custom fitted uniforms worn by airmen were automatically inherited by the survivors of a mission.

They sat and stared, made idle conversation, asking repeatedly, "How do you feel? Do you want something to eat?"

With long periods of silence between questions, I groped for a way to break the tension. I beckoned to my wife of one month (two years before) to my side, only to find that the tension that filled the room was more apparent in her. The sign above the door, "Welcome Home," produced no great revelry.

My mother-in-law announced dinner was ready and we moved with almost funeral speed to the dining room. The dinner was excellent, although any home cooked meal would be a welcome change. I had the feeling that I was the stranger who came to dinner. The conversation remained sporadic, and the words uttered were carefully chosen. My bewildered and questioning looks must have been obvious, and the uneasiness that prevailed remained apparent.

Suddenly, in the loud booming voice he possessed, my father-in-law said, "What the hell, are you going to sit around here forever like a bunch of ghouls, treating this poor kid like he's some kind of sick freak? Now that he is here safe and sound, I don't know about you, but I'm anxious to hear what the hell happened to him."

I had to laugh when it dawned on me what was happening. They were afraid to ask me about my experiences. It seemed that the papers played up the returning veterans as possible neurotics to be treated with kid gloves. I explained to them that it didn't bother me to talk about my experiences, but that on my first day home, I would rather drink in some home life, and thinking, as I looked at my wife, some married life.

The rest of the day was spent more relaxed, consuming good food, and enjoying informative conversation. Friends and relatives dropped in and out all evening, and although I was pleased and honored by their concern for me, I was wishing away the hours with great anticipation as I gently squeezed my wife's hand, causing a crimson shade to appear in her cheeks, with the feeling that everyone in the room was reading my mind.

The next few days were spent reacquainting myself with friends and relatives, visiting old haunts, demilitarizing myself in general. Running into friends who had returned from the wars, and noticing their complete disinterest in having you relate your experiences or discussing their own, made the task of forgetting and readjusting so much easier. This was not the case of non vets or servicemen who didn't see combat. They seemed obligated to heap praise upon you, either for honest concern or as conscience cleansing, but you made yourself believe that it was sincere curiosity. At home with relatives, you knew it was a pride that they could only share if they knew the facts, and I possessed the facts.

It was the sound of the mailman dropping the lid on the mailbox that awoke me from a nap, and the sound of the door bell that bolted me upright.

I greeted the mailman with, "Good morning," and he responded with, "Welcome home," as he handed me the mail.

Although I didn't expect any mail addressed to me personally, I unconsciously looked through it. A postcard caught my eye, and realizing its origin, I laughed aloud, more in disbelief than joy. My exclamation brought the rest of the household to my side, from sheer curiosity or concern for my hysterical behavior. Reading it over and over to myself, and shaking my head in disbelief, only encouraged those about me to prod me for an explanation.

"What is it? What is it?" they all asked in one voice.

"I'll be dammed, I'll be dammed," was all I could say, as I examined the postcard from every angle.

I was holding a card that was smuggled out of Russia, informing my wife that I was safe and sound. It wasn't the information that it possessed which caused my anxiety, but the fact that it arrived at all, in perfect condition.

Explaining to those around me what the card represented was telling the end before the beginning. Here I was holding a piece of evidence which had completely evaded my memory, and just as quickly jogged my memory back to the past, when I was the guest of an ally...

CHAPTER 2 — THE BEGINNING

It was cold, crisp, and dark, very dark. The darkness of war is a deep void punctuated by unidentifiable voices, and flashing fingers of light searching for obstacles. Otherwise one becomes a non-combat casualty.

I had checked crew assignments for next day's flight before going to dinner, and my crew was listed to fly. With this in mind, I made an early departure from the non-com's club, and flashlighted my way towards my quonset hut. I can't explain why I detoured to the administration building, which seemed automatic when you were assigned to fly the next day. As I approached the administration building, I could see fingers of light searching out the pennant atop the flag pole which signified by color mission on, standby, or scrubbed. I always found myself with mixed emotions as to what pennant I hoped was flying. I knew as everyone else knew, that each mission completed was one closer to home, but we also knew that each one we didn't fly, was one less chance of becoming a statistic. The mission was on.

The usual sounds, strains of mingled selections of music, undistinguishable voices, could be heard as I entered my squadron area. The voices of self-acclaimed Carusos were heard as I passed the cinder block building that housed all the lavatory facilities, and there were sounds that proved this a man's world, for no barrier existed to afford a man his privacy.

Although the wattage of light that struck me as I entered my quonset hut didn't challenge a cloudy day, it warranted an optical adjustment after the total blackness outside. On focusing you look for identifiable features. Recognition of a familiar face, assures you that you are in the right hut, for this is a community of conforming comforts, and discomforts.

The fifteen men who inhabited these quarters were part and parcel of three crews, and were as different in thoughts and actions as you would expect to find if you traveled to the places whence they came. Their reactions to a scheduled mission varied, but apprehension was apparent in all. The one crew of the three which wasn't scheduled to fly was obvious. They were playing cards, or planning a visit to the non-com's club.

The scheduled airmen were engaged in mixed emotional endeavors (the hurried letter home, the fitful sleep, the quiet prayer, the incessant chatter of false bravado) to lessen one's anxiety. Not to forget the complacent, but respectful attitude of the fatalist, which was I. I believed, or made myself believe, that one's life was predetermined, come what may. The will of God was my belief, and I prayed only that I be spared a crippling injury that would curtail my active life.

The routine of combat living was unique in that regimentation was non-existent, and housekeeping was on a voluntary basis. Thus where Godliness existed, cleanliness wasn't necessarily a partner. The only hard fast rule that broke the monotony of this easy existence was bestowed upon the heat corporal. It was his duty to keep the ominous pot belly stove a glowing red throughout the cold winter nights. We had such complete faith in this man, chosen from a non flying crew, that everyone slept in his flying gear.

There were great adventures attached to combat living other than combat flying, and one was the urge to go in the middle of the night. I thought that anyone who dared the journey from their hut to cold detached latrine should be credited for at least half a mission. It didn't take long, either by simple logic or experienced know how, to beat at least half of nature's unwelcome calls by placing an airplane relief tube next to your bunk which led to the flower beds outside. Another great adventure was the air raid alert, and the strict adherence to the rule of going to your designated air raid shelter located in the rear of your hut. This was emphatically pointed out to you by a Sergeant, when assigned to your quarters the night you arrived. The experience of your first air alert is accentuated by the absence of a mad dash to the shelter by everyone but the newly assigned crews. It didn't take long to appreciate their reluctance, when you found yourself floundering in neck deep water. The procedure adopted thereafter was "the hell with them"; you put on your tin hat, crawled under the covers, and went to sleep.

Sleep to flying crews is a must, and varies in degrees of benefit. To some it posed a night of subconscious thoughts of the forthcoming mission, or the reliving of a previous one. The apprehension of a rude awakening in the middle of the night was received as such by the sound sleeper, but was a blessing in disguise for the troubled, for it was only when awakened to reality that his mind and body became rested.

Some of the usual occurrences of home life were still available under combat conditions. One could shave and shower before retiring; one could, but most didn't. One could indulge in a bedtime snack, one could, and most did.

For some unknown reason in both fact and fiction, when a group of men are thrown together from all walks of life, there is always a guy from Brooklyn. We had such a guy. I only mention him, not because he plays an important part of the forthcoming story, but because through the ensuing escapades, I felt from past experiences, and his reaction to touchy situations, I would have felt more secure with him at my side.

This guy from Brooklyn loved to eat, and mail from home wasn't mail unless it included a package of food. Such was the case and cause of his missing a page of Air Force history. His bedtime snack consisted of consuming three cans of "Chicken-Ala-King" from a package he received that day, for his theory was finish it to-day, for you may not be here to-morrow.

Reciprocal courtesy prevailed, and non flying crews honored lights out, by either retiring or retreating to the day room to complete letters home, and card games. It was amazing to see the many non flying crews who retired early so they could make early breakfast call. Flying breakfasts consisted of fresh eggs, styled by request, bacon, ham, etc., fresh and individually served, not production line style like that found at the later breakfast for non flying personal.

Since this was a clear night, I anticipated the drone of English bombers as they crossed the coast on their way to the Continent. I lay my head upon my pillow, and prayed myself to sleep with, "Please God, no buzz bombs to-night." We were located in what was called buzz bomb alley, and every one directed towards London passed over our base. If they were winged by the coastal anti-aircraft batteries, they could, and sometimes did, drop onto our base. As long as you could hear the putt-putt of its motor, it was long gone, but when the motor cut out, I would think, "No, not this way", and a feeling of relief would accompany the tremor of the shock wave, as it impacted into the ground in the distance.

The drone of engines being tested by ground mechanics, readying our birds of destruction, seemed to trigger the base into life. My awakening was always just before the day Sergeant reached my bunk, and I would save him the trouble of making the rounds to awaken the flying crews by doing it for him. By now the pot belly stove is an ominous black, and the cold on the outside of the hut is now attempting to finger its way under your blankets, and through your flying suit. I reached for my fur lined parka, climbed into it hurriedly, then quickly placed my double stockinged feet into my fur lined boots. Now I was ready to awaken the flying personnel.

The curses that were directed towards the heat corporal were automatic, and were used only to unfreeze vocal cords, for each of us knew our day of being on the receiving end would come, if you lived long enough. It was about this time that a great decision must be made, separating the men from the boys, as it were. Does one wash before or after breakfast? Believe me there were more boys than men on these cold mornings, for most wanted to absorb some of the fine heat of the mess hall, before venturing to the latrine.

CHAPTER 3 — PREPARATION

Preparing the mind, body, and soul were the three requisites before a mission. Each were attacked with different degrees of fervor by the individuals concerned. Yet when the body was being prepared at the flying crew breakfast, Sunday morning breakfast habits prevailed, and the only degree of difference was the capacity of the individual.

I had braved the elements, washed and shaved before heading to breakfast. Making my way in the early darkness the persons I passed going and coming from mess were unidentifiable shadows, which in a very short time would be molded into significant crews, amassing a great air armada, to rain death and destruction upon a common enemy. They too were unidentifiable shadows, molded into a death dealing machine against us, their common enemy.

I entered the mess hall, accustomed my eyes to the light, and made my way to the chow line after picking up a tray. As I moved along the line, time was consumed unconsciously looking about the hall. Greetings were exchanged, and gentle pokes in the ribs and slaps on the back were common place; serious thoughts were only directed towards food. I couldn't help but notice the eager faces of the newcomer, but the absence of the missing was more prevalent. It only took one mission to make a veteran out of you, and the gung-ho attitude disappeared, as you became part of a machine, and went through the motions of one.

As I sat there surrounded by a multitude of people, I felt alone. With all the chatter of intermingled conversation nothing was intelligible, and the persons I sat with were just so many people, like the Automat at home. I recognized or identified each as being a member of Lieutenant's so and so's crew. Very few close friendships were established. The only ties that represented anything resembling a friendship were between those who might have attended the same technical school in the States, and by chance were assigned to the same Bomb Group. As I sat and prepared my body, I mumbled a prayer in place of Grace. "God we who are about to fly into your sky, over land and over sea, if we fail to return, please take our souls unto Thee." For I felt that a friendship with God was a necessity.

The preparation of one's soul was also an individual endeavor, but somehow the feeling of reverence was apparent even in those who didn't declare themselves openly. A visit to the Chapel of one's particular denomination was a must, as far as I was concerned. The rules and regulations of my church were relaxed as far as penance and abstinence were concerned, so that Communion could be received any time before a mission. The church atmosphere was missing in Army chapels, and Stateside I would always visit a church in town for Sunday Mass, if possible. The Army Chaplin, in his desire to be one of the boys, lost some of his reverence, but when he was garbed in his vestments distributing Holy Communion, the feeling of a blessed aura of protection seemed to envelop me; my soul was prepared.

The preparation of one's mind was fulfilled in the briefing hut where all crews gathered, and the cogs of the machine were assembled into a cohesive unit of destruction. It was here that one realized the purpose of his being, and apprehension set in. There was an uneasy shuffling of chairs and evidence of chain smoking. Voices attempting a whisper would crack into a childlike shriek, which brought snickers as a substitute for laughter.

The podium with its curtained covered map of enemy targets lent its ominous presence to the conjecture of your mind. Where do we go today? The wild guesses originating from scuttle-butt, and overheard dialogue in the company latrine, had the newcomer believing he was in the midst of a G-2 meeting. A milk run is the wish of most, especially the crew member who was completing his tour of duty. A milk run to me was any mission completed without personal loss, for what may be an easy one for you was the toughest for the one who was killed or injured. I realized there will always be killed or injured on most missions, but I believed in my heart that it would only happen to the other guy.

I glanced about the room attempting to locate my crew, especially Brooklyn, whom I could normally find relating his past experiences to an interested newcomer. He would always crown his glory with emphasis on how he, after failing to release our bombs on time while flying as a toggelier, had the strike photos of a late bomb burst which proved a direct hit on the target. Brooklyn readily claimed he had dropped the bomb by aiming off his big toe.

When I finally located him he was obvious only because of his peculiar shade of green, and the doubled up sleeping position he was in. The command of "attention" halted me in my tracks as I was making my way towards Brooklyn. The Briefing Officer was entering the room. The scrambling to an erect position, the "as you were" as you were between sitting and standing, the scraping of chairs, the accidental knocking over of one in hasty obedience, failed to arouse Brooklyn.

"Wake that man in the corner, Sergeant." The order interrupted my act of doing just that.

My gentle nudge aroused a green faced, bleary eyed individual to a semblance of attentiveness. He muttered, "I'm sick."

The usual preliminary speech of the Operation Officer welcoming the replacements, and emphasizing the importance of their presence and their duty, only tended to build up the apprehension of the target for today. The morale building utterances of the group commander depicted the importance of the forthcoming mission and the heritage bestowed upon the new crews, with references to the gallant men since departed who instilled such heritage with their courage and dedication. To the new crew, it stiffened their spines, and they held their heads high with pride. To the veteran of even one mission, the pride and dedication was lost with the faces of those gallant men who only yesterday, had their spines stiffened, and held their heads high with pride.

A game was played every day, for what purpose I'll never know, but while the usual talks were being made, and anxiety was building, some indiscernible creature would slowly and slyly draw that ominous curtain. The first portion of the map exposed was the British Isles, stopping abruptly at the location of our group, and displaying just a hint of the three colored ribbons, and their general direction to the probable target sites. The different colored ribbons designated the Primary, Secondary, and Alternate targets. Targets of opportunity were left to the flight commander's discretion, if failure to make contact with the three prime targets was for any reason imminent.

Each individual had his own idea and personal wish as to where the ribbon ended, but in his heart, as in mine, experience and common sense proved to be factors for determining the potential target. Progress bulletins of allied actions and the movement of the enemy could usually enhance a calculated guess as to what type of target was probable. Being a heavy bomber group it went without saying that such concentrated power was not to be wasted, and to those participating, only the exposure to enemy defenses in the essence of time duration was important.

The usual but important instructions were recited by the Operation Officer, designating Group, Squadron, and Flight Commanders, assigning take off positions and assembly altitudes. Emphasis was given to identifying colored flares representing particular groups for formation position. With hundreds of planes assembling over England, the importance was multiplied, especially if the weather forced a high altitude assembly through heavy cloud cover, which was common place over the British Isles. The ascent through heavy cloud formations was at times more nerve wracking than the mission itself. A sudden flash of light, with an accompanying roar of an explosion, usually signified a mid air collision. We had lost without confrontation with our enemy.

The weather over the target area was announced by the Weather Officer; the types of bombs and fuel load were designated by the Armorer Officer, the latter causing a stir, with a consensus that the mission was important, and lengthy. Suddenly the guessing game came to an end, as usual with a sweep of the curtain exposing the enemy held continent. The concern felt by all was apparent by the stillness that befell the room, as all eyes followed the primary target ribbon to the far reaches of eastern Germany...Dresden.

"Gentlemen, we have reached that phase of the war where we will attempt close and direct support of our ally, Russia," conveyed the Operations Officer.

"The English have," he went on, "succeeded in a night raid over the same target, and have assisted immeasurably in the Russians ground offensive on that key city. We have the honor of being part of the longest mass day-light raid against a common enemy, by participating in this close tactical support with our eastern ally," he concluded.

The reason for this mission was made to appear militarily sound, but one couldn't help but feel overtones of a politically inspired gesture.

The groans and grumbles of complaints that were common place after the announcement of the target were missing. A muffled silence, like a church congregation, was substituted. The distance to the target was obvious, but what was more apparent was the almost direct line of flight from base to target. When the flak concentration and their locations were pointed out you could understand that the distance and fuel consumption to cover same wasn't giving us any margin to circumvent the enemy flak corridors. We were afforded one consolation: our fighter escort P-51's with their wing tanks should be able to ride herd on us almost to the target area. On previous missions, enemy fighter interception had been sporadic and without great concentration.

With the order for the Radio Operators to remain for a special communication briefing, the remainder of the crews were dismissed, to pick up their parachutes and proceed to their respective aircraft. It was now that the grumbles and complaints were exchanged as they filed from the room. However the complaints were presented, the unscrambling and reassembling spelled a feeling of unconcern for the Russians. Veteran officers and men remembered the shuttle flight to drop supplies to the beleaguered Poles in Warsaw during their uprising, only to have the Russians fail to come to their aid as promised. They also remembered the confinement and lack of hospitality to the crews who terminated their flights in Russia. The complete devastation of Warsaw by the Germans, because of the failure of our Russian ally, not to mention the loss of American airmen, was a bitter pill to swallow.

The radio briefing, as usual, was to receive codes and recognition signals for the day, but to-day it was more detailed because of our close proximity to the Russian lines. The possibility that a situation for immediate identification might be necessary magnified the importance.

I made a hurried visit to the Chapel, then proceeded to pick up my parachute, which was borrowed and returned with an air of indifference - just another piece of equipment to be lugged about. As I waited for the truck to take me to my aircraft, the drone of warming engines cracked the total darkness, and I knew before long we would be heading into the rising sun. I wanted to feel a military justification for this flight, but however I tried, it appeared politically motivated. When I reached the hardstand where my plane was located, the activity immediately relegated me to my status, Radio Operator Gunner, trained and educated to believe that whatever we must do is right and just.

CHAPTER 4
HARD STAND TO AIRBORNE

"You're loaded up to the hilt with fuel," the ground engineer directed to the Pilot. "All engines are purring like kittens," he added, referring to the four engines.

The armorers were hoisting the last of the bombs into place, through the underbelly of the plane, into the bomb bay. The tail gunner, ball turret gunner, and the flight engineer, were installing their guns into their respective positions, as I entered the plane to make my way to the radio room. Obliged to pass through the waist, I was surprised to find the waist guns not installed, which was the duty of our toggelier, Brooklyn. After depositing my gear in the radio room, I inquired of the ball gunner, who was emerging from his position, "Where the hell is Brooklyn?"

"He was cleaning his guns in the tent, the last time I saw him," was his response.

Although one gun of the two waist positions was the responsibility of the radio operator, it was a common courtesy of the toggelier to install both. This would afford the radio operator time to set up his frequencies and tune his equipment. With thoughts of the forthcoming mission, its length and its dangers, welling up in my mind, the lack of cooperation drove me wild in quest of Brooklyn.

On entering the tent it was obvious even to a non-medical person that Brooklyn was a sick man. The beads of perspiration reflected the shade of green of his face, and his doubled up position, with his arms wrapped around his middle, gave the impression he was squeezing the poison from his innards, which was in evidence around him. I ran from the tent to inform the Pilot of my find.

"Damn it, we'll need a replacement quickly," was his only response.

A quick call to operations brought simultaneously an ambulance to remove Brooklyn and a Jeep depositing two replacements, one for Brooklyn and another to man the waist gun, since we were using a toggelier and not a Bombardier.

As they placed Brooklyn on a litter, I reminded him, "Be here when we get back, you lucky fakir," attempting to ease his discomfort, never realizing for him to comply would entail a wait of four months.

The replacements were from a career pool made up of those removed from crews for one reason or another, to be used under circumstances such as ours. Little did they realize, that by an act of fate, they would become a part of Air Force history. They would be placed in a position of non-appointed diplomatic envoys, to wage a personal war with an ally.

The hard stands are patches of concrete, scattered about the country side on the perimeter of the airfield. Each was a busy beehive of activity, with ground crews readying equipment that when unified, would create an awesome unit of destruction. This destruction, vented upon targets of names and places, relieved the airmen of personalized combat, and gave one the feeling of material killing, not human killing. Even in air combat, your target was an aircraft, not the man flying it, and the kill was one plane, not one pilot, and all records read as such.

All equipment was in place, all the men were combat ready, and this great bird was ready to join other birds in flight. Men will plot their courses, but God will plot their destiny. His destiny for the members of this crew would continue long after these words, and subsequent words, are written.

Etched against the sky, the lumbering planes snaked their way from their secluded hardstands to the runway approaches. Their cumbersome silhouettes belied the grace they possessed when in flight. The squeak of brakes, the squeal of rubber against concrete, the revving of engines in a stop and go pattern as we fell into takeoff position was the background of sound dimmed by the roar of the lead aircraft as it released its brakes. Full throttle, it bolted down the runway, straining against gravity, and became airborne.

Sweating the takeoff was a prime requisite, and tenseness built to the breaking point as we approached our turn to takeoff. Carrying the maximum fuel and bomb load added to the anxiety. All men are not heroes, and the mission at hand sometimes causes men to act out of self preservation, and the stigma of self preservation befell the pilot who ground loops on takeoff, inadvertent or not. This form of aborting a mission was one of many used by those whose glory of achieving their wings was tarnished when the inevitable was faced.

We were next in line, and the preceding plane streaked down the runway as we settled into takeoff position. Suddenly a malfunction of man or machine, and the plane plummeted to earth in a ball of fire. We had, once more, lost before we encountered the enemy.

The plexiglass-enclosed nose compartment was emptied of Navigator and Toggelier, as all crew members assumed takeoff positions. The tension builds within your body, as the tension builds within the structure of the plane, straining against the power of engines begging to be released from their braked captivity. The roar of the engines becomes a whine, and the plane shutters and vibrates to the point of dismantling itself.

When the brakes concede to the engines, we are streaking down the runway challenging gravity. The black rubber streaks on the runway created a weird pattern as they passed under the left wing, while I watched in silent prayer. The end of the runway loomed closer and closer, and I found myself raising from my seat in an attempt to get both myself and the plane airborne. Suddenly the wheels tear themselves from the concrete, and this lumbering monster is an enlightened bird soaring gracefully to its destiny.

Now we became a team, as each crew member proceeded to his respective position. Even while assembling into position each man became eyes for the Pilot, to prevent mid-air collisions. The first to locate our group's colored flares sounded off their location by clock position.

"Two o'clock high," and we slip into prearranged flight patterns, as we circle and climb to our desired altitude. What appear to be straying birds suddenly form into units of flights and squadrons of complete organization, a fighting team.

The assembling of squadrons into groups, groups into wings, and wings into bomber trains, afforded time to check equipment, or have that final smoke before going on oxygen. The spiraling climb to assigned altitude was boring under normal grouping procedure, but on this particular day the cloud cover was extremely thick, and seemingly never-ending. This condition called for constant alertness from all crew members. We were the eyes and ears for the Pilot. The intercom was alive with constant chatter, as scanning crew members alerted the Pilot to positions of approaching aircraft seeking their respective squadrons.

"Watch it skipper, there's a jerk trying to ride our back," screams the Engineer, as he pulls his head out of his revolving upper gun turret, grossly exaggerating the closeness of the descending aircraft. The ball gunner in the under belly in the descending aircraft was probably relating at the same time to his Pilot, "Look out, that jerk under us thinks he's an elevator, coming straight up."

Meanwhile the tail gunner remarked, "That guy behind us must be queer, I think he's trying to kiss our ass." Of course the Toggelier, or Navigator of the "queer plane" must have related to his Pilot, "That son of a bitch in front of us is flying backwards."

All this was making light of a very serious situation, and if the closeness of death can be exposed through jest, and alert us to the importance of doing our job, we would live. Those who hadn't jokingly do their jobs, would agree, if it were possible, that it was no joking matter.

Somehow the white puffy clouds lost their beauty when they enveloped you in a swirling fog that cloaks the dangers of nature, and the dangers of mechanical and man made failures. You strained your eyes not to locate the enemy, but a stray member of the flock, who, by inexperience or malfunction of instruments or simple error, has drifted from assigned sector. It was now easy for him to become a non-combat statistic. The swirling fog that enveloped you also muffled the light and sound that accompanies the flashing light and reverbating concussion of a mid-air collision. The attempt to locate the holocaust, and evasive action to be spared falling debris, was a blind reaction of the inexperienced Pilot, which, if reacted to in like manner by all, would be a catastrophe.

"Hold your positions and altitude," the Command Pilot ordered.

Eyes strained to locate parachutes of survivors through ever-swirling clouds. The group frequency rackled with damage and injury reports.

"Number one feathered, caught some falling debris, request permission to abort," reports one plane.

"Have injured Bombardier, struck by debris," reports another.

"Have dead Engineer in upper turret," one added to the confusion. He was crushed when a plane pancaked atop his plane in a lower echelon during violent maneuvers after the mid-air collision.

The air waves were filled with jumbled requests and orders.

"Clear the air," ordered the group Commander, following that with a blanket order. "All planes unable to complete mission due to damage or injuries, are granted permission to return to base. Use abort procedure. Good luck."

The strain of assembly, the thought of the long and hazardous flight ahead, and the reason for same, tempted many to imagine physical ills, both mechanical and personal.

Suddenly from a grey, sickening mass of fog, we were blinded by a bright sun, reflecting off a white oasis of billowing clouds. It was hard to imagine that this sea of tranquility could conceal such dangers. Breaking out on top safe was often described as a "better feeling than getting laid," or from the more prudish, "a good shit."

It was a thing of beauty to observe plane after plane poking their noses into the blue out of the billowy clouds, like divers breaking water on return to the surface. Flares began to appear and group colors were called out, and when our color was spotted, we headed for same. Head counting took place at rendezvous, and missing planes were reported to the group commander. Reassignment within the group was made to adjust formations for bomb run and fill voids for enemy fighter protection. As we closed into our new positions there was a fleeting search to determine the identity of missing planes. For then we could only prepare for the job at hand, and with all deference to the missing, the thought inevitably passed through your mind, "Better him than me."

The drone of the engines, muffled by your head set, afforded a constant background of harmonious music. Subconsciously you listened for a bad note, for this symphony must be played without a mistake. By now all planes were in their respective positions, and all personnel within each plane should have been at their assigned posts. At oxygen altitude it was imperative that position reports be verbally given every thirty seconds, and a visual check be made of each other whenever possible. It didn't take more than thirty seconds to render you unconscious, and then dead, if your oxygen supply is cut off. Lack of oxygen at over ten thousand feet afforded little margin of survival for earth dwellers.

The assembly completed the lead plane, carrying the lead navigator, set the heading for the primary target. Like sheep we followed, and like sheep, we had better not stray.

CHAPTER 5 — FLIGHT TO TARGET

All information transmitted from home base command was relayed to the Pilot by the radio operator after it was decoded. Radio silence was maintained, and only very important messages were transmitted. Lengthy signal transmissions would afford the enemy a means of triangulation to pin point our group, as a target for anti-aircraft guns or fighter interception. Contact between group commander and squadron leaders in flight was maintained by uncoded voice transmission when necessary. Fear of enemy interception was remote because the range of the equipment used was limited.

There were a number of requests to abort due to mechanical failures, and after all efforts to rectify same were exhausted, a reluctant permission was granted to return to base. The distance of this particular mission limits the penetration of fighter cover, and every plane less when we are on our own, cuts down our fire power for defense.

As we approached the English Channel, the order to test guns was given. This necessitated the repositioning of planes to prevent the possibility of being struck by empty shell casings ejected from the ball turret gun. Because of the close quarters, the planes hadn't the luxury of a facility to catch and store those casings. Flying into a falling shell casing could and did cause crippling damage with potentially the same effect as falling flak. The short burst from your gun to insure working order was a weak assurance of protection.

"Approaching the French coast," came over the interphone, from the Navigator.

Now the body tensed as you realized enemy attack was possibly imminent. Eyes peered into the sun and also attempted to penetrate the clouds, and the trailing contrails of our own planes, to seek out the hiding places of the attacking planes which you knew were sure to appear.

"Flak at 2 o'clock high," crackled the interphone. "The 100th is catching hell."

"Someone caught it," informs another voice.

I strained to see the plane that "caught it," counting chutes as I located the plane in a flat spin, trailing smoke and flame.

"One, two, three," I counted as I prayed. I unconsciously screamed, "Get out, damn you, get out!" as the plane became more and more like a falling meteor, suddenly exploding into fragments of debris, both man-made and God-made.

"Close up, close up," crackled orders from the lead ship. "Bandits, bandits at 10:00 O'clock," prompted my dash to my waist gun. I plugged in my oxygen mask, and cleared my gun. Off in the distance I could see a wave of black specs peeling off in an attack on a distant group. It was a strange feeling, to find how much you wanted to destroy the enemy, hoping it was you under attack. It was like sitting in a theater watching a tremendous production. I never felt air war was man against man, but plane against plane. It was only when a plane was going down, that I comprehended human life was being destroyed.

Watching our fighter escort intercept the enemy, the graceful maneuvers of both friend and foe were a sight to behold. You found yourself admiring this spectacle as a spectator. The violent maneuvers of our plane, and the crackling of gun fire, awakened me to the realization that we were under direct attack. The intercom utterly shrieked with directions of approaching enemy planes.

"He's coming under, under, there's the bastard, get him, get him."

The plane vibrated as his slugs tore into us.

"We're hit, we're hit," came from the ball turret with a tone of apprehension.

"We're O.K., We're O.K., station report," reassured the Pilot. All stations reported O.K.

The attack was over as quickly as it started. Damage reports and abortion requests, directed to the command plane, filled the air waves.

"Evaluate damage, and ability to remain airborne. Report in squadron sequence," came as a direct order.

Its purpose was twofold: unscramble the intermingled communications, and enable Pilots to ascertain the feasibility of reaching the target area, dropping their bomb load, and making it to Poland or Russia. The other choice was to return to England, before we reached the point of no return.

The continuing drone of our engines was broken by the intermittent chatter of position reports, and the Pilot's instructions to remain alert. The distance to our primary target Dresden was such that we could not afford to circumvent known flak areas, because of fuel consumption. The flak was sporadic, and enemy fighter interception was not expected, as long as our P-51 escort was with us. With the innovation of auxiliary wing tanks, the escort covering capability was extended far into enemy territory. The target Dresden was beyond their range, and we knew the enemy would be waiting the moment they turned for home. The inevitable happened, and the command to tighten up formation came as our guardian angels tipped their wings in a good luck salute, and headed home.

We knew now as we prepared for our bomb run the flak would be intense. It would start with tracking flak, attempting to pick off our chaff dropping planes, which gummed up their radar controlled anti-aircraft guns.

"Hold formation, hold formation, tighten up," was ordered as we prepared to enter our bomb run.

As empty positions appeared jockeying aircraft attempted to fill the voids. Mid-air collisions, or planes hit by flak, caused close-by aircraft to scatter to safety. Regrouping became time consuming and fuel wasting.

The flak barrage, before, around, and after the target area, was a solid wall, an ominous black cloud, ready to consume, digest, and spit out each plane. There was no deviation, no option, but to fly straight through, if you were to reach the target, which was what the mission was all about. Not having a Bombardier, the man assigned as toggelier would jettison the bomb load the moment the lead squadron Bombardier dropped theirs. This was called saturation bombing, and had proved very successful.

"Open bomb bays," was the first command, and apprehension set in, not because you were not susceptible to a direct bomb bay hit before, but now with the bomb bay doors open, and the bombs nakedly exposed, you felt every anti-aircraft missile was headed straight at you. You were not aware of any action around you when you are on the bomb run, but after "bombs away" was sounded you turn to the rallying point. It was then you were awakened to the chattering of machine guns, and the bandit positions being called over the interphones.

"Close up, close up," was the order from the command plane.

Darting enemy aircraft raised hell, actually flying in our formation, using our crossfire as protection. One suddenly split out and took one of our planes as he spiralled through our formation. Parachutes filled the air, and planes in various states of distress plummeted to oblivion, with their human cargo becoming a statistic.

"Feather one," ordered the Pilot to the Co-Pilot. This moment, and those words, were actually the beginning of the mission for this crew.

CHAPTER 6 — TRUTH WILL OUT

"Bombs away," reported the toggelier.

"Bombs away," I echoed, as the bomb bay emptied its innards on the target below, Dresden.

The Pilot turned to the rallying point attempting to regain formation position. The feathered engine was a drag; we began to fall back.

"Runaway prop number two," came from the Co-Pilot.

The plane began to shudder, and a sickening feeling enveloped the crew.

"Position report?" the Pilot asked the Navigator.

"Somewhere south of Dresden," was the reply.

The returning formation were distant specks by now, an a shrill scream from the tail-gunner, awakened us to an enemy fighter streaking in the kill of a wounded bird. The Pilot went into evasive action, with what power he possessed, and made for a bank of hopefully concealing cloud cover.

"Give me a heading for Russia," requested the Pilot.

"We're in a cloud somewhere over Germany," was the immediate response, "your guess is as good as mine!"

Smoke and flame enveloped the runaway engine. The congealing oil emitted from under the cowl of the feathered engine caught in the slipstream and gave the impression that the engine was throwing up its guts.

The Pilot directed me to radio our home base, "We are afire, under fighter attack, will attempt to make Russian lines."

The words "see you in Russia," were ringing in my ears. These words were uttered by my Pilot, to another crew Pilot, as we left the ready room. Before the situation that presented itself could dispel my thoughts, I wondered, "Could this be by design?"

I reeled out the trailing antenna, to increase the strength and distance of our signal. I proceeded to radio our base in England our situation, uncoded, as directed by my Pilot. As I was transmitting, the toggelier emerged from the bomb bay into the radio room. His face was strange to me, for he was one of the last minute replacements for Brooklyn.

As he passed, I was banging out our distress message. He said,"They all bailed out up front, I'm going out the waist."

I hadn't heard the bail out buzzer, and working the radio blocked out any voice order to bail out. The appearance of the toggelier saved my ass.

I looked through the bomb bay towards the cockpit. It was empty. The Pilot was just about to exit from the nose hatch Seeing me, he waved me to go, as he made his exit.

I was about to exit from the aft end of the bomb bay, when by God's will, I looked towards the waist compartment. There was our toggelier, in a sitting position in the waist door, holding frantically to the door frame. By this time the plane yawed in a slow flat spin, and it entered my mind, "Would I be able to reach him before we hit the ground? Are we at a high enough altitude for our chutes to work?" We had been off oxygen for a long period of time, which meant below ten thousand feet. We had been flying through cloud bank after cloud bank; the sight of ground was not visible, therefore our altitude was a calculated guess.

I started to exit from the radio room to the waist compartment, only to realize that I had forgotten my GI shoes, which I retrieved and attached to my parachute harness. I reached the toggelier, only to remember my gold pen and pencil set. I returned to the radio room to get them; it was like a God send. I remembered to set the detonation apparatus, which destroys all the radio equipment.

The toggelier must have thought me some kind of nut, as he looked at me like he was a forlorn puppy. I pried his hands loose from the door frame, placed his right hand on the ripcord ring, yelled, "Count ten and pull," placed my flying boot into his back, and kicked him out.

I saw him once, a distant speck, as the plane circled. His chute hadn't opened yet. "God," I thought, "maybe he passed out," as I dove head first into Air Force history.

CHAPTER 7 — THE INVITATION

The feeling of floating free, the gentle hiss of the friction of air penetrating your ear drums. "Son of a bitch, I forgot my fucking hat," I yelled. This was in reference to Joe DiMaggio's baseball cap, which he gave me when I was voted the most valuable player in the American Legion League, in 1935. I was permitted to wear the cap in place of the regulation cap when wearing fatigues, or flying gear. I had to remove it when donning my oxygen mask, causing me to forget it, but the loss was soon forgotten when I realized where the hell I was.

I recalled asking my instructor at primary flight school, "Could you accidently dump me? I always wanted to make a parachute jump."

"I'll dump you right out of the Air Force, if you pull that shit on me," was his retort. How true were his words, "When you use your parachute, it will be to save your ass."

I attempted to penetrate the clouds that enveloped me, for the sight of the ground. "How much time do I have to free fall," I thought, "before I hit the fucking ground."

As an answer to my question, a white mass of earth appeared, with a cluster of buildings in the distance. "I'm low enough," I screamed as I yanked the ripcord ring; I pleaded gently, "You better work, you bastard."

My pilot chute flew upward, trailing the main chute from my chest pack. The impact of the main chute inflating caused a severe pain in my right testicle, as the leg harness jerked upward into my groin. I felt I was going sideways faster than I was descending. My thoughts were to get to the ground as quickly as possible, because I wanted a chance to hide. To be captured by the military afforded a chance of survival; being captured by civilians was a no-no, especially Dresden civilians, where the only known military targets were Dresden doll factories.

I recalled the chute instructor's words: "Don't try to steer your chute, you can spill the air, and straight down you go."

With this in mind, the course I was taking was directly towards a little cluster of buildings, swiftly approaching my swaying body. Suddenly everything seemed to happen at once. The buildings were a small village, people with guns pointed skyward, and a church steeple, which appeared to be my landing area.

The wind wasn't a gentle hiss of air at this point, and the swirling snow looked ominous, as dark clouds rolled across an open expanse of snow-covered earth in the distance. I coiled my body into as small a target as possible, awaiting the impact with the church steeple, or a bullet from a searching rifle.

At a moment such as this, believe me, your life does not pass before your eyes. You don't think of your parents, wife or other loved ones, You look to a supreme being, your God, or any God, and pray aloud, "dear God, please save my ass. As in foxholes, where there are no atheist, there are no atheists in the Air Force.

I glanced off the church steeple, my left leg taking the impact. The impact caused a catapult effect: I was rising instead of descending. It appeared at this point, I would clear the town, and a wide expanse of open ground would be my landing area.

"Oh shit!" I cried, as I saw the wide expanse of open ground to be a snow covered lake or pond, with patches of open water.

"Before you hit the water," these words rang through my head, "release yourself from your harness, just before impact, to prevent entanglement with the chute."

This was a fucking joke. With the harness pressed so tightly to your body, and heavy insulated gloves tightly clasped in prayer, these instructions, were just that, instructions.

"How the hell do I get to my Mae West," I asked myself, "sandwiched between the harness, and my flying jacket."

I envisioned myself trapped beneath the fucking ice, so I asked mother nature for help, and screamed aloud, Wind, blow you son of a bitch, blow."

Someone heard me. I cleared the water and braced myself for the return to mother earth. The lateral speed into snow covered terrain was like landing on skis. It was ass over head, and no way was I even thinking of emptying the air from this chute. The chute dragged me bouncing in and out of snow drifts across the field. I lost one of my fur lined gloves when attempting to release a thigh strap. Thank God for the nylon gloves we wore underneath. We didn't have quick harness releases; the releases we had were hard enough under the best conditions With the cold, and bouncing situation, the fear for survival clouded even your best intentions.

Somewhere between a bounce and a drag, I managed to release one thigh strap which runs parallel to your testicles. Before I could release the other, a gust of wind made me airborne again, and the remaining thigh strap caught my left nut in a squeeze play. The pain blinded me, but not enough to blot out the wooden fence that suddenly appeared directly in my path. At this time, believe it or not, I thought, "At least this fucking fence should end this bouncing shit."

The chute cleared the fence. I didn't. I glanced off the top, and slammed to the ground on the other side. The chute caught in some brush, and I thought, "You son of a bitch, we made it."

I lay there, wet, cold, with a numb feeling in my leg enlarging the nauseating feeling caused by the pain in my left nut. I struggled out of my harness and yanked on the parachute to dislodge it from the brush. I rolled it up, and half walked, half crawled towards the wooded area that presented itself.

I wondered how long it would take for the people in the village to find me, and where the hell were the Russian lines. The snow was heavy, and the drifts were high and concealing, which afforded hope of escape, for I knew the Russian lines were close to Dresden, our target.

Find a good place of concealment, gather your wits, your resources, then plan, were my immediate thoughts. I moved deeper into the wooded area, and suddenly found myself falling. It wasn't a long fall, but the involuntary suddenness evoked a "What the hell?" as I landed in a snow covered ravine, with my parachute caught in the brush above me. I pulled the chute from its captivity; with it came an abundance of snow, which cascaded upon me. Clearing myself from my entombment, I was greeted with what appeared to be a nature-made escape tunnel. The ravine with its snow covered roof formed a natural barrier from the weather, and searching eyes. I gathered up my chute, and proceeded to follow this God send, praying it would lead somewhere close to the Russian lines.

After making my way, which seemed like hours, and many miles, I stopped to rest, hoping to locate myself. Since I hadn't been discovered by this time, I felt I could afford this respite. I opened my escape kit, retrieving the compass contained therein. It was a miracle: the route I was taking was in an easterly direction, towards the Russian lines in Poland. It soon became apparent that the snow roof was getting darker, which signaled night was approaching. In my mind I was reaching the point of no return. Should I break out of my concealment, and risk capture, for I realized my clothing wouldn't withstand too many hours of the cold which was beginning to effect my thinking. Whatever choice I would make, was soon made for me, as two bodies cascaded through the roof. I screamed, "Oh shit!"

Like the old west, I clumsily fumbled my forty five from my shoulder holster, and bolted a round into the chamber. Their lack of military garb resolved my thinking. "Civilians, pitch forks, dragged through town. I'll take a few with me." I released my safety, and pointed my weapon at the intruders.

"Amerikanski?" one asked, as he pointed to the American flag on my flying jacket sleeve.

"Popolski," the other added, thumbing his chest, and making no effort to disarm me, or a show of fear, they turned, and gestured to follow, an invitation I gladly accepted.

CHAPTER 8 — REUNION AT THE BUNK HOUSE

It was dark when they led me through the snow and brush. They beckoned me to close up, and it was easy to understand their reasoning. I could have easily lost them if I kept falling back. I holstered my weapon when I realized I still had it in my hand. I extended my hand to the one offered me, and clung on as I felt a slight pressure of reassurance. Occasionally a finger of light emitted from the leader, as we groped our way through what appeared to be a densely wooded area. Not a word had been spoken, but a few grunts and groans were mumbled that sounded like "ah shit" as we bounced off a tree, or slipped and slid on the icy, snow-covered ground. Suddenly all motion ceased, and I could hear whispering between my two companions. One held me back as the other disappeared from sight. My companion mumbled something, and placing his hand over his mouth told me I had received my first Polish languish lesson, "Be quiet."

The one who disappeared, suddenly appeared, and each taking one of my hands, led me through the trees to what appeared to be a clearing. My eyes were becoming adjusted to the darkness, and what reflection of light there was off the snow, made me aware of cords of wood stacked neatly in an open area. A snow-covered building was barely visible at the far end of the clearing. I could smell the Christmas aroma of burning wood as a door was pulled open, and I was literally yanked into a dark void. The door behind us was closed, a second door was pushed inward, and the light therein blinded me for a split second. As I blinked my eyes into focus, I recognized my surroundings as a typical western cowboy bunkhouse. Rows of double deck bunks, the pot-bellied stove, the wooden table with attached benches, and finally the smells of working men. There were about eight men in this room, and one walked towards me. He appeared to be the foreman. He extended his hand in friendship, then surprised the shit out of me as he said, "Welcome to our simple abode," in perfect English.

"You are safe here, for the time being. We are trying to round up the rest of your friends."

"Where are we," I asked, "Poland or Germany?"

"This is a German lumber camp, inside the German lines. We are Polish prisoners of war, working this camp."

He explained how when visiting relatives, he was caught up in the German invasion of Poland, volunteered into the Polish army, and subsequently captured.

"There are usually German military personnel supervising us, but they are retreating all along this line, as the Russians are advancing without opposition," he added.

"There are sporadic pockets of resistance, so it won't be too hard to by-pass them, and get you into the Russian sector," he concluded.

I suddenly realized that the warmth that thawed my mind and body was emitting from the pot bellied stove, and without thinking, I sort of pushed my way through my welcoming committee, with a mumbled "Excuse me." The stiffened outer garments became damp as they thawed, so I hastened to remove them. The numbness in my toes was apparent as they thawed into burning, then itching annoyances. I removed my fur lined flying boots and heat slippers, to massage my toes into life.

As my numbness, fear and apprehension disappeared, my ills came to fore. The cut on my jaw began to ooze blood, as nature's coagulant began to thaw. Someone handed me a pressure pad of gauze, and as I placed it over the bleeding laceration, the jagged edge of a broken molar pierced my tongue. I jutted my jaw to inspect the tooth with a probing finger, I knew then it was more than a broken molar.

"You can't win them all," I thought, as one of my saviors beckoned me to what appeared to be a bowl of soup he was placing on the table. It was some kind of beet concoction, with other kinds of greens I could not identify, and remained a mystery throughout my stay in Poland and Russia. It was a substantial dish. The black bread with its lard spread and apple butter was and never will be a diarrhea remedy.

I sipped the soup and nibbled the bread, which at that time tasted like Mom's home-made minestrone and freshly baked Italian bread.

The others joined me at the table, and I felt like a celebrity as questions were asked through the English-speaking worker. Most of the questions were about the United States, and to the last man, his desire to go there some day. It was odd, not one question of a military nature, only that they (the Poles) felt the war would end when it became known that the Americans had entered the war. It was a nice feeling to be a welcomed guest. It soon became apparent that the endurance I sustained during my ordeal was motivated by fear, and the desire to survive. Now that I had the feeling of security my mind and body requested sleep. I accepted the bunk offered me, and without shedding another article of clothing, I curled into a ball, responding willingly to the call of my being.

I was awakened by a gentle nudge to my shoulder, which startled me, I was in such a deep sleep. Forcing open my sleep-laden eye lids, I focused my bleary eyes on the face of our toggelier. My heart was consoled; he had made it.

The English speaking worker briefed him, as he did me. Our future was in his hands, and we accepted his position. I didn't know how long I had slept, and since there was no way of looking outside, day or night was a calculated guess.

I asked, "How long have I slept?"

"Through the night, it is now morning," was the reply.

"Do you have any idea where the rest of the boys are?" asked the toggelier.

I repeated what they told me. "They are trying to locate the rest of our crew."

I conveyed to the toggelier my fear for him, when I didn't see his chute open. He laughed sheepishly, and told me what happened when he pulled the rip cord, I had placed in his hand.

"The pilot chute bubbled out, but the fucking main chute, nothing. I pulled the main chute out by hand," he added, "and it was bang, bang, the chute popped open, and I was on the ground."

"I thought I'd had it, when I saw these two men in civilian clothes approach me before I could even attempt to clear myself from my chute. It was like they followed me right to my landing. Without a word," he continued, "one pointed to the flag on my sleeve, and hugged me.

"They detached me from my chute, rolled it up, and without another spoken word, literally dragged me towards a wooded area which was at the perimeter of the clearing where I had landed."

He continued, "I was taken to a small building in a clearing, where men were trimming fallen trees, and horses were hauling them away with chain slings."

I interrupted with, "The building was like a western movie, line shack, right?"

"What?" he queried.

I kiddingly explained my visual impression of our surroundings. He laughed, and readily agreed.

We endured hours of boredom, hidden way during working hours, and time passed without any reference to our fate. We were informed they may have located another one of our crew. Without any advance notice, in walks our engineer, a little beat, but wearing a happy smile.

He told how he was snagged in some trees when he landed, and broke through some ice and snow over a culvert, submerged up to his chin in freezing water.

"Sprechen se deutch?" someone had asked, putting pressure on the engineer's shoulders in a downward direction.

Being a Pennsylvania Dutchman, he responded with one of the German words he knew, "*Nein.*"

With a shudder, the engineer described the results. "That was the wrong word. He commenced to submerge the rest of me. I started to scream, 'Amerikanski, Amerikanski,' praying I was in Poland, and at the same time grabbed the parachute shrouds in an attempt to pull myself out of that watery grave. In my struggling pulling on the shrouds, the American flag on my jacket was exposed. 'Amerikanski, Amerikanski,' was the signal to yank me from my watery demise.

"I was hidden in the oddest places - lean-to's, tents, wagons - and I was freezing my balls," he explained.

He had been informed they believed two other of his crew were safe, and would make every attempt to join them, after checking their location. Thus, his arrival at our camp.

Later that day we were told, and with great joy, "Three other of your crew are safe, but too far from here to risk moving them at this time. We will start making plans to move you into the Russian sector, after we determine when, where, and how."

While absorbing the information fed us, we conjectured as to who the three other crew members were. We settled into a patient but restless waiting game; three were still unaccounted for. The next day we were informed that an attempt would be made to cross us into the Russian sector in Poland.

CHAPTER 9 — THE INVASION OF POLAND

We were awakened the next evening and informed that they were ready to move us through the German lines into Poland. We started to gather what belongings we had, when we were advised to return to sleep.

"We will move you only in day light, when we are allowed to move about, especially now when supervision is almost nil," their spokesman explained.

We exited the building at daybreak and a train of five horse drawn sleds greeted us. We were separated, then placed in an opening constructed in the sled, which outwardly appeared to be log filled. We moved out in tandem, and still thinking western, I felt like pioneers in covered wagons, and like the pioneers I prayed we would encounter no Indians.

Our movement was slow and uneventful, and it was obvious that the routes were commonplace. The only apprehension was at checking stations, where the cargo was casually checked. After a time, we arrived at an area which appeared to be a collection station.

Suddenly, a voice was directed toward me, from alongside my sled. "This station is too far from the Russian lines. We will have to get our orders changed, which may be hard to do. Sit tight."

"Sit tight?" I thought.

The cold was beginning to penetrate my hiding place, and I wondered how long we would have to "sit tight."

A voice said, "We have permission to remain overnight and move out in the morning, to a location ideal for us. You will have to remain where you are, probably until dark, before we can get you inside the building."

Without warning, a hand stuffed a piece of clothing into my hiding place with instructions, "Put this on, it will keep you a little bit warmer."

Unfolding the item, I found it to be a quilted vest, wrap around style, with tie strings. As it grew darker, the cold penetrated to the bone, and the protection afforded by the vest was welcome. It passed through my mind that catching a cold at this point was not one of my priorities.

Time crept by, the absence of activity exaggerated by the darkness that soon surrounded us. The faint whispers that motivated our release us from our hiding places were received without question. The warmth that greeted us in the bowels of the building we entered was immediately effective, and was also received without question. We were given some hot liquid, which could only be described as just that, "hot liquid," but it served its purpose. We were directed to three mattresses, with pillows and blankets.

"Sleep," said a man I had never seen before, as he pointed to the welcomed beds. It came as a surprise, and we looked at each other with a simultaneous response. "Straw," we muttered, as our bodies became imbedded in pleasant repose. It felt like feathers to me, as I settled into a restless, yet welcome sleep.

"What?" I asked as I was awakened, when it seemed I had just fallen asleep.

"It is time to move, we have to put you back in sleds before daybreak," we were told.

We had reached the most crucial point of our escape, crossing through the German lines, into the Russian sector. Since we realized that we had to be separated, we exchanged, "good lucks," and followed our leaders out into the cold dark morning, to our concealment aboard our respective sleds.

It was a long wait before daylight, and my mind turned to God. "Please Lord, after coming this far, guide us the rest of the way to safety," I prayed.

The light of day joined the cold that seeped into my sanctuary, and I prayed to God to protect it as such.

I could hear the horses as they were positioned to be attached to the sleds. A voice bellowed something in Polish which sounded like "move out," and the resulting motion of my sled confirmed my translation. I could feel the horse strain, as it dug into the snowy terrain to effect a start. With the help of some manual pushing, we were soon on our way.

Visibility from within my hiding place was limited at best, but did afford 360 degrees of piecemeal sight of the surrounding areas. After about a half hour of slow uneventful travel, we suddenly came to an abrupt halt, which was punctuated by a command which needed no translation. Peering from my hiding place, I could see fragments of three armed men. Pressing my eye closer to the opening between the logs gave me a broader field of view. If these were German soldiers, they surely were not the picture of the German soldier I had implanted in my mind. They appeared as the old Revolutionary War soldiers at Valley Forge, ragged, ill dressed, and cold.

One of the soldiers apparently asked to see some papers, which one of our Polish friends produced. A difference of opinion was soon obvious, as one of the soldiers yanked the halter from the man driving my sled. It became a screaming tug of war, and it became increasingly clear, these men wanted one of the sleds. As a soldier started to remove the logs from my sled, he was grabbed from behind by one of the other Polish sled drivers. Now it became clear, we were no longer in the Air Force, as I reached for my forty five, and prayed my two companions realized the situation, and acted accordingly.

The soldier who had been grabbed from behind, shook himself loose, unslung his rifle, and pointed it at his assailant. The English speaking Pole stepped between them, and smilingly said something. It must have been effective, for the soldier lowered his rifle. The Polish leader pointed to another sled, and with a voice command, the other poles began to unload the logs from that sled. After the sled was emptied, the soldiers climbed aboard, and departed much to our relief.

The English speaking Pole stood beside my sled, and explained the reason they were satisfied to take another sled. "I told them the horse pulling your sled was pregnant, and would barely make it to our next station, let alone their distant destination," he related.

I exclaimed how surprised I was to see German soldiers so ill kept. He told me that when the German soldiers first appeared in this sector, they were the very elite, but were turned into the remnants of what I have just witnessed by the impact of our entry into the war, and the stretched out support line on two fronts.

"The Germans were killing seven Russians to one German, and were not overwhelmed by superior fighting men, but by sheer numbers," he continued.

"You will never see a Russian soldier laying dead, unless you see him fall. They are immediately buried if possible, or at least removed from sight in any manner available. The German dead are first stripped of his boots, and usually hung from a tree, or any structure where he can be suspended, and seen," he concluded.

The personal war for survival during our ordeal seemed to have negated the real war around us. What brought this fact into focus was the sudden increase of deafening noise by exploding shells.

"We are getting close to the lines of combat, keep fingers crossed," was directed into my hiding place, by an unidentifiable voice.

I don't know why, but I had the impression that they were just going to drive these sleds up to some imaginary line, and voila, there we were, in Poland.

The next directive came as a surprise. "We may have to fight our way through the German lines. There is much confusion, with disorderly retreating Germans and slave laborers seeking refuge clashing at the borders. We will seek a hiding place and wait until dark. We can not expose you at this time."

To be near, and yet so far, produced an uncomfortable situation, but I felt time was on our side. Patience was a must. I must have dozed Darkness had arrived, and my sled began to move. Peering from my hiding place, I was made aware the other sleds were moving in different directions.

"Damn," I thought, "being separated cuts down our fire power." Being on my own caused me great concern.

The sled moved slowly. I could hear two voices, and wondered which of the Poles was with me. Although I felt comfortable with any of those I met, I felt more secure with the speaking one.

Since we were instructed not to speak from our hiding places unless spoken to, I refrained from seeking information from the man walking alongside my sled. He must have read my mind, for he said something in Polish to the man driving the sled.

The driver spoke. "We will have to lay up until morning, and then make our move to cross into Poland."

The voice of the English speaking friend, relieved some of the tension. "What about my friends?" I asked.

"There is no way of knowing. They were taken to different areas, so if anything went wrong, we would not be all together. There is no guarantee of all of us making it," he concluded.

A horrible thought ran through my mind. I volunteered for the Air Force because ground fighting wasn't my bag, and here I was invading Poland as an infantryman.

CHAPTER 10 — SURRENDER

In broad daylight, we wandered over what seemed to be a winding course. There were times when, peering from my hiding place, I felt that we had passed here before. There were occasions where we encountered small remnants of the German army, clustered together like they were waiting to be captured. They paid us only a casual concern, and at times waved in a friendly manner.

It happened suddenly. The driver of my sled dismounted, grabbed the halter, and jerked the horse into a vigorous run. The panting horse slipped and stumbled, the driver's determination relayed through the halter, as we made our mad dash to freedom.

We broke out of our wooded concealment into a snow-covered clearing. The driver gave a triumphant jerk on the halter, sending the sled into a sideways skidding halt. He threw his hands into the air, and knelt in prayer; "We are free!" he shouted.
I started to throw off the logs that prevented me from throwing my arms into the air, but the logs didn't prevent me from saying, "Thank God."

We were suddenly surrounded by rifle bearing soldiers, and all their guns were pointed at us.

"Shit," I said, as I raised my hands into the air, "are we still in Germany?" The uniforms didn't look German, nor did they resemble any Russian uniform.

"Who the hell are they?" I whispered out of the side of my mouth to my companion.

"They are Polish soldiers and Lithuanian officers," he responded.

"Popolski, Amerikanski," my companion threw at them.

Their faces remained sullen, as they moved closer, close enough to prod us in the gut with the business end of their rifles. My companion said something in Polish, which appeared to cause a more relaxed attitude, and wry smiles etched their faces. Although they appeared less hostile, we were motioned to proceed in the direction they suggested with a wave of their rifles. Being surrounded by an armed escort produced an uneasy feeling in my gut. My companion did not outwardly suffer the same feeling. He was carrying on a running conversation with one of the Lithuanian officers, and the conversation was punctuated every now and then with a smile, and sometimes a haughty laugh. I found myself unconsciously smiling, and laughing along with them, which relieved the tension I had acquired.

The war suddenly became a reality, as we approached an area which appeared to be a bivouac encampment. There were tents as far as the eye could see, and they were augmented by rows upon rows of armored equipment, permeated with the utterances of thousands of soldiers. A close look enlarged two aspects of frontline combat on the Russian front. The first was the presence of women and children - not combatants, but family units. The second discovery was the fact that all the armored equipment was American, and the Katusha rocket launchers were mounted on Studebaker or Dodge trucks.

We were escorted to a small structure which appeared to be headquarters, and were greeted by a smiling, medal-bedecked Russian officer with an outstretched hand. The word of American Airmen must have reached him; he seemed genuinely pleased. He invited us inside, then spoke in an ordering tone to a soldier, who saluted in a affirmative manner, and left the room. He returned shortly with a bottle, which appeared to be water. Producing three glasses, the officer proceeded to fill them with this clear liquid.

"What is it?" I inquired of my companion.

"Potato whisky," he answered.

Believe me, the last thing I needed at this time was a drink, but realizing it was a gesture of friendship, I accepted it as such.

He raised his glass in salute, "Amerikaynet," he bellowed, and proceeded to take a small taste. My companion and I did likewise. The taste to me was mild, and went down easy. He then proceeded to utter, "Popolski," and barely wet his lips, as he raised the glass to his mouth. My companion and I followed suit. The next salute offered by the officer indicated the significance of the quantity of liquid you consumed to a specific toast.

"Russki," he bellowed, as he chug-a-lugged the remaining liquid from his glass.

My companion poked me in the ribs with his elbow,and whispered, "Amerikanski, Popolski," and downed his drink, I did likewise.

I was told by my Polish friend, "We will remain in this area for a few days in hopes that your friends will arrive safely in this same area."

We were led to a heated tent furnished with cots, blankets, and some food already set on a table. The heat was surely welcomed, but the food presented nothing new from the other delicacies presented on the other side of the battle lines.

Hours later I was informed that the engineer and toggelier were safe further north, and we would be united in Turek, a Polish town, safely occupied by Polish and Russian troops. The next morning as we readied our departure to Turek, an earth shattering barrage of rocket fire was launched from the Katusha-carrying Studebaker and Dodge trucks. They emblazoned the sky as far as the eye could see, in an never ending scream of death searching missiles. It was hours later when the din of the rockets appeared to subside, and the voice speaking over the loud speaker system became the focus of attention.

There was a mad dash by the multitude of humans, in what appeared to be the reaction to a command over the loud speaker of, "Fall in."

The pushing and shoving of a Macy's day sale, or the New York subway during rush hour, would be a true replica of the activity, if multiplied ten times over. There was one last scattered barrage of rockets, as if they found some they didn't know they had.

The loud speaker bellowed in Russian in what sounded like a pep talk, and responses of what sounded like "hip, hip, hooray" filled the air.

The cheering was followed by sporadic bursts of gunfire into the air. It appeared the main weapon carried by this army was a Burp Gun, and the staccato bursts filled the air with a feeling of mass hatred. The loud speaker came to life once again, with what sounded like, "Go get them." Another cheer was the response. They now moved as one mass of humanity, men, women, and children, like sheep to a slaughter.

We mounted our sled, my companion and I. This time I rode as a free man alongside the driver. It was about an hour before we reached our destination, but the sights of destruction and death on the way will forever live in my memory. The total absence of Russian dead was as I had been informed. The visual presence of German dead was gruesome, hanging from trees, half buried in snow, with arms frozen in grotesque positions, reaching upward as if pleading for forgiveness.

"You will notice, not one German soldier has his boots. The Russians remove them, even before they check to see if he is dead, and the lucky Russian with the right size foot gets the boots," my companion related.

What appeared to be civilization greeted us about an hour later. Amidst some shattered buildings in the outskirts, there were clusters of what resembled intact buildings that was a town.

"Turek," my companion blurted.

It is amazing, that every cluster of buildings you encounter that makes up a town, the church steeple is the most prominent, and it gives you a feeling of sanctuary and safety.

It was as if word of our arrival had preceded us. There was a welcoming group, led by a Priest, that awaited us at the edge of town. The word "Amerikanski" was easily understood. The hugs, pats on the back, and kisses on my cheeks made me feel like I just ended the war by liberating these people, when it was I who was grateful for the gratitude they displayed for our involvement in their cause for freedom.

I lost sight of my English-speaking companion, and an uneasiness struck me as I was led to what appeared to be either an apartment building, or an office building in the past. A banner, stretched above the entrance, was etched in Russian. The two Polish soldiers framing the doorway popped into a "present arms" attitude, which conveyed to me this was headquarters I was about to enter. I passed through a series of doors into a large room, decorated with pennants, flags, and a large photo of a man I didn't recognize.

A well decorated officer emerged from behind a large desk. He walked towards me with outstretched hand, clasped me in a bear hug, planted a kiss on both my cheeks, backed off, grasped my two hands in his, and squeezed, either in genuine friendship, or power of authority.

I was directed to a chair in front of his desk with a wave of his hand, and a smile on his face. As I seated myself I wondered how I was going to converse with him, wondered where my English speaking buddy was. It was as if my mind was read, for entering the room was my buddy, and a highly decorated officer, their arms locked, laughing and chattering in perfect English. The uniform was other than Russian or Polish, but its identity was soon revealed, when my buddy introduced him to me. "This is an old school chum of mine, now an officer in the Lithuanian army," he explained.

I followed the actions of all present in the room, and rose to attention. He ignored everyone but me, and his handclasp and hug felt sincere, and genuine.

Our conversation was one-sided: he asked the questions, I answered them. To my surprise the questions were of a personal nature "Where do you live in the United States? Do you have children?" he asked.

He didn't ask one military question; he just made a confirming statement: "We have the krauts on the run, it won't be long before we all return home."

The bottle of clear liquid soon appeared. It was beginning to imprint on my mind as a sign of friendship, or a valid excuse to have a drink. The raising of one's glass in salutation at this occasion, didn't have the connotation of one's status as in the past. "To victory," was consistent.

I was informed that my two companions who crossed into Poland with me would arrive soon. Also, three others were picked up by other Polish laborers, and crossed into Poland through the German lines. Three others picked up by the Germans were rescued by the advancing Russians before they could be moved to a stalag, the information continued. All nine were now accounted for. "By the grace of God," I thought. A feeling of comfort and security enveloped me.

Early that evening, our toggelier and engineer arrived, I informed them of the good news concerning the balance of our crew. I also relayed the wonderful treatment and attitude of our hosts. It was after dark when the information relative to my crew was confirmed by their presence. All were accounted for.

After exchanging heartfelt greetings, we exchanged tales of fear and concern for each other. Our English speaking host listened with what appeared to be genuine interest, and even injected questions of concerned nature.

We were directed to toilet facilities, where nature's calls, both internal and external, were heeded. We were led to another room where a table of what appeared to be food greeted us. We ate what was offered. It satisfied our needs, which we conveyed to our hosts with the American signs of contentment and satisfaction, patting one's stomach while pinching one's cheek. The intermingled chatter of Polish and English, both in conversation amongst ourselves and requests for interpretation, reminded me of my family gatherings, when intermingled Italian and English posed the same problem.

We were assigned rooms for the night. It was then we were afforded the opportunity to speak among ourselves without the presence of our hosts. The presence of an officer gave me a comfortable feeling for further negotiations, and the same feeling appeared to impress our saviors, when the officers first arrived. The feeling was short lived, when the Pilot questioned me as to the reason I didn't leave the plane when he did.

Before I could answer, the toggelier volunteered, "It's a good thing he didn't, I would have probably rode the plane right into the fucking ground."

"What are you talking about?" the Pilot asked, "I saw you enter the bomb bay, long before I left the controls to jump." "I just thought it would be safer if I left by the waist door," the toggelier informed the Pilot.

"Just let it be known that you and I left at the same time, and that's an order," he added as he pointed a shaking finger into my face.

"Don't make a big issue out of the circumstances that prevailed. It could have happened to anyone. Besides, we should thank God we all made it," I directed to the Pilot.

Since I had been the one who asked questions before the arrival of our Pilot, I asked the Pilot to question as to our status.

"You mind your fucking business," he growled, "I'm in command here, I'll do the thinking for this group."

His attitude was a far cry from the respect he had for me stateside, when no one was allowed to enter the plane before I made the sign of the Cross at the waist door. There were training missions we made where he would ask me to obtain a radio heading home, and ridicule the Navigator over the intercom to embarrass him. He would dismount the Co-Pilot and have me practice simulated landings, with instrument proceedings, to prepare for an emergency, if he were killed or disabled. Then there was the return from a mission to Hamburg, Germany, where we were shot up and anticipated a water landing. Some of the crew were ready to bail out over the Hegoland islands, and he called me to ask if I would ride it down with him up front.

This faith he had in me must have disintegrated, because I inadvertently left the plane after him. His behavior and language towards us was totally unlike his normal behavior. It required no interpretation by our hosts, and their reaction needed no interpretation to explain their embarrassing withdrawal.

Days passed, and I wouldn't enlarge on the uneasiness that prevailed, by asking questions, content that we were safe, and being cared for.

One day I mentioned the absence of Russians to my Pilot, and suggested that we should inquire who was in command, to make arrangements to return to England.

"Mind you own business. Time is on our side. If we bide our time, this war could be over before we get back," he said.

I looked at the faces of the rest of the crew, hopeful for some sign of resentment to such a directive. Their faces showed no concern one way or the other, and hoping for some contest from the other officers proved as futile. I retreated to my room with an uneasy feeling of alienation from my crew.

The next morning began with the same congeniality as before, but after breakfast, an air of indifference became apparent with an attitude of reverence towards military decorum. We were informed that a Russian officer with an interrogation team was arriving to question us; thus, the reason for the change was discovered.

We were gathered in the main office, greeted by a beribboned officer, and positioned before his desk.

"Officers up front, non-coms to the rear." He spoke in broken English, but was easily understood, because his voice was one of authority.

We were standing in an "at ease" position as he said something to a Lithuanian officer, which was relayed to us in a curt, meaningful, "Attention."

The Pilot repeated "attention" with an accompanying salute. We responded accordingly.

"What the fuck?" I said to myself. Many "what the fucks" would be uttered before this day was over.

We were asked who was in command. The Pilot stepped forward, with another snappy Air Force salute. The Russian officer said something in Russian with a smirk on his face, and I ventured he said, if translated, "Jerk." The translation was only a wild guess, but the ensuing incidents proved the translation correct.

The first question directed to our Pilot made me think "he must be kidding," with a questioning looks at each other.

"What was your target in Poland?"

Before the Pilot could answer, he was interrupted with, "Was this a bombing mission, or a parachute invasion?"

The look in the Lithuanian officer's eyes was one of disbelief when ordered, "Separate these men for individual interrogation."

"Didn't anyone tell this guy we are American airmen?" I inquired of the Lithuanian officer.

"Do as you're told," the Pilot injected.

"Why don't you make a protest? What the hell, are we prisoners?"

Here we are with American flags on our jacket sleeves, and thinking, we wouldn't be here if we weren't bombing to help their advance against the Krauts.

The Pilot was the first taken to an adjoining room, and he returned in about fifteen minutes with disbelief etched on his face. He was in the process of replacing his clothes. "What the hell goes on here?"

Almost in unison, we responded, "You tell us."

I was the next one directed to the interrogation room, and it didn't take long before our question was answered personally.

"Strip!" was bellowed at me.

"What?" I asked unbelievingly.

The prodding by the business end of a Burp gun speeded me into compliance.

"Raise your arms, spread your legs." The order preceded a physical frisk, included scrutiny of my arm pits and testicles. The next order was the most degrading.

"Bend over and spread your cheeks."

"What the fuck are you looking for?" I asked.

"Do as you are told," was emphasized by a slap on my shoulder from a soldier standing behind me.

This jerk actually prodded my asshole with a naked finger. I would have liked to fart in his face.

"Nothing," was all he said.

The only excuse for an examination such as this would be if we were considered enemy, and cyanide pills for suicide were secreted in one's rectum. The rectal compass was another item, but everyone knew about them, a part of our escape kits. Shit, mine was in my flying jacket, I would have told them that, if they asked. I could have avoided the asshole-prodding by a total stranger.

The verbal interrogation was loaded with idiotic questions. My thinking was maybe they aren't sure who we are. My gut feeling was they realized we were allies, and were playing games or attempting to embarrass us.

"Where did you come from?"

"What is the strength of your force?"

"Where was your drop point?"

"Is there a ground force follow up?"

These questions were thrown at me from all sides. I was never given a chance to answer any one of them. What surprised me most was they never asked me my name, rank or serial number. They gave me no opportunity to even volunteer it, and the question I thought most likely to be asked was never asked: what outfit I belonged to.

When we all had been through this unbelievably demeaning occurrence, we remained in the main office, and discussed the ordeal amongst ourselves. The interrogators huddled in a corner of the room with a most jovial attitude, and appeared to be passing judgement.

"We are sorry for this inconvenience, but we must be sure of the people we are dealing with. This is war, you know," was directed to us by the commanding officer.

"Tell him it's a lot of shit," I pleaded to my Pilot.

"Let me handle this," he replied, and added, "It's OK. I mean, it's all right, we understand." He accepted their lame excuse.

The next request from the man in charge, was the most demeaning gesture of contempt to compound the disrespect shown up to this point. The only conciliatory change, he used the word "please."

"Please surrender your weapons to the Sergeant," and pointed to a soldier approaching us.

All of my crew were removing their forty-fives from their holsters, when I injected, "What the hell? Are you all crazy? They're not getting mine! We're allies! To give up your weapon is a sign of surrender."

It was amazing. The Sergeant by-passed me with a smile, and the rest of the crew surrendered.

CHAPTER 11 — THE GOOD AND THE BAD

The atmosphere changed with the presence of the Russian military in command. In the presence of the Russians, we were treated as friends at arm's length, with the emphasis on military decorum, but it also was apparent that the Polish and Lithuanian personnel were only acting as robots, with tongue in cheek.

We were eventually assigned sleeping quarters in an adjoining building. It was suggested that we rest and freshen up. We would be notified when and where we would eat our next meal.

In early evening we were rounded up, and believe it or not, we were escorted by two armed guards, single file through the street into a rear entrance of the headquarters building. We were led into a large room, where a large banquet table was visible. There were many military personnel milling about, casually talking, smoking, with glass in hand. Our appearance caused all heads to turn in our direction, and in a token of approval, those with glasses, raised them in a salutation of welcome.

Those officers who spoke English were mostly Polish or Lithuanian, and they gathered around us in apparent genuine friendship. The Russian officers, predominantly remained aloof, but there were some who ventured into our conversation, by prodding the English speaking officers to translate their questions to us. It wasn't long before we were seated with the highest ranking Russian officer at the head of the table. It seemed odd but their was no one seated at the other head of the table. Other Russian officers flanked the head Russian, on both sides. Polish and Lithuanian officers faced each other in the adjoining seats. We were placed opposite each other with officers preceding the non-coms, with two empty seats separating us.

It wasn't long before our glasses were filled with that clear liquid, "potato whisky," with toasts of status being imposed upon us.

It suddenly dawned on me, that our English speaking escort was missing from these festivities, and I mentioned it to my Pilot.

He agreed, saying, "He'll show up, don't worry about him."

We never saw nor heard from him again.

The food was placed before us, a mixture of meat with vegetables, but the toasts between each bite offered by our host appeared to be the main course, which negated any real taste for food. It could only be said that the minor sipping of whisky to the Polish, and American participation in the war effort, was overridden in importance by the chug-a-lugging of large quantities of whisky, when the toast was directed to the Russian efforts.

After a few of these obvious Russian toasts, my resentment was being encouraged by the quantity of liquid I was consuming. I grasped the opportunity for a fresh refilling to short-stop the Russian's toast with "Amerikanski," and downed the full glass in one swallow, which gagged me.

"What the hell, are you nuts?" my Pilot screamed.

Before I could answer, all the Polish, and Lithuanian officers rose as one.

"Amerikanski, Popolski," they toasted, omitting Russki, with the downing of their drinks, then smashing their glasses. Their action first brought a frown, then a snicker, which turned into a hardy laugh from the Russian, as he smashed his glass in agreement, the bad turned to good.

The English speaking officer left the room, and his absence was only explained when he returned with two persons, a young girl and boy. They were seated in the two empty chairs. No immediate reference to their being was offered.

The boy was in his early teens and the girl in her late teens, from their outward appearance. The girl's presence amongst all these men without us knowing the reason made her the focal point for our inquisitive eyes. The boy was slightly built, with a gaunt look of emaciation. The girl was more robust, with a comely look, and when our eyes met, her smile was enhanced by a set of perfect sparkling teeth.

Food was placed before the new comers, and the boy charged his plate with a vengeance, while the girl gently poked at her food with a ladylike exploration. While our new guest were being served, idle chatter permeated the room in an unintelligible drone. Suddenly there was a strain of music from a string instrument, which came from a far corner of the room. A close inspection revealed two men strumming what appeared to be Balalaikas. From my youth I always connected the music of the Balalaikas with the Cossack dance. My youthful interpretation was substantiated with the appearance of two men garbed in authentic Cossack uniforms. They commenced to entertain us, with their systematic and acrobatic gyrations. We all joined in by clapping our hands and stamping our feet to the beat presented. Suddenly, as if we were back in New Jersey's Meadowbrook Lounge, sounds of Glen Miller's "In the Mood" were being beat out on a piano by our Pilot, demonstrating a talent unknown to us.

I kicked off my heavy fur lined boots, grabbed our Engineer by the hand, and commenced to toss him into an American jitterbug. He broke free, kicked off his boots, and away we went. The Russian dancers stopped dancing, and relinquished the floor. His being of small stature afforded the means to really toss him about, which astounded all present. The Pilot commenced to play one number after another with increasing fervor. Without hesitation, everyone, some with, some without partners, attempted to join in the rollicking gyrations of the American jitterbug.

The next few hours were spent dancing and drinking, and believe it or not, I wore a hole in my sweat socks. In all this revelry there was a loss of individual personal contact with those present, and the potato whisky began to take its toll. I had found a chair to sit and rest my weary legs, when without warning my sweaty brow was being patted dry with a soft cloth, in the hand of our female visitor. She made mention that my exuberance when dancing had caused a flow of blood through the bandage on my jaw.

I assured her it was ok, and I would redress it the first opportunity I had.

"It looks swollen. It may be infected," she added. or badly bruised when I bailed out," I informed her. "The pain has lessened each day," I added.

Her concern appeared genuine, but I wondered, "Why me?"

The festivities began to wane, as the whisky and the dancing produced tired, staggering, non-military appearing personnel.

"Come here, my comrade," beckoned the head Russian to our Engineer, and without hesitation, he complied.

As I had previously mentioned, our Engineer was a diminutive, cherubic sort of guy, who wouldn't say shit if he had a mouthful. The next action and reaction brought the party to an end.

"Sit here on my knee," the Russian requested, as he yanked the Engineer to his knee.

The laughter that accompanied the Russian's actions when he said, "Charlie

McCarthy," while grasping and shaking the back of the Engineer's head, made my blood boil.

My crew sat frozen, and their forced accompanying laughter drove me into action.

"Get your fucking hands off him, he is an American airman, not a fucking dummy, you dummy," I screamed.

He released the Engineer, and the room fell silent. The ensuing laughter from the Russian, preceded his apology, "I meant no harm," then qualified it with, "I respect his station in your Air Force."

The Pilot looked at me with daggers in his eyes, and although his lips were puckered to speak, all I could hear was what sounded like, "you, you, you," in an exasperated whisper.

The rest of the people present sort of passed it off, with salutations of Amerikanski, Russki, with raised glasses. Although some of them tried to rekindle the party, a pall of uneasiness prevailed. A Lithuanian officer attempted to help the situation, by encouraging the Cossack soldiers to play and dance. The attempt was futile at best, and the exiting of the revelers brought the party to an end.

The Russian officer spoke to the English-speaking Lithuanian officer, and he smilingly asked us to follow him to our assigned rooms. The long hallways and adjoining rooms confirmed my previous concept of this building as an office or apartment building in the past. My Pilot couldn't wait to corner me before I entered my room.

"You better start showing some respect to our hosts. We're a long ways from home," he chastised me, with a shaking fist under my nose. Then he added, "I'll have your ass when we get back to England."

"Back to England?" I queried. "If we don't gain some respect from these pricks, and make some demands, we'll be lost in the shuffle. God knows if and when we'll ever get back to England.

"Can't you see they're demeaning our importance at every opportunity? You officers are the couriers of leadership, and must act accordingly," I suggested.

I couldn't believe the response to my words. "We are under their jurisdiction, and can't make demands. Besides, like I said before, as long as we're safe, I'm in no hurry to return to a flying war."

CHAPTER 12 — HOUSE OF ILL FAME AND ASSIGNATION

With these words ringing in my ears, I entered the room assigned to me. It was furnished with a bed, chair, bureau, and barred windows. The click I heard sounded like the door lock was engaged.

"What the hell?" I said aloud, and tried the door. It was locked as I suspected.

I was tempted to pound on the door, and make a protest, but the drinking and dancing had sapped some of my belligerence. Besides, the bed looked inviting. It appeared exceptionally high, so I used a chair as a step stool. Removing my outer clothing, I entered the bed with a cloudy and wondering head. The mattress gave way with the weight of my body, and I found myself engulfed in a soft acceptable repose.

The click of the door lock being disengaged half-awakened me, and the ensuing incident was vague and fleeting. So much so, I had to have it substantiated the next day to prove I wasn't dreaming. The door opened slowly, and through veiled eyes, I thought I could see a beautiful blond girl entering the room with an open kimono, exposing a nude body. The door closed behind her, and the clicking lock engaged.

In my half awakened stupor, I recoiled as she shed her kimono, used the chair as I did, and entered the bed beside me. Since I had not crawled under the covers, her bare body was offered to me without concealment.

Two things entered my mind. I had promised myself that I would refrain from my premarital practice of promiscuity. The vivid colored film at preflight, depicting the actual results of diseases contracted from indiscriminate sex, was and will be forever my guide line.

I exited the bed from the opposite side, pushing her from the bed, and said, "Get the hell out of here."

She must have understood my request. Without a word, she replaced her kimono, then proceeded to knock repeatedly on the door. A few moments later, a Polish soldier opened the door. She turned and smiled, as she made her exit.

"Did she make you happy?" the soldier asked, in perfect English. "It did not take you long," he added.

"It was fine," I lied. I could only think of getting back to sleep, and I didn't want to offend their generosity.

The next morning produced some descriptive stories, with mixed emotions, as the heads were now clear, and the stories were at best vague memories. The stories and descriptions of the services provided by these Aryan German women was the topic of conversation, and everyone agreed, they were all real blondes. I just nodded in agreement with all the action that was to have taken place, and didn't commit myself to any questions concerning my personal behavior of pleasure or displeasure. My non committal provided my cohorts the opportunity to challenge my masculinity

"He must be saving it for his wife," was my challenge to rebut my lack of a factual or fictional sex orgy story.

I attempted to educate them to the dangers of their acts without vilifying them. I reminded them of the vivid colored documentation of venereal diseases available to all the sexual heroes, and my hope of surviving this war without a blotch on my service record, especially one of a sexually contracted disease.

This stand only added to my alienation from my crew. The Pilot added to the growing intensity by making my actions and words personal affronts.

"He doesn't want to be one of us, we're all bad guys, he's a saint," was his means of rubbing it in.

"Being a saint has nothing to do with it, I would fuck a snake, if someone held it, but at least I had an idea where the snake came from. These broads must have been viewed, screwed, and tattooed, by every German, Polish, and Russian officer who needed rest and recreation. This place is nothing but a whore house," I concluded.

"Listen to his shit," the pilot continued, "here we are safe from the shooting war, and he complains about our enjoying ourselves."

"Enjoy yourselves, but don't belittle my actions, as long as it doesn't interfere with yours," I offered.

We were assembled for breakfast, and led by an armed guard to the dining room where we partied the night before. One table was occupied by Russian and Lithuanian officers. Another was occupied by the civilian boy and girl who made their appearance at the party, whose presence was never explained. The Lithuanian officer whom we befriended through our English- speaking Pole arose from his table and directed us to our seats, at the table occupied by the two civilians. He then proceeded to introduce them to us, not by name, but their function as interpreters.

"They are proficient in Russian and Polish, in all dialects. They will accompany you in your travels through Poland. We expect to have you on the move shortly," he informed us.

It was this sitting that our segregation as allies became obvious, and unbelievable. The food served to our table was definitely picked from a different menu than the food served to the other table. We received the same unidentifiable liquid, and black bread with the lard and apple butter spread. The other table was served peach halves, eggs with sausages, and tea. The most interesting item was the butter, real butter. The package was the one with the pretty Indian Maiden, "Land-O-Lakes," which was very popular in the states.

"Can you believe this shit?" I commented. "We are fed this crap, and they have the nerve to eat our food right in front of us, without one iota of concern," I added, loud enough to cause heads to turn.

"They may have an allotment, rationed, with no extras," my Pilot injected.

These words may have satisfied us at for a moment, but shortly thereafter, seconds were requested by some of the officers, and the quantity set upon the table became leftovers at the end of breakfast.

"Come on," I directed to the Pilot, "asking for food shouldn't alienate our standing, which is practically zero anyway."

"You're really intent on causing friction with our ally. Well, you're not involving me. Like I said, time is on our side, and survival with safety, is O.K with me," was his response.

"But we're Americans, and you are an American officer, and rate some respect. You give the impression that we are the enemy, and are satisfied with the treatment we are receiving," I pleaded.

"The guards are for our protection. This fucking area was crawling with Krauts just a few weeks ago, and who knows who or what was left behind," he injected with an air of appeasement.

"The fucking Krauts were running like scared rabbits, and behind-lines infiltration may have been Hitler's wishes, but it was the furthest wish of the retreating Germans, trying to save their asses," I countered. "Come on, stop making excuses for their crummy attitude, and exercise some balls. If you won't I will," I declared.

There were affirming nodding from most all the non-coms and the Navigator, but no verbal commitment. This almost constituted a mutiny in the mind of the Pilot, and his retort was repetitious.

"If and when we get back to England, I'll have your ass," he screamed.

The rest of the crew remained non committal, one way or the other, but our civilian guest nodded with a smile of agreement at my dialogue. I felt that any satisfaction from the Pilot was impossible. His attitude was apparent: sit out the war. The rest of the crew, by not speaking out, gave him the justification for his actions, so I let it rest.

It would have remained "at rest," but the Lithuanian officer came to our table, and commenced to explain the duties of our civilian interpreters.

"As I have previously explained, they will accompany you wherever you travel from here, until you reach Russian territory," he instructed us.

Before he could expound on their presence, the female extended her hand to each of us with, "I am Helena," then pointing her finger towards the male, "this is Novak."

I was convinced that she was the leader of this team, and wondered how these two, who were miles apart in their appearance, were joined together in this capacity.

Novak's response was a feeble, mumbled "hello."

"They look like rags, and riches," I whispered to the Pilot. "I would like to find out the connection," I added.

"It's no concern of ours, mind your fucking business," he threw back at me.

"Damn, don't you want to know who we're traveling with? She has all the earmarks of a collaborator. I'm going to ask the Lithuanian officer," I countered.

Before I could accomplish my intent, my question was answered by Helena. She directed her remarks to the Lieutenant, but they were designed for our benefit.

"As you have witnessed, Lieutenant, Novak and I have eaten the same food as the Americans, to establish a trust between us. Their eating of obviously American food in the presence of these men is no way of effecting such a trust," she suggested.

The Lieutenant didn't agree in so many words, but his response, "These things you speak of, are out of my hands," placed the blame where it belonged.

I looked questioningly towards my crew, hoping for some sign of understanding. A shrug of their shoulders said, "Who gives a shit, anyway."

The next instant confirmed the attitude of our Russian ally, and their respect for our presence or the help we were contributing to their war effort. A bag of shredded tobacco was placed on our table, with paper not unlike our paper towels at home, to be used to manufacture our cigarettes. The Lieutenant, placed a pack of Russian tailored made cigarettes on our table, when he realized, as one, we were looking at the table next to ours. They were opening a carton of American Lucky Strike cigarettes, in the olive drab colored packages, which had been discontinued in the United States. "Lucky Strike Green" had gone to war.

CHAPTER 13 — BEFRIENDED
BY ACTIONS

The next few days were anxious ones for me. I wanted to move, or at least have some knowledge of when we would so. I was afraid to suggest to my Pilot that he inquire of our status. The tenseness was apparent in all, and the last thing we needed was an air of individual concern. Leadership was missing, so collective bargaining was still our strength.

My thoughts turned to home, and I wondered about the notifications to my wife and mother. Knowing my mother's reaction to tragedy, I feared the worst. Both my mother's and wife's religious beliefs and faith in God certainly would be needed to soften their anxiety if some official notification made them aware of our safe status.

"Why don't we ask someone in authority if a message could be relayed to our command in England to inform them of our situation?" I asked the Pilot.

Surprisingly, all took up the request, which prompted an immediate response from the usually pugnacious Pilot.

"OK," he responded. "But we'll discuss it with the Lithuanian officer only, so it doesn't appear so demanding," he added.

"I can't believe what you're saying. We're here because of these bastards. They should be licking our boots! You have it the other way around," I retorted.

His response was a look of displeasure when the rest of the crew backed my words with a "Yeah, yeah."

He mumbled something that sounded like, "My day will come."

The next morning, he made his request to the Lithuanian officer. His answer was the lack of a facility in Turek to fulfill our request.

"Maybe in Warsaw or Lodtz, we will find the necessary equipment," he added.

One piece of unsolicited information resulted from these conversations. Warsaw, and Lodtz were mentioned as cities we were to visit. It was obvious, plans were being made to move us.

After breakfast, Novak approached me.

"I overheard your Pilot's request for a message to be radioed to England. Do not tell your Pilot, because I can see he is afraid to ask for anything. I can smuggle a card out of Warsaw, to the United States. I will get some cards, but only give them to ones not afraid of consequences if Pilot finds out," he cautioned.

Novak supplied postcards that evening, with the same precaution posed earlier. I thought we should all have the same opportunity, and requested the Co-Pilot to inquire if the rest of the officers, including the Pilot, wanted to participate. To my surprise, all agreed. At breakfast, we slipped our filled out cards to Novak, without the knowledge of the Lithuanian officer or Helena.

It's funny how one can acquire a feeling of mistrust for a person you hardly know. That was the feeling I had for Helena, but not for Novak. Maybe his willingness to help us, bought him a little more respect. Helena's demeanor was smug, and full of outward confidence, as if she had a free hand afforded to her by a higher authority. The fact that she ate the same crap as we, and confirmed my complaints to my Pilot, only added to my suspicions that we were being placated.

Days of the week were just that - days, one following the other. Saturday night we were asked if any of us desired to attend mass after breakfast. We who agreed were escorted by an armed guard through the snow covered streets to a small building with a Cathedral architectural appearance. The ornate design of the interior spoke to the obvious skills of the builders.

We were seated in a pew at Altar level, with Novak seated next to me. The old Priest who was saying Mass came over to shake our hands, and said something in Polish to Novak.

Novak in response looked at us, and asked if any of us was interested in assisting, by serving Mass as an altar boy.

I nodded in the affirmative. The Priest smiled graciously, and made the sign of the Cross over me as I arose to take my place at the foot of the Altar. To be part of the Mass placed a feeling of security in my heart, and I prayed the feeling would be instilled in all of us.

After Mass, all the parishioners approached us with heartfelt warmth and affection. Hugs and kisses were commonplace, and their unexpected knowledge of the English language fortified the strength of their friendly behavior. We ventured out of the Church into the cold, and they followed, surrounding us with a cordon of loving gentleness.

The cold was beginning to penetrate to the bone, when I realized my head was uncovered. My ears were beginning to smart. I couldn't remember when I lost my flying helmet. I had no fatigue hat, but I knew where my Joe DiMaggio hat was, and it made me sick.

As if my predicament was emitting from my numbing brain, a Polish soldier, nudged his way through the crowd to me.

"Here take this," he said, as he placed a fur hat upon my head.

I recognized it as a Polish officer's hat, which I removed to examine more closely. Its warmth was readily visible from the fur-lined makeup. The Polish Medallion affixed to it was an added surprise. For some reason the hat upon my head and my flying gear must have had a comical connotation, they all seemed to be pointing to it, and smiling with an air of satisfaction.

"Why are they smiling?" I asked Novak.

"They are smiling because you now appear as one of them. They believe more Americans are coming to free them from the Russians." He concluded with, in a whispered voice, "We were better off with the Germans in command."

I didn't have time to pursue his statement any further, but it rang with a tone of discontent.

As we were led down the street to our place of confinement, we were detoured to the side of the street as a column of raggedly dressed men and what appeared to be young boys with arms raised over their heads, approached us. The armed guards were definitely Russian, and their presence caused a retreat by the civilians, in all directions, as we remained alone with our escort.

As the guarded group reached our position, they stopped, and the fact that they were lashed together by a chain identified them as prisoners. The lead Russian walked towards us. His rank was not identifiable to me, but the row of ribbons adorning his chest, made him at least a combat veteran. He asked he Pole who was guarding us a question in Russian which needed no interpretation. The questioning tone, and the word "Amerikanski," made the query clear: "Are these the Americans I heard about?"

Then as if to establish his authority, he bellowed a command to his contingent, and they nudged their prisoners to a semblance of attention. These prisoners weren't in the best of shape. They appeared tired, cold, and most of all, frightened. Some appeared at least in their late fifties or sixties. The young ones looked like our grammar school kids.

We never found out what was said to these poor wretches, or what action brought on the next incident. They were suddenly recoiling into a protective retreat, and appeared to be begging for their lives.

The Russian officer laughed haughtily. This prompted the guards to commence poking the prisoners with the business ends of their Burp guns. We felt this was all a show for our benefit, but the next incident left a sinking, sickly feeling of contempt for the Russians engraved on my mind.

One of the shackled prisoners threw himself to the ground, and crawled as far as his chains would permit towards the Russian officer. With his arms outstretched in a pleading posture, he grasped the officer's leg. Without a feeling of compassion, the officer drew his leg back, and kicked the man directly in his face. The man flew backwards into his companions, blood gushing from his mouth and nose. He regained his feet and again attempted to approach the officer. He dropped to his knees, with hands clasped as in prayer. The sounds emitting through his smashed mouth and gushing blood were the sounds of a man fearing imminent death. His fears were soon realized, as the officer snatched a Burp gun from one of the guards and readily cut the prisoner in half, discharging a steady burst right up his middle, from his groin to his face. His body was catapulted back into his companions, who scattered as far as their confining chains would permit, but who could not escape the blood, flesh, and bone of one of God's children.

"He was not going to be killed, he was frightened because they were told by retreating German officers to fight to death. The Russians will kill you if you are captured." Novak went on to explain, "The Russian officer was annoyed by his persistence, and your presence embarrassed him. He had to show who was in command. The Russians only put the young and old prisoners to work, to free the able bodied Poles and Russians to pursue the retreating Germans," he concluded.

It was a bitter pill to swallow. We relayed the incident to the men who weren't present, and as one, they were happy not to have witnessed the scene.

Our discussion of the callous disregard for human life by the Russians prompted the Pilot to use the situation as a tool to chastise me.

"They could just as easily blow us away if you continue to press them and disregard their authority," he whispered in an almost frightened voice.

I made no attempt to qualify his continuous utterances that belittled his role as an American officer, our existence, and purpose for being here. Out of nowhere Helena appeared, and approached me with an attitude of unconcern for all the others present. She took me by the hand, led me to a chair in the far corner of the room.

"Sit down," she ordered, and I obeyed, knowing I must have had a look that said "What the hell?"

"I have noticed the laceration on your jaw appears infected," she volunteered. "I know where I can obtain medicine to help healing, but I will have to travel to Gydenia, by train.

"You will have to help me to get seat on train. Since the Russians have over run this area, the released prisoners of war are returning to their respective homes. The railroad is main means of transportation, and is loaded to capacity," she continued.

"If I wait for military clearance, it will take days, and rumor has it you will be on move in a few days. There will be no opportunity to obtain medicine, when we leave Turek."

"How can I help?" I asked.

"The Polish military control the movement of trains in this area. You know how much they respect you Americans. They would without question assist you in any request you made, if humanly possible," she insisted.

She concluded with, "Novak will come with us. He will escort you back, if we are lucky and I get seat on train."

The endeavor meant leaving our sanctuary and alienating my Pilot. To ask his permission, and possibly be refused, decided our format. We would make our way to the railroad marshaling yard in early morning the next day; it was within walking distance.

It was a cold but beautiful clear morning. Blue skies were accentuated by white puffy clouds and snow-covered earth. After breakfast, as always, everyone returned to their rooms for their morning defecation. We used this opportunity to exit discreetly from a rear door, led by Helena, after obtaining the necessary clothing.

The walk was uneventful, cold but exhilarating, and a feeling a freedom prevailed as I crunched through the snow. A flash of this scene jogged my memory to my days on Staten Island, as I crunched through the snow, dragging my sled to the top of a hill, for a cold, but exhilarating ride of free living.

Our arrival at the railroad yard presented a sight we could not imagine in our wildest dreams. There were three trains side by side, standing on spur tracks off the main line. They were surrounded by armed soldiers, beating back the thousands of people, men, women, and children, who dragged their meager possessions, and pleaded, begged, for a place on the train.

The inner bowels of the trains were filled to and beyond their capacity. How they survived suffocation was only God's will. Every conceivable area which could hold a person and his earthly possessions within and outside of the train had a human being clutching on for his or her life.

Helena located the train headed for Gydenia, and singled out a Polish officer, who appeared in command. She told us to remain where we were, as she made her way through the milling crowd to the officer. We were unable to hear the conversation, but the smile on the officer's face, and his glance towards Novak and I with what appeared to be a consenting nod, indicated success. The officer and Helena made their way to us. He pointed to the American flag on my sleeve with the acknowledgement "Amerkanski," then shook my hand. Then with almost a childlike giggle, he pointed to my headgear, with the Polish Medallion, then hugged me with a feeling of satisfaction.

Through Helena he informed us he couldn't possibly get her a seat inside any of the cars on the Gydenia train. The passengers all had military passes; to remove anyone would ensure a riot. He hoped to find a place on the coal tender, close to the Engineer, where she would be protected from some of the scum who robbed and raped the poor refugees every chance they get. The Engineer and his crew were protected by an armed escort, and he would attempt to get Helena within that protected area.

He disappeared for a short period, and returned with a smile that spelled success. We all walked to the front of the Gydenia train, where Helena was lifted by two Polish soldiers to the confines of the coal tender.

The Gydenia train was the first to move, with a blast of its whistle. We felt a feeling of safety for Helena as she waved good-bye. The Polish soldiers raised their arms in the form of a "V," the sign of victory.

The blast of the whistle, the belching of steam, the spinning wheels seeking traction, turned the scene into utter confusion, turned humans into animals. They rushed the cordon of soldiers protecting the perimeters of the train. The soldiers first responded with shots into the air, and found themselves overrun. They resorted to shooting point blank into the wave of humanity, causing the white snow to be blotched with blood.

The train left its siding and entered the main line, with screaming men and women pulling others from the train in an attempt to get aboard. The train's armed guards and the posted soldiers opened fire as the train picked up speed, leaving dead and wounded in its wake. The soot-laden smoke of the engine obliterated the sight of its clinging human cargo, and cast a shadow over the pall of death left behind.

Witnessing this carnage, and realizing the sacrifice Helena was making for me personally, befriended her to me.

CHAPTER 14 — INFAMY: THE DEATH OF A CITY

It was late the next day when Helena rejoined us. She had a broad smile on her face, extending a package towards me as she approached. All felt a feeling of relief at her presence, especially after the horrible picture I painted of the marshalling yard at her departure.

Helena explained how much easier it was to obtain passage on her return: "The trains were almost empty, except for Polish soldiers, who gave me no trouble."

Even though I witnessed what appeared a sacrifice on her part, her attitude of complacency somehow revived the feeling that she was playing both ends from the middle.

When I opened the package she presented, the first objects that were obvious to all were the tailored made cigarettes, and a bottle of Brandy. The cigarettes were Russian, somewhat like an English cigarette, a hollow tube of cardboard with a slim portion of paper-wrapped tobacco attached. The tobacco was thinly packed, and we found, those of us who smoked, that smoking two or three at a time afforded you a small resemblance to American cigarettes.

Helena reached into the package, retrieving a smaller one contained therein, and with the same motion grabbing my arm and leading me away from the others. She gleefully produced some salve which looked like zinc ointment. She immediately applied it to the laceration on my face. The gentleness of her touch, which appeared loving, confused my thinking. I really wanted to fully appreciate her actions as platonic, and not subterfuge.

She modestly slipped the toothbrush and toothpaste into my jacket pocket. "I am sorry, but I could get but one toothbrush," she whispered into my ear. I would swear it was no accident, that I felt her kiss my ear as she whispered.

The next day at breakfast we were informed of their intentions to move us out. Where to wasn't clearly specified. The feeling that we weren't forgotten was received with mixed emotions.

"Shit," the Pilot said, "I could sweat out the war right here. The action is moving away from us, we are being treated well...why move?"

His reasoning may have been selfish, or self-serving, but his comment "being well treated" was a negative exemplification of our future treatment.

The possibility of being moved became official when our friend the Lithuanian officer asked us to gather our belongings and prepare to move at a moment's notice. Our belongings were meager, but his intent was accepted.

About an hour later, we were directed to proceed to the front of the building, where a vehicle would be waiting for our trip to wherever. The vehicle was easily identifiable: a Dodge 5X5 troop carrier. We climbed aboard, I with an air of "let's get going," the others with "only because we have to."

The driver appeared a veteran of the wars, but not a veteran of chauffeuring. Starting the vehicle was accompanied by a continuous stomping of the accelerator which produced the flooding of the engine. The odor of gasoline substantiated the end result. His utterances were in Russian, but interpretation weren't necessary.

The Pilot, seated beside him, conveyed the idea to wait for the flooding to subside by removing his right foot from the accelerator. Waiting a minute or two, the Pilot, with a wave of his hand in an OK attitude, suggested the driver try again. As the driver prepared to stomp the accelerator, the Pilot grabbed his leg, in an almost comical situation. The Pilot was holding on in an almost desperate life-saving struggle, the driver continually attempting to free his leg to reach the accelerator. The engine started. A look of contentment was etched on the driver's face, and there was a curling at the corners of his mouth, which could almost be considered a smile.

It suddenly struck me: the absence of Helena, Novak, and most of all, the replacement waist gunner. I looked to the Pilot for an explanation.

"I forgot to mention it, but the Lithuanian officer told me he came down with a high temperature. It was diagnosed as Scarlet Fever. They will treat him, and move him out as soon as possible, with the chance he may catch up with us before we leave Russia." He concluded with, "I asked if I could remain behind, but they thought it best I remain with you, since I was the ranking officer."

I thought to myself, "Some shit." It must have killed him to lose the opportunity to kill some more time.

The motor was running, but it was apparently not running on all cylinders. We chugged along for a few blocks before the absence of Novak was rectified by his presence on a corner.

He looked pathetic in a quilted jacket three sizes too large. The rags wrapped around his feet "are to insulate my thin soled boots from the intense cold anticipated during our forthcoming travels," he explained.

"Where is Helena?" the Pilot asked.

"She will meet us at our next destination, but I do not know where that is at this time," Novak answered.

After witnessing her ordeal at the railroad yard, th inconvenience of riding in an open truck could not be her reason for not being here. My mind again was doing an about face: friend or foe?

The grinding of the gears announced the attempt by the driver to get the truck moving. He succeeded only when he remembered to depress the clutch, and his coordination of clutching was akin to body action prior to an orgasm. It was but a moment later when all movement associated with the truck's mobility ceased.

We were dead, not in the water as the cliche goes, but dead in snowy sub-zero climate.

The driver opened the hood as if he knew what he was doing. This thought was obliterated from our minds when he removed the radiator cap and peered inside. His automotive knowledge was exemplified when he checked the water in the battery, then returned to the cab and blew the horn. I wondered if we had fuel; this idiot probably didn't have any idea what made the engine run. I checked the fuel gauge; it read full. Someone at the motor pool knew enough to fill the tank before issuing the truck.

Through Novak, the Pilot instructed the driver to acquire another truck. We would return to our quarters, since we were only a few blocks away. His suggestion was reasonable, but his motive seemed self serving to me. Whatever his intent, it was soon crushed when the Engineer, seated over the gasoline tank, noticed the absence of a gasoline cap for the filler tube. The absence of the cap wasn't the cause of my laughter, but the substitute being used. There was a rag stuffed in the neck of the tank's filler tube, but even that wasn't the apparent cause of the vehicle's demise. It was when I started to remove the rag cap that the necessary surgery was being performed to instill life in this dead vehicle. It became obvious that the yards of cloth I removed from the gas tank hindered and finally blocked the fuel flow from tank to engine.

Novak suggested to the driver that he attempt to start the engine after the cloth was removed from the tank.

"He says the Pilot ordered him to get new truck, and he will do so," Novak explained.

"Tell him the problem is fixed," I retorted.

The officers were the only ones dismounting from the truck as Novak convinced the driver to hit the starter. The roar of the engine stopped everyone moving in their tracks. A haughty laugh from the driver, along with a jubilant clap of his hands, joined the roar of the engine as it coughed and sputtered to life. It was like he had just won the war. It was music to my ears, but I had reservations about the feelings of the others.

We had been traveling a few hours, when the driver pulled into what appeared to be a sentry post guarding the road. The gun emplacements now abandoned, the massive bomb craters and the German dead scattered about the area depicted a scene of heavy fighting, not too long before. The lone sentry approached our driver, and they exchanged a few words.

The conversation was interpreted by Novak. "We are approaching Warsaw, it has been cleared enough for us to pass through."

If we had known before hand that we would witness this devastation and the desecration perpetrated upon people and a city, in what we were to believe was a civilized world, we certainly would have bypassed this symbol of unforgiving horror.

In a very few minutes, Novak exclaimed aloud, "In the distance you can make out the silhouette of Warsaw."

If the silhouette etched against the blue clear sky on the horizon was Warsaw, my eyes were seeing something that I not have imagined. What faced us was a pile of rubble, with bulldozed paths to afford passage. Even the great cities bombed incessantly by our heavy bombers were not so completely obliterated, and the stench of human dead permeated the area, even in sub-zero weather.

Whatever respect I'd had for the Russians became a lie, when I realized the architect of this infamous act of destroying a great city was the Russian refusal to assist the beleaguered Poles and Jews when they revolted against the Germans, with the expectation of advancing Russians to assist them. The Russians had thumbed their noses at them, as the Germans gathered up the equipment we had dropped to them in preparation for their revolt. The Germans then proceeded to systematically, block by block, destroy Warsaw, burying the dead and living into what remained: a garbage heap, a monument to the courage of a free people, and a monument to an infamous act, both by enemy and ally.

CHAPTER 15 — BE OUR GUEST

As the carnage of Warsaw faded from sight, the stench of the dead remained in our clothing, and appeared to cling to the hairs in our nostrils. A good bath and change of clothing would probably reduce the physical ills, but nothing could erase the picture indelibly imprinted in my mind of what man could do to man and the reasons he conjured up to absolve himself from the guilt of his actions.

We passed through some small clusters of buildings, which were not unlike temporary dwellings set up by the military during occupation. The driver guided our vehicle to a large cinder block building, which emitted steam from a stack on its roof. We dismounted from the truck, stretched, and as one, looked questioningly at each other as if to say, "What's next?"

We were escorted into a dimly lit room, which was damp with moisture laden air. Through the dim light I saw military clothing hanging from hooks on the far wall.

I approached the clothing, pulling Novak with me. "Russian?" I asked.

"Russian tank commanders," he answered, then added, "You are in for rare treat, believe me."

Before I could question his remarks, a man wearing a fatigue jump suit spoke to Novak, who repeated his words almost simultaneously in English, "Remove all your clothing, and hang them on the hooks at the far wall." These instructions were followed with the issue of a towel.

Novak instructed us to use them, let them dry and keep for our travels, then added jokingly to guard them with our lives.

We all stripped down and wrapped the towels around our middles. We were led through a double door, which when opened emitted a cloud of swirling steam. Novak was in constant conversation with the fatigue wearing individual, who certainly was the custodian of this operation.

"Move to the room to your left, where we will be deloused," Novak directed, then added, "Our clothes are being treated at the same time."

We obeyed as instructed. I wondered what condition our electrically wired suits would be in after delousing. We were sprayed with some powered ingredient, then led to a room containing showers, which were graciously received as they washed away the residue of the delousing powder and the odor of death.

From the shower room we were led through another set of double doors, and it was here that Novak stated, "Now comes the rare treat."

"What the hell are you talking about?" I asked as the doors were pushed open.

The swirling steam was, as expected, warm to the feel, and obscured our sight. The most obvious surprise was the feminine voices permeating the steam, from silhouetted figures in a variety of relaxed positions. The motion of the swinging double doors, and our physical movement entering the room, caused a swirling disruption of the steam-laden air. This action, and becoming accustomed to the dimly lit room, presented a picture of what Novak called "a rare treat."

I didn't know, nor did I venture a guess, what was his definition of the word "treat."

The sight of nude women, some towel draped, others naked as jaybirds, might have instilled a amorous arousal in our limp genitals, but the sight of these gargantuan, unfeminine appearing persons effected a retreat of both body and body parts.

Almost as one, their reaction was one of friendliness, as they approached us with outstretched hands, smiling with giggly laughter. Our reaction was an abrupt halt to our retreat, and an extension of our hands in salutation. Their response was to continue past our extended hands, and reach for our private parts. My thoughts of what they were thinking seemed obvious; we were scrawny compared to these muscular unfeminine tank commanders, and it was a comical situation as we attempted to withdraw from their advances. They gleefully pinched our buttocks, and grabbed us in lovingly bear hugs. This all ended when out of nowhere, a masculine voice bellowed a command in Russian, which caused an immediate response by all the women to exit the room.

Our conversation turned to the physical appearance of the departed women, and all but I felt their actions were of ridicule. I explained that as a worker in a shipyard as a welder prior to being called up for Pilot training, I was witness to Russian ships coming into the Bethlehem Shipyard on Staten Island, for repairs. Their crews were almost entirely made up of these masculine women.

Novak substantiated my statement with, "He is right. There are few pretty women in service, only because the Russian Government forbids the production of beautifying essentials. The women must be war productive."

Our Navigator was a real good looking guy, and from past experiences was the real lover of our crew. His conversation after returning from leave to London was always sex related.

"How was your stay in London?" someone would ask.

Before he could answer, we in unison would answer, "I don't remember. I hit the first pub, got drunk, tied into a gorgeous blond for a couple of Hershey bars and a few sticks of gum. Got laid, relayed, and parlayed, with all the pop corn I could eat."

His response to our description of the Russian tank commanders was, "They are probably good at blow jobs."

We laughed, but Novak added, "Do not be surprised if you get your chance. We will be here a few days, and they will come looking for you."

We remained in the steam room for about twenty minutes, just milling about in an apprehensive mood, but appreciating the beneficial results of the cleansing steam. We were instructed by Novak to exit the room and retrieve our clothing. They were a little damp, but the smell of death was missing, to our collective relief.

We were escorted by armed guard to an adjoining building and a second floor room, dormitory in appearance, with rows of bunks.

Novak instructed us, "Stow your gear. We are to be fed in the mess hall downstairs."

Again escorted by armed guards, we were led to a large room, similar to the mess halls associated with the military of all branches. We were assigned a table next to a table occupied by only Russian officers. Looking about, I was surprised to find this mess hall wasn't only for the military; more than half was occupied by civilians.

"What are civilians doing here?" I asked Novak.

"This is a way station for displaced persons, being routed to their respective home areas. Most are released prisoners of war, others are civilian workers used by the Russians in behind the lines occupation, and are no longer needed," he explained.

"From now on we are under Russian jurisdiction, and must comply with their every order."

As an aside, Novak added, "Do not forget the fact that you are an ally, and your status warrants respect. Please remember my respect for you Americans. I never suggested any advice contrary to the instructions from the Russians I conveyed to you."

It soon became obvious that our presence adjoining the Russians made no impression on them. If they felt any comradeship, or even plain inquisitiveness, they sure as hell concealed it.

We discussed the situation amongst ourselves, and all but the Pilot agreed that the treatment we received from the Polish command, even with Russians present, was more congenial.

"Don't get involved in controversy, they are probably acting under orders," the Pilot directed.

"Yeah, orders to shit on us. Don't you realize to them we're no more important than the displaced persons we are thrown in with, and they want us to know it?" I suggested.

The Pilot bellowed, his tone and loudness causing heads to turn by everyone within hearing distance, which appeared to effect the whole mess hall. "You watch your fucking mouth. Pretend we're just another group of displaced persons and we'll sweat out the war traveling."

Novak, who understood English, glanced at me with a look of concern. The others of the crew neither showed consent nor dissent. I felt I may be attaching too much importance to the actions of the Russians toward an ally, especially we Americans. However, it didn't take long for their actions to cause even the Pilot, and those who may have agreed with him, to reconsider their evaluation of our position.

The food was in the process of being served, and without a doubt the table of the Russian officers was served first, as was expected. The next action was obviously one of disdain, substantiating my words "shit on us." They served the whole mess hall before even setting up our table.

Wine was served to the Russians, and the Pilot volunteered, "They haven't received their food yet. We'll probably be served the same thing they get."

"We'll probably get the same crap being served the displaced persons. It's no different from the shit we've been getting all along," I responded.

After the second wine serving, the Russians, in a "fuck you" attitude, turned as one and raised their empty glasses in our direction. It was at this juncture that utter contempt was displayed for our status, and a bullet through the heart would have been more acceptable.

Placed on the Russian table was a canned ham: "Armour."

"Why still in the can?" I asked myself.

"Except to rub it in," I answered myself.

Their intent was realized when the canned ham was removed, and a platter of sliced cooked ham replaced it, with accompanying plates of vegetables.

The rest of the people present, both military and civilians, were being served the type of food that was not as appetizing as the food served the adjacent table, though it appeared as palatable as the food usually served at mass messes of military establishments. We felt that the food served us should be at least the same calibre.

The table of Russian officers were being served what looked like tea, or what might be ersatz coffee. The accompanying service of peach halves caused an inquisitive glance to be exchanged between us, which was punctuated with a simultaneous, "Can you beat this shit?"

Almost without warning, a small portable serving cart appeared beside our table. It was almost with disdain or as an after thought that food was placed upon our table. This belated action caused all heads to turn in our direction, as the food was obviously intended to demean our status in the eyes of the beholder. The food wasn't the type you would serve your enemy, let alone your ally.

Here again were the unidentifiable greens, beets, potatoes, black bread, with the accompanying lard and apple butter. Those who were close enough to witness the food served us began to murmur amongst themselves. The murmuring grew in intensity throughout the mess hall. The intensity grew when word spread that Americans were present, and the feeling was that we were being mistreated. A Russian officer, feeling the uneasiness that prevailed, arose from his adjoining table with a glass held in a toast facing our table.

He spoke in both Russian and Polish. His words were interpreted by Novak.

"We have with us some American airmen, whom we welcome as our guests," he bellowed, then sat down.

We all felt belittled: not one word explaining the reason for our presence, not one mention of being an ally. It was apparent that the Russian displaced persons knew better than to applaud, but the Polish people stood as one and applauded with sincere enthusiasm. which only subsided when a gruff order to desist came from the Russian officer.

As we poked through our meal, the final gesture of contempt was exposed. Placed on the adjoining table was a carton of Lucky Strike cigarettes, boxed in the original color that created the cliche, "Lucky Strike green has gone to war." Our hopes for a similar treat for we who smoked were dashed by the bag of shredded tobacco and paper towel paper placed on our table.

The attempt of any civilian to approach us was thwarted by a cordon of armed guards, who suddenly surrounded our table.

CHAPTER 16 — MISPLACED DISPLACED PERSONS

The guards herded us through the milling, pushing people who were trying to reach us. Although we were happy to be escorted out of this chaotic condition, we stopped almost as one when voices were heard above the din that was meaningless to us. Salutations of, "Good luck, we'll get together, we're American and British" were heard. Straining to locate these voices was almost impossible, as we were ushered out of the room with an attitude bordering on violent. As I scanned the crowd, the closest I came to any resemblance of a voice matching the body of an American or British origin was a couple of jumping civilian-dressed individuals to the rear of the hall.

We were escorted to our dormitory, and Novak translated to us what was a gruff order from our escort: "Remain here until further orders." As the guard exited the room, we could hear the door lock being bolted.

It was hard not to feel the embarrassment, indignation, and the need to vent your feelings regardless of the consequences.

"How long are we going to put up with this crap?" I directed to all, hoping for some sign of agreement.

There was no outcry of agreement, but the questioning looks towards the Pilot seemed to spell out, "Where do we go from here?"

Feeling somewhat pressured to furnish leadership, he responded with, "This appears to be a temporary juncture in our travels. Let's wait until we feel a more permanent situation."

His words made sense; we accepted. What was more acceptable to me was his demeanor towards our hosts. He readily admitted that the stories circulated after the shuttle run to supply the beleaguered Poles and Jews in Warsaw, by returning airmen, were not exaggerated; the Russians were not great hosts.

It's hard to describe the activities of eight men thrown into a situation of uncertainty and mistrust. The conversation was sporadic, and usually with no substance constructed to appease the situation. The status of the war was a mystery to us, except that the Russians never missed an opportunity to inform us of their almost unhindered slaughter of the retreating Germans.

We would attempt to calculate the missions we would have flown, had we not been shot down. Of course the bottom line would be, had we survived the rest of our missions, we would have completed our combat tour, and we would be on our way home.

I had dozed off while lying on my cot, trying to kill some meaningless time. I was awakened by a voice of Russian origin, which was being directed towards Novak.

"Believe it or not," Novak translated, "we are invited to an impromptu entertainment session in the mess hall, in about an hour.

"You do not have to attend, but if you do not, you must remain in this room locked in. Those of you who choose to attend, must remain in close proximity of each other, and station yourselves to the extreme rear of the hall. You are forbidden to converse with any of the other people attending," Novak concluded.

"They must feel there is some danger, and are taking every precaution to protect us," the Pilot volunteered. "I for one am not going."

"I'm going. Anything to break away from this confinement. We might just as well be prisoners of war. Who else feels a break is needed?" I asked.

The Engineer and ball turret gunner followed my lead, and agreed to accept the invitation. Novak also accepted.

We were escorted to the mess hall, which was jammed to capacity. The only vantage point remaining was just outside the double doors which afforded entrance from the rear of the hall.

The guard suggested we remain there, and left us to our own devices with, "Remain here. I will return after the show. Be here," he ordered through Novak.

Since there was no elevated stage, the performers were at floor level, causing the audience to be constantly shifting position to get a piecemeal view of the act in progress. Most of the acts were acrobatic in nature, or Slovak and Russian dancing Their actions appeared from our vantage point as so many bobbing heads and waving arms.

The accompanying music, although not of American origin, had a Polka beat, which was acceptable. The professed comedian could have been the funniest in the world, but the language barrier was only breached when those who understood the lingo laughed.

With the response of laughter and applause came a feeling of being anywhere but the situation we were in. It was like attending a movie on a military base when the lights went out. The lighted screen obliterated the mass of military garb, placing you in an imaginary world coinciding with the make believe world on the screen. It was only when the show ended, and the lights came on, that reality was restored.

As time passed, and the odor of smoke permeated the air, I felt the urge for a cigarette. The paper and tobacco we had was back in our room, and although we desired a smoke, none of us felt the urge badly enough to return to our room. I looked around, hoping to discover a friendly smoking face. We resigned ourselves to the fact the only taste of smoke we would have was the smoke inhaled by breathing deeply of the smoke laden air. We all agreed that the odor was familiar, not foreign, but American. Our suspicions were soon visibly substantiated when a man removed a canvas bag tightly vised between his ankles. He unbuckled a restraining strap, threw open the flap, then searching through its contents exposed the open end of a cigarette carton. With a pick pocket's deftness, he removed one pack of "Lucky Strike Green" cigarettes. In almost the same action, he quickly glanced about him to insure no detection, and secured the bag with a slight of hand that was a wonder to behold.

"Do you think he would give us a couple smokes, if we asked?" I inquired of Novak.

Novak's response was odd: "Possibly if I identified you as Americans, but you know the Russian's orders. I would chance losing my assignment."

Not wanting to place Novak in any jeopardy, we dropped the issue, but I was personally seething inside. My only thought was of a feasible plan to share that man's good fortune.

We arrived at the point where the appearance of our escort to return us to our room would be welcome when out of nowhere appeared two men in civilian clothes, who grasped our hands in friendship and hugged us like we were lost relatives.

"Maybe we'll get some action now," one said in perfect English.

The other added, "You have officers with you, Air Force officers. They should carry some clout." His accent was undoubtedly British. "We are the guys who yelled to you in the mess hall. We hoped to get close to you, for we need your help," he pleaded.

"How come you are in civilian clothes," I asked, "and traveling with displaced persons?"

"There are thousands of us in the same circumstances. We were prisoners of war, in Germany and Poland. As the Russians overran the Stalags, they just turned us loose and pointed in the direction of freedom, with the instructions, 'You are on you own.'"

"The only transportation available was the transportation afforded the displaced persons. Men in uniform of any allied country were given no courtesy or guidance of any kind. As a matter of fact their actions bordered on belligerency and disdain," the American explained.

The American identified himself as an infantry Staff Sergeant, captured in Italy.

"I had a head wound, a fractured skull, caused by an anti-tank shell that bounced off my tin hat without exploding," he explained. "Left for dead, I was picked up by the Germans, who operated on me, and saved my life," he continued.

To document his story, he removed the cap he was wearing to expose a shaved portion of his head replete with the stitched scalpel wound, and the indentation reinforced by a steel plate.

"From the way we have been treated by the Russians up to the present, I thank God that the Germans picked me up," he said in almost an unintelligible whisper.

The English soldier was a rugged looking red head who related the story of his capture in Africa, and how he escaped once, returned to his command, was again captured in Crete. He escaped when confined to a Crete Stalag, was recaptured again, and removed to a more secure Stalag in Germany. There he was isolated as a trouble maker, and spent most of his time in solitary confinement.

"I am regular army, a professional soldier. My intent is to kill the enemy to get this bloody war over with. I have no intention of shirking my duty," he related with an air of pride.

"As my friend the American sergeant will testify, there are many released prisoners of war who are using their new found freedom to plunder, rape, and even kill, not the enemy, but anyone or anything which will satisfy their lust sexually or materially," he concluded.

We listened in awe, I with mixed emotions: disbelief, disgust, and an inward fear for the future.

We belatedly introduced ourselves, and explained our plight in regard to the lack of assistance afforded us by the Russians to return us to our command.

"The only difference between we and you, is our being kept together under guard, and our movements are controlled. This format is a lot easier to stomach than being on your own, unless you are in the class of the degenerates you previously described," I offered.

Their motive for approaching us was being volunteered, but the arrival of our escort within hearing distance broke it off. Realizing that being seen together might cause a problem, we separated discreetly. The escort asked if we would like to return to our quarters.

We responded in the negative. "We would like to remain for the balance of the show." My companions nodded in agreement, and Novak relayed our decision to the guard.

The escort shrugged his shoulders in an attitude of agreement, and walked off.

After a few minutes the guard faded from sight, and our new found friends eased their way through the congregation of cheering and laughing people. If not placed in the right context in your mind, it could be misconstrued as a totally happy event. They explained that they would shed their concealing outer garments and readily identify their military assignments if we would assist them in requesting from the Russians permission to travel with our group to wherever we were designated.

"All we can promise," I answered, "would be to convey your request to our Pilot, then get back to you."

This promise ended the conversation in that light, and all I could think of at this time was the Lucky Strike cigarettes so near, and yet so far. I conveyed my thoughts to our new found friends. The Englishman asked that I point out the target, and I did so. Before I could stop him, if my intentions were to do so, he had sided up to the target. He appeared to have waited until the cheering, and jumping throng were intent on viewing a group of acrobats performing on the stage. His slight of hand, and the deft cut he sliced in the canvas bag, could be described as a surgical masterpiece. It surely wasn't an appendix he removed, but had it been, the patient wouldn't have felt a thing.

He sided up to us, nudged us into the hallway, slipped the carton of Lucky Strikes under my jacket, and departed with, "We'll get together soon."

I went out into the show area, after giving our new found treasure to one of my companions, to locate our escort. He was in the process of locating us, and the bedlam behind him caused him great concern for our well being.

"Let us get out of here, where are the rest of you?" he asked through Novak.

"In the main hallway," Novak responded.

"What the hell is going on out there?" I inquired.

The answer was relayed through Novak. "Someone had his cigarettes stolen, and he is challenging everyone with a very large knife, causing a mass riot."

God, I thought, have we become no better than the degenerates described to us?

CHAPTER 17 — JOIN THE CLUB

The escort ushered us to our dormitory, and believe me, when we entered our room and the door was locked behind us, was the first time I accepted being locked in.

The anxiety showed, and the comment, "Let's have a real smoke," as he produced the pilfered cigarettes from beneath his jacket, caused a swarming mass of bodies to witness the exposed treasure.

"Where in hell did you get them?" the Pilot asked, with a look of surprise that reeked of anger.

Not wanting to go into detail, I volunteered before the others could speak. "An English soldier and an American Sergeant, traveling with the displaced persons, gave us the cigarettes with a string attached. We are to discuss it with you," I added.

"String attached? Discuss with me? What in God's name are you talking about?" the Pilot asked, with that usual "what have you involved me in now?" look.

"They are what I said they are, an English soldier and an American Sergeant, released prisoners of war, liberated by the advancing Russians, instructed to find their own way. They are wearing civilian clothing to hide their military identity, thus being able to travel with the displaced persons. The traveling facilities are somewhat shoddy, but at least controlled, is the way they explained it," I repeated what was told to me.

"What do they expect from me? We're not even able to help ourselves as yet," the Pilot queried.

"They would like you to intercede for them with the Russian authorities, to get them permission to travel with us. Not only to live their real identity, soldiers, but to disassociate themselves from the scum that has festered from embittered form of humanity," I pleaded their case.

I was surprised when he responded with, "I'll see what I can do. I have no idea where we are headed, but I would like to speak with them, before I stick my neck out for two strangers."

"Strangers?" I thought to myself. Not allies, "strangers". The Russian ideology must be catching, like a communicable disease. At least he didn't shut them out completely, which pleased me immensely. There is strength in numbers, and these two men in my mind were true soldiers who possessed more military skill than all of us put together.

As those who smoked enjoyed the taste of real tobacco, we told the sick story about the freed prisoners of war, vividly described by the two men we just met.

"You must realize that they may be playing on our sympathy, trying to use us to cover up their own misgivings," someone suggested.

The remainder of the evening for those who smoked, was spent framing visual memories in hallowed smoke. The next morning at breakfast the remnants of the activities after our discreet departure were visible, by the piles of broken chairs and tables against the far wall.

"What the hell happened here?" the Pilot asked.

The same question was framed in the faces of the others not privy to the cigarette episode, or the ensuing brawl. Remaining mute at this juncture delayed the threatening and haranguing speech we would receive if the Pilot knew the real cause of the incident. It was then our new found friends introduced themselves to the Pilot, who still remained curious about the remains of the brawl, ignoring their introduction.

"Do you guys have any idea of what happened here last night?"

His curiosity was so intense, I really believed he hoped their answer would implicate me.

"We know about as much as your crew members present. We left about the same time as they," the Sergeant replied. "All was quiet at that time."

"Yeah, until some bloody goon started to accuse everybody of clipping his bloody cigs. They were American smokes. The way he carried on, you would think he had his bloody name on them," the Englishman related.

"Where does he get the nerve to have American cigarettes? He must have stolen them," the Sergeant added.

The Pilot still wasn't going to let go, intent that the presence of the cigarettes we possessed placed at least me in the middle of the cause.

"Did you give cigarettes to any of my crew?" the Pilot asked, in a Clarence Darrow interrogation mode.

He was, in a way, attempting blackmail: the right answer if you want a favor done was the connotation, which thank God, our guests realized.

These two pros, as I had believed, politely and conclusively dispelled our involvement by stating, "We had an extra carton. All displaced persons were given cartons at our last stop by the Red Cross. Those who did not smoke bartered theirs for food or clothing."

The subject was dropped at that moment, but I could read his mind. "Wait until we are alone, you're not getting away with this shit."

The Pilot's attitude wasn't conducive to favor giving, and I realized that our friends were aware that their position at this time was very tentative. Feeling that this controversy might negate any opportunity for the Pilot to accede to their request, they admitted their part in the theft of the cigarettes.

"You jeopardized the safety of my crew, and now you want my help?" the Pilot responded in a chastising tone of voice.

"Come on," the Sergeant stated, "we're allies in a strange country. We must stick together, and most of all challenge their treatment of us."

"We don't want incidents such as this causing us to become the focal point of attention," stated the Pilot.

The Englishman volunteered, "The Russians will use these incidents to belittle you Americans, at every opportunity. They will attempt to discredit your importance in the war effort, by placing you in a humble, weak position. Your reluctance to challenge them adds credibility to their ridicule of you Americans."

"Well, I have no idea where we're headed. I'll try to find out. In the meantime, keep in touch. I'll let you know as soon as I have any worthwhile information," the Pilot informed them.

They thanked him for his concern, and we all proceeded to enter the chow line for breakfast.

It was during breakfast that the Pilot's curiosity about the disgraceful actions of the released prisoners of war while roaming through the German and Polish countryside was displayed. His interest prodded our new found friends into describing the most unimaginable, descriptive picture of man's inhumane treatment of another to satisfy one's greed or sexual lust. They told of robbing the dead, pillaging homes, committing cold blooded murder of civilians or isolated remnants of retreating Germans, stripping them of their valuables after they surrendered, killing them with their own weapons, raping the woman regardless of nationality, and thanking them in kind, even when welcomed as liberating saviors. Their reasoning for such degenerate behavior was to repay all the things perpetrated upon them during their incarceration.

As to the treatment of women, the contention of the renegade American POW's was that they were nothing but unpaid whores, having been screwed by anyone who controlled the area they were in.

We listened in utter disbelief, and the Pilot asked, "If what you say is true, why haven't the Russian or Polish authorities taken action?"

Without hesitation, the Sergeant answered, "Because they perpetrate the same crimes. Their actions are explained as spoils to the victors, and what's good for the goose is good for the gander.

"If and when you are moved, and by chance it is by train with the displaced persons, all that we have described will become vividly real. Any doubts you may have will be dispelled," he added emphatically.

"Well, fellows?" the Pilot asked. "We know where we come from, Airmen, how do you feel about having these guys join us?"

I was surprised he even considered our feelings. He was always so adamant as to who was in command. We all responded in the affirmative, and as one: "Join the team."

Somehow I felt the unanimous agreement, including the Pilot, was the result of an inward personal conviction. These men would add strength and fortitude in the ensuing days of travel.

CHAPTER 18 — THE INTERLOPERS

The rest of the day was spent locked in our dormitory, cat napping and talking idly with casual reference to the absorption of our traveling companions. For the first time during our position of what should be mutual trust and unanimous agreement at all times, we found ourselves solidly united. The Pilot consented to approach someone of authority at first opportunity.

The Pilot asked Novak if he would be able to get permission to leave our dormitory for the purpose of reaching out to someone of authority. We could then present our request with some chance of success. Novak knocked on the locked door; after a few minutes with no response, Novak pounded harder, and accompanied his pounding with a verbal tirade that needed no translation. Just his tone and facial expressions spelled out Polish or Russian demeaning epithets.

The door opened. There stood a menacing Russian, burp gun poised in a threatening manner. His bellowing voice seemed to say, "What the fuck do you pricks want?"

Novak, shielding his face with his hands, said something that sounded consoling in Russian, which caused the Russian not only lower his weapon, but etched a semblance of a smile in his otherwise ugly face. They exchanged dialogue, in what appeared to be friendly in most instances, but there were times it appeared the Russian was not agreeing with Novak - there were too many "nyets." Novak's responded by gesturing with both his hands and pointing to his chest, which I understood as, "Do not worry, I will take full responsibility."

"He is going to leave door unlocked accidently on purpose. Anyone who ventures outside, is on his own, and must accept his own fate," Novak explained.

"What fucking cooperation. If we only had some way to reciprocate," I volunteered.

"Under these circumstances, any action taken will be voluntary, including Novak," the Pilot declared.

Novak immediately stated, "I will go. I will have no problem moving about. His warning was directed to you, which is to protect his own ass.

"I can leave any time I choose. Leaving door unlocked was not necessary. I do not think he had any intention to leave door unlocked, which could be traced to him. He had hope of you doing something foolish, to put you in bad light."

The inquiry to get permission for our friends to accompany us in our future travels was a valid excuse to seek out some responsible authority, with the hopes they had knowledge of our future destination.

A cold, dreary morning was observed from our windows, and wet slushy snow covered the streets. Novak appeared shortly after breakfast, and informed us of his intent to fulfill our wishes that morning. He proceeded to, much to our amazement and disbelief, wrap his shoes with rags.

"What the hell are you doing?" I asked.

"My shoes are worn through. Paper inner soles are not much good when snow is wet," he explained.

"Wait a minute," I said, "we'll correct this problem," as I retrieved my GI shoes from under my cot.

Novak holding them in his hands brought a smile to his face, and haughty laughter from my companions. It was obvious that the shoes were many sizes too large.

"Don't look a gift horse in the mouth," I suggested. "Give them here."

I proceeded to use Novak's rag wrappings to stuff the shoes, thus reducing the extra area in the toes. Watching Novak with his stuffed GI brogues exit from the room, with a Charlie Chaplin gait, caused even the guard to enter into the combined chuckles, and laughter that followed his every step.

As we waited for some info from Novak's travels, we returned to our customary routine of idle conversation, and uneasy apprehension. This I compared to caged animals, out of their natural environment. Without realizing their actions, someone without thinking would try the locked door and finding it as such, would viciously kick the door in an act of retaliation.

Out of the blue, someone asked, "What the hell happened to Helena?"

I personally wondered the same thing, but I felt whatever, wherever, we had no control over her actions. I was grateful for the good she had done for me, but I always felt there was some ulterior motive.

It was hours later, just before dinner, when Novak returned. I think we all prayed for some hopeful information, not if permission was given concerning our adopted friends, but when or where we were to move. Novak's information wasn't very positive. It was the same as usual, conjecture, with the same theme as before: "Be patient," fortified with, "soon," end of message.

It appeared our inquisitiveness about the whereabouts of Helena must have possessed a telepathic intensity, for in walked Helena.

"I have good news for you," she said with a smile directed towards me. I embarrassingly watched all heads follow her words in my direction.

"You will be moving out in a day or two. I believe we will depart for Lodtz. A marshalling yard is located there. It will afford the necessary transportation to connect with other means to successfully get you home," she advised.

She sided up to me, and whispered, "I missed you," as she gently squeezed my hand.

"Please," I responded in a voice so low, if I didn't know what I was saying, I wouldn't have heard it myself.

"What did you say?" she asked.

I took her elbow, and nudged her gently away from the others. Taking her elbow as I did, must have felt to her like an endearing gesture, for her response was a cuddling action which was the opposite effect of my intent.

I realized that our actions were readily observable by everyone in the room. I had to, without the appearance of chastisement, convey to Helena that her concern could not be personal to me, especially in the areas of mutual interest. I emphasized the embarrassment it caused to all, and for her to use better judgement.

Surprisingly, and without one iota of repentance, she responded, as she looked directly at me, "My concern is for all, but my heart responds to you."

What the hell am I getting into? I thought. She must be some kind of nut, especially since somewhere in our conversations, I told her I was a newly married man.

As suddenly as she appeared, she was exiting the room, with a slight wave of her hand. As she stepped over the threshold, she turned gently towards me, touched her lips with her forefinger, and blew the kiss she planted thereon in my direction.

The motive for her personal attention to me couldn't possibly be sex. Our Navigator, single and good looking, propositioned her the first night in Turek, at our first meeting. Without disparaging his qualifications as a Navigator, this guy would fuck a snake if someone held it. He was rejected politely, and the result of his advance was quite a blow to his ego and reputation.

"Hell, her reason for refusing was because, 'I was too drunk, when you are sober,'" he quoted.

Knowing that the condition of all of us that night was no secret, but not being drunk since, belied his reasoning.

We were just milling around after breakfast the next day, delaying our return to our confinement, when we were approached by two men in civilian clothes. They were unshaven and scurvy looking, but their language was unmistakably not only English, but American English.

"Who's the leader of you glorious fly boys?" one asked in a disrespectful voice.

"I am," the Pilot answered. "What can I do for you?"

"My friend and I-" (gesturing towards his seedy looking companion) "-are American soldiers released from a German Stalag. We have no papers, not even dog tags to verify our identity. We want you to vouch for us, so we may travel with you," he added.

Without a chance for the Pilot to answer, he interrupted. "You fly boys seem to rate preferential treatment, and we want in," he concluded, in an obviously demanding posture.

"By the way," he directed to the Pilot, "what rank are you?"

"Second Lieutenant," he responded.

"Well, I'm a Captain in Airborne, so I out rank you. I'll do the talking from now on, and that goes for the rest of you glamour boys," he directed at us with a sneer that bordered on extreme hatred, or envy.

The Pilot didn't challenge him at this time. It was obvious a confrontation at present would solve nothing. The Pilot beckoned to our escort, informing him our desire to return to our quarters.

Once we were secluded in our quarters, we discussed the dilemma facing us, and the consequences of our decision.

"We have no idea who the hell these guys are. They're not the kind of people we want to be associated with, especially after the stories the other two guys related," the Pilot volunteered.

"Fuck them," I echoed, "there are ten of us, counting our friends, and the Englishman could probably eat them up by himself."

This statement brought s snickering form of a unanimous agreement, and a unanimous, vocal, "Fuck them interlopers."

CHAPTER 19 — FOUR & EIGHT

The next morning we relayed our situation to our American and English friends. Their response was, as I expected, to repeat their description of the animal type of men turned loose by the advancing Russians.

"They are attempting to use you as a cover, hoping to avoid any body search to prevent the discovery of any contraband they surely have in their possession. You being airmen, not freed prisoners of war, and under constant surveillance, will pass through any check points along the way," the Sergeant advised.

Although we tried to dismiss the two scum bags from our daily routine, they appeared at intervals of premeditated interruptions. The big mouthed one, who seemed the leader, always exhibited a threatening demeanor.

"When the hell are we moving out?" he would say, closing with, "Don't you faggot fly boys try to fuck us, if you value your ass."

To me this was the last straw. I reached for my forty five, and moved towards them as they were exiting the room. My intent was short lived, as I was surrounded with human bodies.

"What the hell, do you want to face a murder rap for the likes of those two creeps?" the Pilot queried.

"I don't know about you all, but nobody calls me a faggot, especially after what we have gone through," I responded. "You should have at least allowed me to kick the big mouth in the balls."

"Let's keep our cool," was a simultaneous suggestion, with unanimous approval, me included.

An odd feeling engulfed me all the rest of the day. I was willing to bet that moving day was not far off. The uneasy chatter of the others, their strange behavior, such as sorting out their belongings and discarding non-essentials, which were non-existent, except in your mind.

We were in the mess hall awaiting our usual crap for dinner when Novak appeared, with a smile that engulfed his skinny face.

"We are moving out tomorrow, to Lodtz, where after a few days a train will carry you to Odessa. There a Scottish ship will be your first leg to England," he practically screamed.

His verbal outburst of enthusiasm caused all heads within earshot to turn towards our direction. It wasn't the multitude which caused us any concern, but the obvious two, who in scrambling to their feet knocked over their chairs in their haste to reach us.

"Now we're cooking. I hope you had no intention to keep this good news from us," he queried with a scowl.

"You heard it the same time we did," the Pilot replied, in a non conciliatory tone which bordered on contempt and defiance.

His answer must have had the effect intended, because the response came as a surprise, and made me feel their bluff of authority had been negated.

"Look," he said, with subdued reverence, "we're all Americans, and should stick together. We would appreciate it if you could make arrangements to take us with you.

"Lodtz is not too far from here. We'll get there somehow, if you promise to attempt to help us," he asked pleadingly.

Without waiting for the Pilot to answer, I screamed, "Go fuck yourselves, and if you want to make something of it, now is the time, you degenerate!

"You tried to intimidate us, now you want our help. As I said before, go fuck yourselves, and blame your initial attitude for our response," I continued.

Much to my amazement, everyone concerned shouted "yeah, yeah," and Novak was doubled over laughing.

They retreated humbly, and in almost a whisper, the usual outspoken one threw over his shoulder a vehement, "You'll get yours."

We all agreed that constant concern for each other's well being was our number one priority, and we must keep our guard up at all times.

"I'm going to tell our American and English friends the threat of these two scum bags," I volunteered.

"Let's not involve them in our problems. If we can't get permission for them to travel with us, it would make the situation embarrassing," the Pilot suggested.

"I'd leave that decision up to them," I countered.

The next morning at breakfast, our two friends approached us, and to our collective surprise, informed us of our good fortune, plus our problem with the two interlopers. We all looked questionably at our friends, but the Pilot reacted verbally.

"How, who?"

"Novak," was the reply. They added, "Novak told us you actually challenged the bastards, and one of you was stopped physically from killing them." He concluded with, "We never heard any such story."

Feeling secure in our trust towards these two men, the Pilot reiterated Novak's words to them, then added, "We'll be happy when we receive the good news officially. At that time I'll make a formal request to have you accompany us."

"No matter how it turns out, we are grateful for your efforts, and wish you good luck," the Sergeant said with a sincere tone, hands clasped and raised in a comradely attitude.

The following days passed without incident, the hours passing slowly. Feeling depressed, yet apprehensive, we considered the good news that was sure to come. Every unlocking of our dormitory door, which by the time of day coincided with our meal periods, was joined with a heartfelt prayer for good tidings.

I asked Novak to seek out Helena, for some solid information if available. He was reluctant to do so, feeling to put pressure on anyone would cause him to lose his assignment to us.

"I do not have the connections Helena has," he explained to us in his broken English. "My assignment is based on dialects I am capable of understanding as we move into specific areas of Poland and Russia. Helena is not able to converse with the peasants whom we will meet on our journey. It is most important for me to identify myself with you out of military jurisdiction. Helena is your connection with the military, where I have no authority, as I have mentioned before."

I figured this explanation was a cop out. "You little bastard," I directed at him, "you do as we ask."

I hadn't time to enforce my request with a threat before he stated "You give shoes, now you think you own me." He proceeded to remove my GI brogues, much to my embarrassment.

Almost tearfully, I apologetically begged him to reconsider my intent.

Novak continued his attempt to rectify his refusal by explaining the hazards we will encounter in our travels.

"You must understand the further east we go, the military are more concerned in reestablishing normal life. Their concern with transients is not a priority. Direct confrontation will make it impossible to receive any assistance," Novak explained, then added, "Here is where Helena prevails."

Everyone believed that I provoked the embarrassing situation, except the Pilot, to my surprise.

"Now listen, guys, anything he says or does, is for our benefit, so lay off," backing my efforts.

Novak cleared the air with, "I understand your feelings, your concern as Americans in foreign land, your need to face up to threatening situations to protect your existence."

These were the words we interpreted from his utterances, and the case was closed as he relaced his shoes.

"How will we be transported to Lodtz?" I asked Novak.

"By truck or trucks," Novak responded, adding, "The powers that be can not foresee what size truck will be available."

"Shit, I'll walk, if I know it's the right direction home," I kiddingly suggested.

Ignoring my idle chatter, Novak continued. "The long journey after Lodtz will be by train, and going away from front, should eliminate many stops."

With a wry smile, Novak suggested that if there was an opportunity, he would like to show us the type of train we would be traveling in.

The next morning at breakfast, Novak came to our table, and sneakingly placed a photo face down on it.

"What is it?" the Pilot asked, as he turned it over.

"It's a World War One freight car," I volunteered, recognizing it because of its designated identification. "This car is called a 'Four and Eight,' because it was designed to contain four horses and eight men."

Novak continued. "In this part of the world, under existing conditions, these are considered luxury trains, because they have eliminated the horses, and added four more men."

I wondered to myself, there were nine of us, and if we obtain permission for the other two, that's eleven. Would the extra three take the place of four horses?

CHAPTER 20 — OUR GYPSY ENCOUNTER

The official order for movement came early the next morning, conveyed to us in an almost joyous manner by our guard. We as one wondered if his outward exuberance was genuine on our behalf, or relief from his personal responsibility for our well being.

"After breakfast, there will be a truck to drive you to Lodtz, your first stopover. One of many, but from what I was told all stops wherever, will be in the direction to England," he volunteered.

A funny feeling prevailed; it was the odd sideward glances at each other which exposed our unanimous feelings without a word being spoken. I clenched my Miraculous Medal, hanging from my neck with my dog tags, and whispered to myself, "Thank God."

A sudden change was apparent at breakfast. For the first time, our table wasn't isolated from the Polish and Russian officers. One long banquet table with bemedaled officers were standing and applauding as we were led to our seats. This was a complete reversal from the total disregard of our presence, and the disdainful attitude of our past association. We acknowledged our appreciation with a nodding of our heads, and a semblance of a smile.

An added surprise was the arrival of Novak and Helena, who looked as happy as we. Her happiness was conveyed to the others with a gentle pat on the back as she made her way around the table. The embrace and kiss she planted on my lips, appeared, and rightly so, as a farewell, with a "please don't leave me" connotation. The gentle snickers and throat clearing sounds tended to minimize my embarrassment, as I bent her over backwards, ala Rudolf Valentino, and returned her kiss.

"If I only had a camera, I'd own you for life," someone said, in a whispered, disguised voice.

"Jealously, professional jealously." I attempted to defend my actions, but the crimson shade of my face was apparent to all, and I could actually feel its heat.

I could have weathered the whole situation, if Helena would have let go of my hand, and not added to the embarrassment by raising my hand in hers as in victory, with that endearing smile she possessed.

As we seated ourselves around the table, the joyous atmosphere began to sink in. The mixed dialogues of conversation, with Helena and Novak attempting to translate the utterances into a semblance of intelligibility, did not need much interpretation. The sounds of of laughter and comradeship were more obvious by their absence in the past.

I suddenly realized that this was to be a day of surprises.

Packs of Lucky Strike cigarettes were deployed generously about the table, and Land O'Lakes butter made its entrance. When we were asked how we wanted our eggs, a thought ran through my mind: could this be a condemned man's last meal?

In the rear of the dining room I could see our two friends with arms raised and fingers in the V sign of victory. The fact they were standing behind the two scum bags, and the victory sign was converted a thumbs down sign over their heads, and the depressed demeanor of the two pricks, confirmed that our friends had in some manner deprived them of open hostility.

"We have to make an honest effort to get permission for them to accompany us," said the Pilot. "It's the least we can do."

A smile appeared on Helena's face. "It has already been arranged," she volunteered. "But how?"

Helena responded immediately. "Novak finally took me into his confidence. The shoes story is really funny," she added.

"They will not move out with you to Lodtz, and you will not see them again until you have boarded the train. The Russians want to keep you isolated from the displaced persons, and the freed prisoners of war," she said.

"Your friends will not know when or where, but at the right time, they will be spirited to the train, with as little fanfare as possible," Helena continued.

We looked at each other questioningly, but realized this was not the time to discuss the "whys" or the "what fors." The sudden reversal of disdain, and the open celebration in our behalf, certainly presented an inquisitive area, with unanswered questions. This area mixed with the veiled secrecy of our and our friends' travels, and sort of put a damper on what could have been a day of revelry. Whatever the reason or the intent, the breakfast and the actions of our hosts caused me without thinking to blurt out, "Eat and be merry, for tomorrow you may—"

"Shut up," the Pilot cut me off. "What's with you? Don't you trust anyone?"

"Shit no, and I'll tell you why," I said as I sided up close to the Pilot. "Don't you realize, from now on we'll be strictly under Russian jurisdiction, and totally isolated from friendly Polish eyes, or even displaced persons whose visible presence could be a veil of protection?"

"You may be right, but we won't know until we start to move. We must be alert, and take nothing for granted," the Pilot agreed.

The breakfast developed into lunch, and lunch developed into a dinner-show extravaganza. By this time, we all felt relieved, sincerely or alcoholically. Whatever the cause, it felt good.

The festivities continued. Food and drink were plentiful, and the entertainment was spectacular. The Cossack dancers, as I recalled them in my youth, amazed me, but to witness them in person enthralled me. It wasn't a full compliment of ballet dancers that appeared, but the graceful movements of both men and women had to excite even we, who looked upon such dancers, especially the men, as faggots.

Even though my mind was clouded with the potato whisky, I wasn't completely oblivious to the lack of close proximity of the Russians, to us personally. I conveyed my belief to the rest of my crew, and they agreed

"Do you notice, that when your eyes actually meet, it's usually when you inadvertently glance their way? They act embarrassed, with a raised glass, or a slight wave of their hand," the Navigator remarked.

As the daylight blended into twilight, then disappeared into darkness, so did our exuberance and frivolity fade into the area of oblivion. The lights of the banquet hall were dimmed, as a suggestion to depart, and the suggestion was enforced by our escorting guard.

Helena took my hand, pulled me aside, and whispered, "I won't see you until you are situated in Lodtz. Novak will accompany you from here." She concluded with, "We'll have lots of time to get acquainted."

She punctuated her meaning by clasping my hands in hers, and pressing them lovingly against her breasts.

Novak informed us that the powers that be offered any of us who wished a private room with a female companion, instead of the usual dormitory. All but one, the replacement waist gunner, a total stranger to me and the most drunk, declined the invitation. Helena nodded with an affirmative smile at my refusal, which was perfectly clear, even through my bloodshot eyes.

Sleep finally engrossed my befuddled mind, but didn't have any effect on that part of my thinking which kept asking myself, "What is the Russian intent?", and most of all, "What the hell is the intent of Helena?", unashamedly, almost disgustingly declaring a lustful appetite towards me.

I slept a dream world sleep, knowing I was asleep, but disorganized pictures and situations flashed before my eyes. It was only when a sudden interrupting influence shattered my subconscious, that the disorganization of my mind became lifelike.

"It is time to get up." The familiar voice of our guard was the shattering influence.

The clearness of my head was a pleasant surprise: no hangover, and the rest of the crew agreed when I declared my observation. We gathered what belongings we possessed, checked our surroundings, and were led to the mess hall, where the usual crap was served. We were the only ones present, and we were instructed by our guard to hurry,

"We want to depart before the others awaken," he ordered.

It wasn't hard to dismiss one's appetite without fanfare, with the obvious change in diet. We all gulped down a cup of ersatz coffee just to warm our innards, knowing we were to ride in an open truck, and although we rarely discussed the weather, it was fucking cold.

The ride to Lodtz was uneventful, except for freezing our balls. It was during these direct encounters with the weather that we realized the hell one faced in ground combat. As we moved out of the city into snow covered terrain, the hustle and bustle became distant, and the war was with us again. Evidence of death and destruction reared its ugly head. The waste of man-made machinery could be forgiven, but the waste of God's children is unforgivable.

The stench of death penetrated the cold crisp air, which would under normal conditions be invigorating, not convulsive. The remains of dead bodies were covered by snow one day, in frozen slumber, only to be uncovered the next day by the drifting flakes and blowing drifts.

We finally reached the city of Lodtz, and the hustle and bustle was again visible. The normalcy of city living blotted out the hours of travel, and the scars of war. We all as one, wanted to blot the cold that had numbed our bodies, as we parked in front of a building.

"This is it," Novak said.

We dismounted, gingerly, I might add, placing our almost frost bitten feet carefully on the frozen white road. The building appeared as an old brownstone, those landmarks of the Borough of Brooklyn, and was five stories in height. As we lined up on the sidewalk, the front door opened, and a kid of about eight years of age bounded out through our ranks into the street. Behind him was a woman wielding a broom in one hand, and a clenched fist in the other. Behind her was a man, a very large man, suited up in a true Cossack uniform. He laughingly grabbed the woman by the scuff of her neck, which stopped her forward progress in mid-air. Her legs, pretty legs I might add, kicked at empty space.

Out of nowhere Helena appeared, and her presence caused an immediate change of action. The Cossack said something to Helena, which brought a burst of laughter from them, and Novak joined in.

Novak realizing our concern, laughingly explained the situation. "It seems the kid who jolted past us is a Polish kid, and he visits and plays with the son of your house-keeper, who is the woman with the broom. Now the Cossack soldier is your guard, and he provokes the Polish kid to beat up on the house-keeper's son. He incites the situation by reminding the Polish kid that the housekeeper's son has a German father, who is retreating with the German Army, and his Mother is a Polish Gypsy, left behind with a bastard for a son."

CHAPTER 21 — CONFINEMENT

We followed the housekeeper and cossack, led by Helena up three flights of stairs. The hallway was the railroad type we have in the States, with doors leading to rooms on both sides o the hallway. We were led to what appeared to be the sitting room, and there Helena, with an air of military obedience, gave us our orders and expected behavior during our stay here. She assigned sleeping accommodations to each including Novak, right down to her sleeping with me, since she made sure I had the only double bed. She then laid down the ground rules with an authoritative tone.

"You are not permitted to leave the building unescorted. You will only speak to the guard through me or Novak, since he understands or speaks no English. You will follow his commands through Novak, if I am not present, as if I directed you in person. I will attempt to obtain supplies of food and cigarettes more compatible to your desires."

She then continued with the most unexpected rhetoric concerning our sexual behavior. "We will furnish you with a woman, if you wish, but you will not be guaranteed of their good health. Most of these women consorted with the Germans, when they occupied this city."

She concluded with, "If any of you can make it with your house keeper, she has been checked medically OK."

She put the screws to the thinking of our lover boy the Navigator, when she threw in a casual aside.

"She keeps reporting the guard's advances, and he has desisted, because the Russian Officer who is her lover has threatened the guard with a trip to Siberia, whence he came."

All this conversation was one way; the Gypsy was not present.

Helena called to her, "Sonia, come here, I will introduce you to your new tenants," for our benefit, then added in Polish what apparently was a translation.

Sonia's appearance was a pleasant surprise: she was beautiful. Even through her bulky clothes, one could see a pleasing feminine body, a far cry from the Russian women we had encountered in our travels. Her smile was shy, but revealed a genuine friendship when she said, in halting English, "Americans welcome."

"She knows very little English, but is learning from her son, who is taught English in school," Helena revealed.

Our Navigator is a handsome guy, unmarried, and sexy, but like myself, had a fear of contracting a venereal disease. When he saw the Gypsy, and was assured of her sound medical history, his demeanor changed.

"Fuck the Russian Officer, I'm going to get a piece of that," he said, without one iota of secrecy.

Helena, hearing his comments, sided up to me and whispered, "Let them share her if they wish. As far as I am concerned, she is a German collaborator. Besides, you can have me anytime you wish."

I wanted to ask her why she was throwing herself at me in such a demeaning manner, and what have I said or done to make her think I was interested. I could only believe the gratefulness I showed her when she made that dangerous trip to Gdynia to obtain the zinc salve, tooth paste, and cigarettes, was misinterpreted.

As I have declared in the past, I was sincerely grateful to Helena for the help she has given me personally, but her indifferent attitude and smugness still suggested self-interest.

With her authoritative air of importance, she suggested a tour of the facilities. She commenced to direct each of the others to their bunks, separating the officers from the non-coms.

"You will not exchange bunks without permission," she said, then explained why. "Bed check is a must; absentees will be easily identified."

"Two in a bunk had better be one male, one female," she laughingly concluded.

It was received as a bad joke, for no one laughed.

There was only one toilet facility and bath tub, and no shower. Sonia showed us where the towels and soap were located. The towels were good replicas of burlap bags, and the soap was like the brown laundry soap my mother used. We wandered about our new confines, acquainting ourselves with the locations of necessity: personal relaxing areas, and most important, an area where we could inconspicuously discuss our status without the appearance of secrecy.

The heat was furnished by oil stoves, although the best effort at diminishing the bitter cold of the outdoors, only made it less bitter.

The most popular piece of furniture was a large oval table in the sitting room. Sitting around the table in idle conversation brought back memories of family gatherings back home. No matter where parties of people started their assemblies, it was the dining room or kitchen table where it ended.

Helena and Novak suddenly departed without fanfare. The guard lost his air of hostility and regimentation as he flopped into a stuffed chair with a smile and an utterance that sounded like, "Ah shit."

Sonia, who had been shy and protective, suddenly became a smiling joyous person, as she and her son set the table. Her attitude was magnified as she sang in Polish what was definitely, "Roll Out the Barrel." Her voice was beautiful, and surprisingly professional.

Not knowing if she understood, I suggested, "Return with me to the States after the war, where as your agent, we would get rich."

Her son smiled, and said something to her in Polish. She must have been pleased, for a smile etched her beautiful face as she moved towards me. She gratefully placed her hand in mine and uttered one word, "Yes."

"Damn, now you'll have her believing that shit, like you're some god. You have to convince her that I can help her too, or I'll never get into her pants," pleaded the Navigator.

Whatever beliefs or desires I instilled in her, the results were shared by all. A bottle of red wine appeared (from where we didn't ask)., which was offered to us by this beautiful Gypsy. With this loving gesture of hospitality, we would probably survive this confinement. We toasted our hostess, with a rendition of the American version of "Roll Out the Barrel."

CHAPTER 22 — SEDUCTIVE ENCOUNTERS

It was nightfall when footsteps were heard mounting the stairway. It signaled the guard and the housekeeper to return to the rigid demeanor expected of them. The guard buttoned his tunic and returned to his position at the door. The housekeeper quickly cleared the table of the wine-stained glasses. None too soon, if the appearance of Helena and Novak was the reason for their reaction to the footsteps. It was this kind of atmosphere that reminded me of that gut feeling of mistrust towards Helena.Not as much towards Novak, since he withheld the postcard incident from her, and only told her of our wishes to assist our friends when he knew she was the only one who could help us.

"We have been trying to get a requisition for supplies, but the Russian officer who is Sonia's lover is out of town, and the officer in charge of supplies won't even grant us a visit," Novak volunteered.

"When we mentioned the supplies were for American Airmen, they belligerently escorted us to the door," Helena concluded.

"Maybe if one of us would go with you, we could convince them that it is for American Airmen," I suggested. "Maybe an Officer," I added.

"You keep me out of your hair-brained schemes," the Pilot screamed, "and that's an order. If the rest of you have any sense, you won't even listen to this idiot."

Not wanting to provoke an argument in the presence of outsiders, or show disrespect, I bit my tongue in response to his description of me. This was only the first day here, and one could sense the helpless feeling we all shared towards our fate.

The heat of the oil stoves was losing the battle of offsetting the night cold that penetrated the innards of the building. The only defense we had was to dress in all the clothing we possessed, and head for bed. The guard slept on a couch near the door. The Gypsy and her son had a room to themselves, and it was no secret she wanted no visitors, the bolt of the lock being set confirming her wishes.

"Now, wouldn't this be the time to cuddle up to her warm body? The fact that her Russian friend is out of town might have her in a lonely and receptive mood," the Navigator uttered, almost in a pleading tone, as he searched for some consenting faces.

Helena, without one instant of hesitation, said, "Do you really want to sleep with her?"

"You can bet your ass I do," he responded.

"Don't bet my ass, it doesn't belong to you," she answered. "I'll get you into the room, but after that you are on your own, no guarantees."

All I could think was that Helena certainly knew her way around, and our American "slanguage" wasn't foreign to her.

She knocked on Sonia's door, and softly responded to the questioning voice from within, "Helena."

There was a quiet conversation, and Sonia's face showed reluctant consent. Helena beckoned the Navigator to the door, and with a gentle nudge, she said, "You're on your own."

The door closed behind him. Helena suggested we retire to our beds and keep our doors open, to let the heat from the oil stoves circulate throughout, since not all rooms had heaters.

Some, after they had made their descriptive foul remarks as to what was going on in Sonia's room, made their way to bed. I stalled to give Helena time to get into bed; I didn't want to be in her presence when she disrobed. It was odd but there were no remarks about my sleeping with Helena. I believe they realized I was truly embarrassed, and the situation was forced on me.

I thought it wise to relieve myself before retiring, thus offsetting the chance of feeling the urge later, when I knew the cold would be colder. I couldn't believe my eyes, though the odor should have warned me. The toilet was filled with shit, and it was evident it wasn't the work of one man. As I retreated, I held my nose, at the same time pulled the flush chain. It was then I realized, the water was solid ice. I added to the collection, then made my way to my room. All the other doors were open as Helena suggested, but ours was closed. The room was dark except for the oil lamp, set in a low flame, whose light was reflected from the eyes of Helena, who was not asleep, as I had hoped. I made my way to the opposite side of the bed, gently groped for the covers.

Finding two, and without removing any clothing, I slid myself between them, effecting a barrier between Helena and myself. She discovered the subterfuge, but honored my intent, and whispered,

"There will be other nights, my heavenly one."

"Heavenly one"? Where did she dig that up?

The next day started with an unexpected surprise when Novak told us we were going to eat breakfast at a military mess hall. Although we all were ready to have breakfast, we would rather have the Navigator, the lover, relate his conquests.

"Not now," he pleaded, "Sonia may overhear, and I don't want to embarrass her."

I watched as Sonia's son conversed with Novak, and the smile that etched Novak's face meant he had a story to tell.

We all hoped to be able to relieve ourselves in a more sanitary facility at the mess hall. I couldn't help but wonder how Sonia and her son could endure the filthy and odorous condition. My wonderment soon disappeared. Walking down the hall to exit the building, we passed the toilet facility. There was Sonia, scooping the frozen shit into a bucket held by her son. We didn't wait to find out where she discarded it, but welcomed the fresh cold air to remove the sick feeling from our stomachs.

It's amazing how in one's mind the most beautiful woman in the world loses her beauty if in your mind you see her functioning as a normal human being, shitting, pissing, wiping herself, let alone handling shit. I hoped the Navigator, missed the scene; it might curtail his amorous intent, and the bullshit stories that followed, which were needed entertainment.

Three other guards joined us in front of the building, and took position on either side and one to the rear as our guard led us into a single file down the street. The city seemed to be awakening as most cities do early in the morning. Our presence was noticed through half opened, blinking eyes, curious but not understanding.

It was very cold, and crunching through the snow covered street, I thanked God for the sheep-skin-lined flying boots we had. They were the only piece of flying equipment that was conducive to the conditions that prevailed.

We walked about three blocks, which led us to the outskirts of town, and a military encampment. As we entered, it was a replica of what was obvious to we Americans: all the vehicles, but a few, were Dodge or Studebaker trucks.

Curious, I stated to Novak my observation, "It's terrific that we could supply you with American equipment."

"Yes," he answered, "this equipment is made in America, but by Russian workers, while the Americans are defending against invasion."

Everyone within earshot laughed aloud, almost in unison. "Where did you gather that shit?"

"Do you deny that Russia, turning against Germany, saved America?" Novak queried.

It was obvious Novak was in need of an American history lesson. It was also obvious that the populace was easily brain washed.

The mess hall was sparsely populated; that we were still being kept away from the multitudes was apparent. The hall was warm enough to remove the chill that had settled in our bones, which had to be welcome under any circumstance. The food, when it arrived, was a shade better than what we were getting at our confines, but the location too made it more palatable. The Russian cigarettes were a pleasant addition, but the construction of two thirds cardboard, one third tobacco, and the diameter of about one half of ours, necessitated smoking two at one time to effectively retain enough smoke for enjoyment.

Helena appeared, and suggested we remain until the military stationed here arrived, "to absorb some of this fine heat.

"They are attempting to thaw out the toilet facility at our rooms. I reported the condition to Sonia's officer friend. He's back in town, and asked for better food," she concluded.

Now, I thought to myself, an introduction on a friendly basis was a must, before this Russian prick, found out about our Navigator lover and his Gypsy.

Thinking about the Gypsy caused me to make a solemn request of the Navigator, "How about an account of your conquest last night, loverboy?"

He played the part to the hilt, as he beckoned us to close up into a small circle "to escape the ears of the enemy." With a motion of his hand, he directed Helena and Novak to remain apart.

"Let me tell you, this woman is or has been a woman of the world. She knew lovemaking techniques that I never heard of, and used every desirable method of seduction," he related.

Before he could continue, I injected the question, "Where the hell was the kid, through this heavenly bliss?"

A chorus of a questioning "yeahs?" added unanimous strength to my question. His answer was unbelievable. I looked towards Novak, who couldn't have heard the conversation, but the smile he had earlier when talking to the kid was still there. I felt Novak must know the Navigator was a bullshitter, and the kid had relayed to Novak the true facts.

"The kid must be use to these situations. He just curled up on one side of the bed, and went to sleep," he explained. "He didn't make a sound, and Sonia, by gesture and action, suggested a minimum of movement during foreplay." His story continued with the most vivid description of love making, which I believe we had all at one time fantasized about.

"We couldn't relate our ecstasy, verbally because of the language barrier, but I could feel her elation as we performed mutually to the satisfaction of each other. The only time throughout our encounter her kid moved was when we simultaneously enjoyed an orgasm."

CHAPTER 23 — CONFRONTATION

We left to return to our quarters just as the assigned military personnel began making their appearance. As we filed out a strange incident occurred. A uniformed soldier approached our column, walked beside us, and addressed us in perfect English.

"Hi Yanks," he said. "I'm from New York. I used to be a tailor in Queens, but got caught in the German invasion of Poland, and was conscripted."

He never finished his tale. He was rifle butted to the ground by one of the guards. We all automatically moved to assist him, saying, "What the hell are you doing?"

Novak yelled, "Don't!" His warning were substantiated when the guards blocked our movement by lining up abreast with rifles at the ready. It wasn't bad enough to have assaulted a fellow soldier, but as we were nudged back into line, the trailing guard placed a boot into the side of the fallen man.

"What gives?" I asked Novak.

"I don't know if you realized the man was a Polish soldier, but believe me it would have made no difference. They would have treated a Russian soldier the same way," he said, then added, "You just don't interfere with any military formation."

"What if it were a civilian who approached us?" I asked.

"They would have shot him without batting an eye," was his answer.

"What kind of animals are these people?" I pursued this line of questioning with Novak.

"Your description of them is quite accurate. They lived as animals, were self sustaining, lived off the land from whence they came. No education of the modern world. Whatever they know of the world of today is what they learned in the Russian army, and they perform like the robots they were trained to be."

Novak moved up close to me and said, "If they knew the information I have told you, God only knows where I would wind up. When we get to our quarters, I'll tell something you won't believe," he promised.

We were pleasantly surprised when we entered our quarters and found additional heaters were installed. We found the toilet water was unfrozen and the flusher worked.

We were all pleased by the improvements, but I had informed the rest of the special story Novak had promised to tell.

"Everything that has happened to us and about us is a special story as far as I'm concerned," said the Pilot. "What in this part of the world would surprise us?"

One must understand we Americans have a mutual camaraderie, with respect to all who we feel are fighting for a mutual cause. We feel we know our enemies, and respect the rights of our allies. After Novak related his special story, we had to protect his well being by promising never to repeat it ever again or discuss it in the presence of Helena.

It wasn't a long story, but still a narrative of substance which portrayed unbelievable information, and would certainly place Novak in a dangerous position.

"I tell you this because your travels after Lodtz, without me, will be an uninformed encounter, and I think it best you understand the nature of your ally," Novak commenced.

"You have witnessed some of the uncivilized actions of your ally, and the disrespect towards you personally, so the information I will place in your custody will I pray reach the people who will have to deal with them, if and when this war ends.

"It is hard for me to relate this, because I have reasons, personal reasons, to hate the Germans. Friends and relatives of mine have been killed by them.

"You have witnessed the love and respect the Polish people have shown you, whenever the opportunity presented itself and the Russians, took no obvious embarrassing action.

"I want you to know, and through you, the world, that the Polish people, almost to a man, were happier under German occupation and rue the day the Russians appeared as saviors.

"The Germans, after they felt no military problems existed, placed townsfolk, mostly priests, in charge of every day activities, and permitted almost complete freedom of the churches to reopen. The Russians dictated the policies of the church. and attempted to brainwash the people with their atheist indoctrination. There were those such as Helena, who out of either self preservation or collaboration, played both sides of the coin to the mistrust of most.

"Sometimes she used her connections to help someone, which I have witnessed under both occupations. My feelings are mixed at best; you'll have to make your own judgement.

"I don't know how you will accept or use this information, but I feel you should again use your personal judgement." Novak concluded with, "Please respect my trust in you, as we Polish people respect all Americans."

It certainly was an unbelievable bit of information, and reflected attitudes and actions foreign to the reasons we were here. We all agreed there was no reason to even discuss the information entrusted to us; there would be a time and place.

The Navigator pawing at Sonia every chance he had. He became the focal point of entertainment. The mood was lightened by the laughter of Novak and the kid. Every time Sonia swished her hips to evade a clutching hand, she did appear to do it in a provocative manner, and the kid would jump between them.

"What's the connection that causes the kid to laugh. You must know or you wouldn't laugh with him!" His answer was what we all waited for. We asked this of Novak, out of ear-shot of the Navigator; we didn't want to break the lover's stories, without which our confinement would become completely unbearable.

"What did the kid tell you, the morning after?" I asked. "We saw you talking to him."

"He told me he did exactly the same thing he's doing now, jumping between them when he got too close. The funniest part of the story is that he slept between them through the night, and they cuddled up together to keep warm," Novak related.

"The lying bastard, he had me yearning," the Pilot said, "with his descriptive escapades."

"At least he got into her room. Who knows how he'll make out the next time?" someone said.

"It may never happen. Her Russian loverboy is back. Let's hope she doesn't report our loverboy's advances," I wishfully stated.

Mentioning the Russian, and his return as commandant, started my wheels turning: a frontal confrontation. I cornered Novak, and asked if it were possible to duck the guard and get out of the building.

"We may beat the guard, but I don't want to get your Pilot angry. Besides what do you expect to accomplish?"

"I don't think Helena has the pull with this prick. I believe Sonia is the one to approach," I suggested.

"If I would use Sonia, it would be obvious we knew of their affair. A Russian officer and a common Gypsy is a no no." He then added, "If Sonia gets wine or any other things for you, it is given to her secretly, with no direct connection between them."

"The guard seems to have befriended you, especially one of your crew who traded a watch for the guard's beautiful stiletto and sheath. Maybe I can make a deal," Novak stated.

Son of a bitch, I had my eye on that knife, I thought to myself.

I awaited the opportunity to speak to the other crew members, without the Pilot's knowledge. I informed them of my intentions of confronting the Russian officer directly for better food and smokes. I suggested we pool all of our escape money, which was four pounds English each, and maybe bribe him. Though some were reluctant, they agreed with reservations: they would deny any complicity if anything went wrong, which was par for the course.

CHAPTER 24 — TARZAN OF THE APES

I went to bed thinking of my plans for the next day, and the possible ramifications, both for the Russian officer and my crew if something went wrong. All I had to do to bolster my courage was think of who we were and why we were there. Our physical presence was so prevalent: trucks, food, weapons, and us. Where do they get their nerve to deny us a legitimate request? I felt, nothing ventured nothing gained, and without Helena present, I fell into a twilight sleep, wondering where she could be.

Before I completely succumbed to absolute oblivion, my mind trailed off, forming my lingual approach to the Russian officer, realizing through an interpreter there was a possibility of a misunderstanding. Although I felt a need to be forceful to satisfy my personal feelings, I also knew I was in their ballpark, and their rules prevailed.

It was daybreak when Novak gently poked me. "It's almost time," he whispered.

"Where is Helena?" I asked.

"It's best she not be here. I would not want to involve her if at all possible. Let's go," he responded.

Just about that time the kid emerged from his room, and said something in Polish to Novak.

"He wants to know if his mother had returned home. She was not home all night," Novak explained.

Wherever she was (probably with her Russian lover) she could not return home before now because of the curfew, I thought. Like my mind was read, footsteps up the stairs were followed by Sonia. She seemed startled when we were there to confront her. She looked towards the guard, and appeared pleased when she saw he was still asleep. I knew better; he was feigning sleep because Novak had made a deal, so we could slip out before everyone was awake.

It was now or never, as we descended the stairway out the front door into a freezing foreign world. I thought, I must be a fucking nut, or possess some pair of balls. I could feel Sonia's questioning eyes staring at the back of my head.

The cold bit into my face, and before long my ears began to smart. I followed Novak's move, lowering the ear flaps on the Russian fur hat I wore, pulling up the fur collar on my flying jacket and tightening the strings on my wrap around jacket. I said aloud to Novak, "At this point, kid, whatever we achieve is well earned. We're sure as hell paying for it."

We seemed to just mill around. Novak did an awful lot window shopping.

"What gives? Let's get on with it, I'm freezing my ass. I am not interested in sightseeing your fucking town," I injected, hoping a little hostility would speed up whatever his plans were.

It wasn't my hostile questioning that provoked his answer. The way he answered assured me in no uncertain terms who was in charge of this escapade.

"If you think you know what is ahead, and how we proceed to achieve success, I'll follow you. If you don't, don't ask questions, do as I tell you, and maybe, maybe we will get out of this with our skins. We are not playing games," he instructed with a voice of authority that belied his diminutive stature.

He explained that we must flow in with the people casually with as little fanfare as possible and try not to be noticed. It was then I realized the American flags sewn on the sleeves of my jacket were visible. Novak made the same discovery about the same time, as he pushed me into a doorway.

"Sorry," he said as he proceeded to rip the flags from my sleeves.

"Keep them close at hand. We may need them to prove your identity at a moments notice," he said with a sincere voice.

"Why the hell do we have to be so secretive? Why not just go where this fucking Russian is, make our demands, and bail out?" I asked.

"Here we go again. Your attitude is going to get us killed. If you persist in your interference, I'm heading back to our quarters, and you're on your own," he answered, then added in a more conciliatory tone, "I don't fear the Polish police, or Polish soldiers. It's the Russian ingrate soldiers who were taught that anyone who is not Russian or Polish, especially not wearing a Polish or Russian uniform, is an enemy or a spy, and to kill them. There is no possible way to reason with them," he concluded.

"My God," I thought to myself, "for some crummy food. What a way to die. We could disappear from the face of the earth, without a trace, just another MIA."

"Did you get all the English escape money from your crew? How much is it worth?" Novak asked.

"In English pounds, we had four each. Thirty six pounds worth four dollars five cents each American, about one hundred and forty five dollars," I quickly calculated.

"We'll find a bank to determine the exchange rate into Polish money," Novak suggested

"Banks are open?" I asked.

"Most all businesses have reopened. To the people who have returned, this is home. The war is over as far as they are concerned, and life must resume," Novak explained.

"It's too early to make any productive move. We will have to kill some time. Let's see if the movies are open. Sometimes they have an early morning show for the night workers."

Believe it or not, there was a movie theater open. Novak said, "You don't have any Polish money yet, so I'll treat, but you must repay me when we exchange your English pounds."

To actually find a movie theater in a war torn country seemed like a miracle, but the title of the picture showing had to be a mirage. There, big as life on the marquee in bold letters read, "TARZAN OF THE APES," with Johnny Weismuller and Maureen O'Sullivan. Novak purchased two tickets; when we arrived inside the movie had already started. I couldn't believe my ears. Tarzan's grunts could have easily been Polish, but Maureen's voice was definitely English. The sound was English, with Polish subtitles flashing across the bottom of the screen. In the darkness, watching an American movie with English sound, I forgot the time and place, and I felt at home.

CHAPTER 25 — BLACKMARKET-BLACKMAIL

By the time we left the movie, the movement of the people about the street was no different than a city awakening anywhere else in the world, each person with their own thoughts, desires, problems and destinations, all huddled within themselves fending off the bitter cold. It was only when a conversation was necessary, and I was within ear-shot, that reality presented itself: everyone is a total stranger.

Novak was undecided, "Should we go to the Bank first, or seek out. "Do you think a bribe would help with this prick?" I asked Novak.

"You don't know this man. Why do you use such a vulgar description of him?"

"Because I haven't found a Russian officer yet who isn't one, in my book," I answered.

"Please do both of us a favor, and show a little bit of humility if we ever get to see the prick. Shit, now you have me calling him a vulgar name," Novak blurted out.

"It's easy, because you believe it too, and you just keep it in the back of your mind," I explained.

"You have an American explanation for everything. It appears the tales that preceded you are true: Americans make light of the most serious situations, but your attitude never interferes with the job at hand," Novak, volunteered.

"I'll be damned," I thought, "this kid likes us. Maybe I should show him a little more respect."

"I think the bank is open," Novak said as he tugged my sleeve in the direction he wanted me to follow.

As we rounded the corner, Novak made an abrupt stop, and yanked me into a doorway. "Damn," he said, "look at the crowd of people waiting to get in. We had better chance seeing the ff— officer first."

I stifled my laughter as he caught himself saying "the fucking officer," and agreed with his decision.

We approached a formidable looking structure, with a large banner stretched across the double door entrance. It was obvious even to me, a very poor foreign language student, that it was Russian. Of course, the enormous picture of Stalin, made my linguistic deduction easier. The two Polish soldiers stationed as sentries were our first obstacle, but my fears were soon put to rest as Novak placed a restraining hand against my chest.

"Stay put," he ordered, "let me check the land, before I drag you into it."

He mounted the four steps leading to the apron supporting the two guards. He then surprised the shit out of me, and probably the guards too, as he boldly grabbed the door handles and yanked them open. He only got one foot inside the doorway before he was jerked back bodily, like a sack of potatoes, and slammed against the wall with a rifle jammed across his neck. I could hear him gasping for air, and not one sound of explanation was emitted.

I felt I had to make some sort of move before the poor kid was killed. I fished my American flag emblems from my pocket, and with an air of conjured bravery, I ran up the steps yelling, "Americanski, Americanski!" waving my American flag labels. If it did nothing permanent, it startled the one guard into releasing the rifle pressure from Novak's wind pipe, and pointing it into my face. I believe I closed my eyes, as if I didn't want to see the bullet I expected. Novak recovered his voice. I could hear guttural sounds definitely a Polish dialogue. He placed himself between me and the threatening guard, waving his arms frantically.

"Americanski, Americanski," were the only words I understood, but his pleading tone and the protective position he took were effective: the guard lowered his rifle. The immediate threat was minimized, but their hostility was voiced in Polish to Novak, who translated, "Don't move, one of guards is going to find out what they want to do with us."

"Didn't you tell them who we wanted to see, and what for?" I asked.

"Damn! You could see I never had a chance! Thank God they weren't Russian, they would have shot right through me to get you!" he explained. "We'll just have to wait it out."

We didn't have to wait long. The guard returned and said something to the other guard. They prodded us in the back with their rifles, none too gently. We entered through the opened door, and were confronted with another set of imposing doors, with two more armed sentries. "God," I thought, "this must at least be Fort Knox." These doors were opened, and the long marble hallway led to another two impressive doors, with equally impressive armed guards. These were definitely elite Russian soldiers, not the ragged fighting soldiers I had seen at the front lines.

I wondered why up to this time we hadn't been frisked, but this was soon corrected. We were thrown, and I mean literally and physically, against the wall, and frisked with severe intensity. When the guard who frisked me made his way to my testicles, he lovingly caressed them, then with a sadistic laugh, squeezed them in a vise-like grip that caused me to fall to my knees.

"You cock sucker!" I screamed. I didn't know if he understood me, but he responded as if he did, as he picked me up and slammed me against the wall and jabbed his rifle into my gut. My outcry must have reached the inner office, for suddenly a medal-bedecked officer appeared. The first thing that entered my mind was Novak's pleading: show some humility. Novak answered the officer's inquiry, which I had interpreted as "What the fuck is going on here?", before the guards could answer. After Novak spoke to the officer, he directed me to get up, and offered his hand. Novak had told him who I was, and most important, where we were staying.

"Did you tell him how we are protecting his girl friend from the guard at our quarters?" I asked.

"You must be looking to get killed. If I suggested that to him, me, you, and your crew would be witnesses, and would have to eliminated. Why don't you tell him about your Navigator sleeping with Sonia, and his promise to get into her pants?" He concluded with, "Use some sense. He knows our position. It is better we use it as an inference, one hand washes the other".

I couldn't believe all the phrases, cliches, and American slanguage that Novak used, always in the proper situation. The Russian officer waved off the guards as he extended his hand, and led us into a palatial office. He offered us chairs and sat down behind a beautiful ornate desk, where he appeared out of place. I envisioned a German officer behind the desk with a picture of Hitler, and a Swastika flag adorning the wall behind him.

"Does he understand any English at all?" I asked Novak.

"Not a word," Novak answered. "You tell him through me what you want in a reserved tone, not demanding, and I'll take it from there."

We knew that he was aware, through Sonia, that our plight was no secret, and that our needs were, as allies, deserving. Of course I wanted to scream about everyone, even displaced persons, having American cigarettes, and about the American food eaten in our presence while we were given food we wouldn't feed to our pigs. I figured I had better wait to see the response to my request. Novak's voice sounded conciliatory, almost pleading, as he translated my words into Russian. The officer's response, usually a "hmmm," sounded understanding, but Novak's responses always sounded repetitious, and his tone would rise an octave or two, which began to cause a furrowed brow to form in the officer's forehead.

It was hard to tell what was on this smug prick's mind. His smile was arrogant, and he thrust out his chest by placing his hands behind his neck, thus presenting his medals as a sign of authority.

I asked Novak if he knew what the fruit salad represented. "Probably Stalingrad, Leningrad, they were all heroes if they fought there. Important like your invasion of Europe - even if they weren't, they were." He concluded with, "Who would know?"

The verbal fencing between Novak and the officer seemed to make no significant headway. I began to steam, and my Italian blood overrode Novak's plea for humility. "What the fuck goes?" I blurted out. "You arrogant son of a bitch, stop playing games with this kid. Who the fuck wants to look at your fucking medals?"

I didn't whisper, and the tone emitting from my angrily screwed up mouth caused him to recoil as if in disbelief. He spoke to Novak, his demeanor and tone of his voice appearing questioning. The next statement from Novak was surprising, as he said with a look of disbelief.

"Do you know what he just asked me? If all Americans were as crazy as you, and if they are, he was happy we are on the same side."

The next surprise was the Russian grabbing me in a bear hug, shaking my hand, and walking to his desk to press a buzzer, which brought one of the sentries. Talk was exchanged, and Novak was included. The look and smile on Novak's face was a look of victory.

"You crazy bastard, you did it, we're going to be taken to a food storage warehouse with a truck to load up!"

"Now?" I asked.

"Right now," he answered.

"I wouldn't bet on it," Novak countered.

The officer had the guard lead us out a back door to an inclosed area were a small fleet of five by five Dodges were parked, protected by a ten foot fence topped with barbed wire.

"I wonder if this protection is to keep people in or keep them out?" I asked Novak.

"What the hell do you care? Let's just be grateful, reap while the reaping is available," Novak responded.

The guard said something to Novak, and Novak motioned to a truck which had its motor running. We walked to it and climbed aboard. The guard opened a gate for us to exit, and the two massive sentries, armed with Burp Guns, satisfied me that the protection was definitely not just for show.

"You notice the guards are Mongolians, just like the one at our quarters. They are used in all areas where the Russians want secrecy. They are impressive, but stupid," Novak explained.

It was only a short ride. We came to a building which needed no explanation as to its importance. It was surrounded with armed Mongolians. The windows were barred. Steel doors adorned the entrance, and a glance upwards caught fleeting glimpses of sentries patrolling the roof tops. I don't know why, but a flash of the Alamo came to mind. "Geez, if they had half of the protection as here, they could have held out forever."

The driver pulled behind the building. He blew his horn in a manner which denoted an apparent code, and a gate was opened. We entered, and found ourselves facing a wall not five feet in front of us, with a sentry guarding another gate. We were trapped between two walls. Off to the right of us was a line of people at an opening in the wall. We were moved quickly through the second gate, but not too quickly to observe parcels of food being passed through the wall opening to the waiting people.

Novak appeared not to notice. I knew better - he couldn't have missed it.

"The sons of bitches," I whispered to Novak, "they're not protecting against the enemy, they're running a black market! We can't get any of our own food, and these pricks are selling it!" I was so pissed, the loudness of my voice caused heads to turn, with questioning glances.

"Mind your business! You say nothing, just observe. We have our Russian friend by the short hairs - he can't refuse any of our demands!" Novak gleefully directed.

Again, the American slanguage used by Novak, and always at the most appropriate situation, was mind boggling.

The truck stopped. We dismounted and were led through a door, as the truck backed into a loading platform. The door closed behind us, and we were in an office of sorts. Some conversation between Novak and a soldier sitting behind a desk was translated for me by Novak.

"Sit down. We were told the truck will be loaded, and we will return with it to our quarters."

"Come, on Novak, can't we at least choose our own poison?" I asked.

Novak posed the question to the soldier, and the waving of his arms certainly wasn't a response in the affirmative.

"Now is the time to find out if we have any clout with the Russian officer," Novak added, "we'll try a little blackmail." This kid never failed to amaze me. He pointed to the telephone on the desk, and before the soldier could respond one way or the other, picked it up and jammed it into the soldier's hands. His actions were accompanied by a verbal order in Russian. Its effect was demonstrated by the soldier's dialing the phone.

"What gives?" I asked.

"I told him to call the officer who sent us here," Novak replied, then sheepishly said, "I didn't say 'fucking,' although I wanted to."

The results were in our favor. The soldier was nodding his head in the affirmative, and saluting at the same time. He removed the headset from his ear, which signified the voice on the other end wasn't whispering.

"We have scored! The Russian officer realizes the knowledge we possess. We will have him eating out of our hands!" I gleefully conveyed to Novak.

"Damn, don't take that attitude. You are a long way from home. Any sign of a threat of exposure to these mean people would place you and your friends in immediate danger. Please play it close to the vest," Novak pleaded.

We were led down a hallway which opened into a tremendous room, I couldn't believe my eyes, and I could see Novak blinking in utter surprise. There were rows upon rows of shelves from wall to wall, with access rows separating them. If you can't remember shopping in an Atlantic and Pacific or a Butler chain grocery store, this sight would certainly jog your memory. We could just as well been there, with rows upon rows of Premier and DelMonte canned foods, A&P coffee, and all the goodies you longed for at home, in mind boggling abundance. There were large refrigerators loaded with meats of all descriptions. Novak and I looked at each other, eyes full of great expectations.

The service window was outside in the court yard. Money was being passed from the outside to the inside, and food was being passed from the inside to the outside. The war had no meaning here.

The man assigned to escort us carried a clipboard and wrote down the items Novak and I pointed out. We spent about a half hour making our choices before Novak said, "Let's not overdo it. With our connection we can come back anytime."

"You seem to forget we are out on our own. What if we can't make contact again? We're up shit creek if that Russian prick makes sure we can't get out again," I corrected.

We were led from the warehouse, and the soldier in the outer office said something to Novak. Novak shrugged his shoulders, and said, "Let's go. We're walking back. They will deliver the merchandise."

"Wait a minute, lets not go empty handed," I said as I grabbed a couple of cartons of Lucky Strike cigarettes. They were snatched back, and we left empty handed.

CHAPTER 26 — ERSATZ

"Let's try the bank again," Novak suggested. "We may have better luck: fewer people, fewer inquisitive eyes when we produce English money."

I noddingly agreed-anything to get out of this freezing cold. Wearing all of our clothing in the confines of the warehouse caused me to sweat and the cold, along with my damp longjohns, combined to form a bone-penetrating chill. The bank was sparsely occupied when we entered.

Novak whispered, "Make yourself inconspicuous, and for God's sake, don't talk to anyone."

Novak walked to a teller's window. He apparently wasn't in the right place, as the teller pointed to a desk in the rear. I surveyed the area, and found to my satisfaction I would be close enough to witness any transaction between Novak and the man sitting at the desk without raising any suspicion. Not understanding the language wouldn't stop me from checking the resulting exchange of monies.

They were exchanging handshakes with accompanying smiles, which indicated a satisfactory transaction. Novak smiled and gestured to the shopping bag he emerged with, substantiating my interpretation. When we cleared the immediate area of the bank Novak moved into a deep secluded doorway. I followed with anxious thoughts, wondering how much money he had in the paper shopping bag. He opened it gingerly, as if he had a million dollars.

"How much?" I asked.

"I really don't know. It's a lot of paper. What it will buy, we'll soon find out," was his answer.

"We'll head for our quarters down the main street. I know of a bakery store along the way. We'll test its value there," Novak suggested.

By this time I didn't give a shit for any of Novak's ideas, I just wanted out of this bitter cold.

"There's our quarters. Let's just forget the bakery. We'll have plenty to eat when the truck arrives," I practically screamed.

I was almost in a trot. My frozen feet felt like I was running on rocks. It was then, about a half a block from our destination, when it caught my eye: this big cream frosted layer cake in the bakery window. The suddenness of my attempt to stop put me into a Leon Errol dance, legs, arms, and head in every possible direction. Somehow I kept my balance. I think I made up my mind not to fall just to hush Novak, who was laughing hysterically. We were like two kids gaping at the cake. There were other cakes in the window, but the frosted layer cake stood out like a Christmas tree.

"Gee, Novak, with all the money we have, we can probably buy everything in the window, and really surprise the rest of the boys," I wished aloud.

"After being gone so long with no one knowing where we are, I doubt if this surprise is going to please your Pilot," Novak commented. "The truck load of food may, I say may, curtail his anger."

"I'm not really worried about him. It's Helena who isn't going to be too pleased, after the warning she gave us," I countered.

"Don't worry about her. I forewarned her. She'll act out her anger in front of the rest-she and Sonia helped to get our guard to go along," was Novak's surprising answer.

"Don't talk in the store, just mumble and point to the cakes you like. I'll take care of the purchases," he instructed.

When we entered, there was but one other customer who appeared to be just looking and drooling. It was funny to me but this Bakery didn't smell like those at home. I couldn't explain it, but the odor of fresh-baked products was missing.

Novak was having what appeared to be a battle of words with the proprietor. It was without need of translation, clearly being anything but a friendly discussion. I wasn't able to question the goings on without exposing myself. I bit my tongue, and waited for Novak's action. He grabbed me by the arm, and led me out the door into the street.

"What the fuck's the problem?" I asked. "Isn't the money any good?"

"The money is good, but it won't buy much of anything. This guy is a big thief. I can't bargain with him," Novak explained.

"If we were like those scum bags we left behind in Warsaw, we would hit him on the head and empty this fucking place," I suggested.

"You don't realize we are out of the war areas. Martial law prevails, and the crap you can get away with where the fighting is, is a no no now," Novak warned. He added, "You forget who you are, and where you are, which wouldn't help the situation."

"How about that layer cake in the window?" I asked.

"Do you really want to know?" Before I could respond Novak added, "Every bit of money we have, and he wants me to believe I'm getting a bargain".

"Let's buy the layer cake and get the hell out of here, I'm losing my desire. Maybe if you tell him it's for me, an American, we'll get a break," I said.

"You must be out of your mind! Don't even think about it," Novak whispered.

"Ah shit, what have we got to lose? This little fat nothing can't hurt us," I whispered back to Novak.

"If you pull anything like I think you're thinking, I'm leaving," Novak threatened, and started to walk away.

As he stated to leave I walked into the shop, pulled my American flag patches from my pocket, and waved them into the face of the clerk. I suspected he didn't understand English, so with as broad a smile as I could muster, I said, "Listen, you son of a bitch, I'm an American, and I'm in this God-forsaken hole, freezing my balls, trying to help you and yours. All I want is to get the fuck out of here, and all I want from you is a fucking piece of your crummy cake." I said all this with a broad smile through my clenched teeth.

"I'm not any of the names you called me. Your friend never mentioned who you were, he just tried to pull rank on me, telling me of all the Russian officers he knew, so I jerked him around a bit. Shit, take anything you want, it's on the house." He concluded with, "I'm one of many Poles who were caught here during the German invasion, and conscripted into the Polish Army. I was lucky: I wasn't captured. I escaped into Russia. Because of my age and baking experience, I remained out of combat."

Novak retraced his steps, when he realized I hadn't followed him. He entered the store like he expected to find me or the clerk dead, or ready to do combat. I wish I had a way to preserve for eternity the look on his face when he heard our conversation in English. When he saw the clerk filling a box with goodies, and placing the frosty layer cake in a special box, I thought he would swoon.

Almost gasping for breath, Novak asked, "What the hell did you do? what's going on here?"

"I did nothing. I called him some choice vulgar names, and told him I was an

American, showing him my American flag patches. He told me the flags didn't convince him I was an American, it was the names I called him."

"We're getting all that cake for how much?" Novak asked.

"For nothing," I responded, "but you will give him all the money we have, OK?"

"After this escapade, anything you say or do is OK with me," Novak agreed.

When we arrived at our quarters, we climbed the stairs and left the cakes in the hall. I thought it best to survey the atmosphere, then plead our case. It was a welcome sight to see Helena there; her presence calmed the actions of my Pilot, outwardly that is. I could sense his desire to question my actions. I could see in her face that Helena wondered how we made out with the Russian officer and his commissary.

It was time to satisfy all the questions, and placate all the anxieties. I, with Novak's help, vividly told of our travels. We placed emphasis on the dangerous escapades, in an attempt to gain some sympathy from our companions. We then told them of the truck load of hand-picked food on its way, which should arrive momentarily.

"While we are awaiting the truck, we have a delicious treat for you. You may want to eat it as dessert, after dinner, but that will be your choice," I explained.

Novak produced the boxes, placing them on the table. He then opened them, to anxious searching eyes. After the shit we had been eating most of the time, the sight of these goodies, especially the layer cake, produced sighs and moans that made all our efforts worth while.

Before anyone had made a choice of dessert before or after dinner, we were informed of the truck's arrival. The guard said something to Helena, and she responded with, "It's alright to go downstairs and help unload the truck."

When the canvas curtain was opened on the back of the truck, neither Novak, who was by my side, nor I could believe what we saw. We didn't want to believe the sight that was presented to us. There wasn't one tenth of the food we had seen loaded on the truck. Everyone looked at us with disdain, and disappointment.

"Fellows, believe us, we have no idea what happened to the food we saw loaded in this truck," Novak and I said, almost defensively.

I looked at Helena with questioning eyes, trying not to implicate her in our escapade with the rest of our companions, but hoping for some explanation. When we carried what was there upstairs, even Sonia showed surprise at the meager supplies. She said something to Helena, which caused Helena to recoil, as if in disbelief.

Helena pulled me aside and whispered, "Sonia knows the truck was filled when it left the commissary. Her Russian lover told her so. He liked you American airmen."

Sonia removed the supplies to the kitchen to prepare dinner, which would include nothing new to add to the usual crap we endured.

"Well, at least we'll have some fine dessert to offset our food disappointment," I attempted consolation.

The dinner was the best Sonia could provide with the tools at hand. Somehow Sonia always produced some sort of liqueur when it was needed most. We finished dinner and as one awaited dessert. To our surprise, especially those who smoked, Sonia produced with a smile a carton of Lucky Strike cigarettes, with a glass of burgundy. These luxuries lessened the disappointment, but not the bitterness, over the missing food stuffs .

Now came desert time. The goodies were placed upon the table, totally exposed from their confinement in their respective boxes. Sonia produced some coffee, and started to cut the layer cake. It really looked delicious, as Sonia's son placed dishes and forks before us. Someone asked about the coffee. Helena responded with, "It's not bad. It will go good with the cake."

The cake was cut in slices, placed upon the dishes, and each of us forked a piece into our mouths, with expected relish. "What the hell?" was a unanimous outcry, accompanied with a unanimous expectoration of cake in all directions. Those who attempted to rinse their mouths of this foul taste with the coffee, found no relief. The words of Novak filled the room with the only explanation, "Ersatz."

CHAPTER 27 — THE JOLLY RUSSIAN GIANT

The cake episode minimized the seriousness of our unauthorized travels. The rest of the crew's attitude of appreciating our efforts made any attack by the Pilot appear self-serving. His attempt to pull rank by chastising us verbally was weak, but we accepted it as an honest concern for our well being.

We never discussed the hows, or who helped us initiate our adventure, but everyone was interested in hearing the full story. Novak and I answered most of the questions asked with relations to specific incidents. I tried to lessen the gravity of the incidents which in reality were kind of scary. Novak embarrassed me at times when he described incidents in which I felt I acted foolish and irresponsible. He made it out like I was some kind of hero. I dwelled on the movies, the funny things that happened in the bakery, and the response to my wild retorts by the Russian officer and how he was happy all crazy Americans were Russia's allies. When all was said and done, every one knew exactly what we wanted them to know. Novak nor I ever mentioned the black market operation, although we never decided to refraining from disclosing it. The seriousness and possible ramifications were indelibly, automatically, imprinted on our minds, and then just as automatically blanked out.

Helena's absence most of the time caused some concern, but Novak assured us, "Your well being is uppermost in her mind. She'll bring you up to date, whenever she has positive information."

I wondered if my refusal to participate in a love encounter the first night soured our friendship. She hadn't shared my bed since then. Sonia began to show a more friendly attitude towards the Navigator, especially when her son wasn't around. When they disappeared into her room, he was aware that all ears were glued to the door. He would emphasize his grunts and groans in such a manner that a picture couldn't be more vivid. It got to the point where the guard joined in the act of listening, then went one step further. He showed us an adjoining room where we could witness the love making through a transom above the connecting door. The first night we attempted a transom vigil we were blacked out, and only darkened shapes were visible. Of course the sounds were still audible, and you could feel the results of your imagination by a bodily response.

We told the Navigator of the lack of light to illuminate his love prowess. He said he would attempt to convince Sonia there should be light. "Hell, I don't think she ever opens her eyes anyway, she fucking swoons the moment I stick it in," he bragged.

The days passed slowly. Cat napping and idle conversation became boring. We waited impatiently for our lovers' encounters.

"We've got to find some diversion," I suggested. Every time Sonia passed through the room she was mentally undressed and raped. She must have sensed the arousal in the virgin farm boys of the crew. She played a little "now you see it, now you don't," swishing around in her loose fitting skirt, bending and squatting in the most exposing positions. I felt these long drawn out days were boring to her also.

I never thought the guard would present a diversion of a new and sadistic nature. It happened the day Sonia's son brought home the Russian friend we had seen running from the apartment the day we arrived. I suspected Sonia chasing him with a broom meant to get lost and don't return. Apparently they had made up, but Sonia's language and finger-pointing at the Russian boy was translated by Novak as, "If you want to play with my son, you mind how you treat him, or I'll bust your ass."

Everything was normal. We sat around just killing time, as usual. Even the potential undressing of Sonia was eliminated when she left, we suspected to spend some time with her Russian lover. Novak intercepted her at the door, spoke to her, patted her on the ass, and said something that sounded like good luck.

"I asked her to find out, if she could, what happened to the food that disappeared from the truck," Novak volunteered.

"I'm curious, what did you say to her, when you patted her on the ass?" I inquired.

"You know me by now, I haven't a vulgar mind like you. But under the circumstances, I didn't wish her good luck. I said have a good fuck. Now I'm like you," he added.

"Get off that shit, you're no saint. I see you taking your turn getting off when Sonia points her pussy in your direction," I countered.

The laughing of the guard disrupted the conversation, which was going nowhere. The screams in Polish needed no translation: the one screaming was getting hurt. We all dashed into Sonia's bedroom. The Russian giant was holding the Gypsy's hands behind his back, and the Russian kid was taking pot shots at the Gypsy's head. The guard was uttering some kind of encouragement. I asked Novak what was he saying.

"Hit the German, hit the Nazi, and the big bastard means it," Novak said, as he yanked the Gypsy from the guard's grasp. The Russian was taken aback; he responded with the release of his stiletto from its scabbard. As he raised it in the direction of Novak, we all as one moved between them. The guard smiled as he lowered his weapon, and replaced it in its scabbard.

"As I have explained, these Mongolians are so brainwashed the only enemy they know are the Germans, or anything that represents a German," Novak reiterated.

The guard appeared genuinely embarrassed. Maybe the days of being in our company, and the crazy things we do, had broken through the military shell that encased him. We all agreed, his next action not only substantiated our belief but proved not all Russians are pricks. He proceeded to call the Russian kid to his right side, and the Gypsy to his left.

"Geez, he's going to have them make up," we all thought aloud.

Then to our disbelief, and with a smile on his face, he grabbed the Russian kid, locked his arms behind his back, and proceeded to encourage the Gypsy to belt him.

"He wants to be friends, and this is his way of making amends," Novak explained. "He wants us to believe he's fair."

"Shit, tell him just to leave the kids alone," I suggested, "he don't have to prove a thing."

Before Novak could tell him anything, he had the two kids squaring off in a boxing stance, but with open palms. He began to instruct them the art of self defense without any contact. He also included wrestling, and a form of jujitsu. Each and every day the two kids were together, the instructions they received and their performances were entertaining. We really looked forward to it. The guard became more friendly, and his relaxed attitude was to our advantage. It gave a chance to exit the building for some fresh air, even though we didn't venture off the front stoop. The stench of the oil heat saturated your clothes, and impregnated the hairs in your nose as a permanent part of your being.

It got to the point where the guard would sit down with us when we ate, and through Novak, he would ask questions of a personal nature. His curiosity was enhanced by the relaxed attitude of all concerned, and our willingness to answer all of his questions. He never asked questions of a military nature, and if he did Novak never let on. We were apprised through Novak that he had very little geography knowledge. America was just the name of a far away land, and he was helping to fight their war.

One day his curiosity centered on the equipment we either wore or stacked in a corner of the room. The heated suits we wore were equipped with plug in wires; the boot wires plugged into the pant leg at the ankle, the cuffs had lead-ins to the heated gloves, which all in turn was plugged in to the electric source aboard the aircraft. Now all these wires were nothing but dangling encumbrances, and a topic of inquiry for the guard. Novak's explanation about electricity excited him as we allowed him to finger the dangling plug and run his fingers along the imbedded heating wires throughout the suit. Through this mutual admiration course we did a little brainwashing of our own, and used this new found Russian ally to not only provide us with whatever news he had concerning our future, but as a source of cigarettes - Russian, but better than the usual.

His curiosity was centered on the Mae West jackets piled in a corner of the room. He questioned Novak about them as he picked one up.

"One of you explain - although I know what they are for, I have no idea how they work," Novak requested.

The guard always had his Burp gun slung across his back, which would be in the way if our plan of demonstrating the Mae West would be effective.

"Tell him to get rid of his piece, if he really wants to see how a Mae West works," I directed to Novak.

His *nyet* was easily understood, and the negative nodding of his head left no doubt he wouldn't comply.

"Come on. Novak," I pleaded, "explain that we won't hurt him, we're friends, he'll get an education."

"What the fuck do you have in mind?" the Pilot asked, as he had just entered the room after taking a nap. "It's got to be some devious shit, if it's your idea."

Novak explained the curiosity of the guard. "We are just displaying our friendship by visual and physical demonstrations."

"Just don't create any situations that will embarrass or alienate our host," the Pilot ordered.

Novak finally convinced the guard to discard his weapon, and we placed the Mae West over his head. As I have said he was a very large man. The Mae West was very snug, but we managed to secure the tie strings.

What happened next wasn't planned or rehearsed, but it can't be told until the whole stage is set.

The day was dreary and gray; it had warmed a little, and the snow-covered terrain had thawed. A light wet snow was falling, adding to the rivulets of water that ran in the gutters along the curb. All was peaceful and serene, as well as any city under martial law could be, with weather conditions as they were.

All this unpleasantness was locked outside. We were snug in our quarters, with nothing but fun and frolic on our minds, and all kinds of time to enjoy it. What happened next displays what can happen if the educated beguiles the uneducated.

The Mae West was snugly in place, in the deflated position. The lanyards attached to the C20 cylinders used to inflate the Mae West were dangling within easy reach of any idiot who didn't know what they were. Of course we surmised the action of our Mongolian idiot: he pulled on both at the same time. The results of that, we didn't surmise. The Mae West inflated fully, and the collar snapped up in the back of his neck, jolting his head forward into his chest. His reaction was one of defense" he removed his stiletto and proceeded to slash the Mae West.

Novak tried to stop him, verbally and physically, to no avail. During all this confusion, the Pilot was screaming, "You sons of bitches, I'll have your asses for this," but he made no move to help.

The inevitable had to happen: his stiletto finally reached the packets of orange dye to be released when you are floating in the ocean, as a marker for rescue operations. It is a bright, almost iridescent orange visible for many miles. It is stored in powder form in packets attached to the Mae West. When our Russian giant slashed the packets. The powder spewed all over the room. He slashed and ripped until the Mae West was completely removed from his person. Then before anyone could prevent him, he opened the window and threw the remnants of the Mae West into the street below. Getting rid of this mystery weapon appeared to calm him. Novak soothed him with what sounded like conciliatory talk, and did everything but pat this big ape on the head.

"Damn you bunch of jerks, look at the mess you caused! Clean it up." The Pilot almost had a smile on his face when he concluded, "It could have been worse."

The pounding of heavy booted feet bounding up the stairs froze us in our tracks, and the door being kicked in by gun bearing soldiers meant "it was worse."

Novak, the courageous little bastard, stepped between us, as we automatically backed against the walls. What he was screaming had some effect; at least no shots were fired. One of the soldiers, apparently an officer, raised his hand and blurted out what appeared to be an order that relaxed the rest into a less combative attitude.

Out of nowhere, Helena burst into the room. "What the hell is going on here?" she asked in English, Polish, and I presumed Russian, because everyone froze in place.

The officer certainly knew Helena. He responded with a salute of respect and recognition. They had a short conversation which ended by the open window. During the mass confusion, with the shouting and screaming, the noise of shouting and screaming outside the building went unnoticed. Now with the forced quiet of the room, the noise outside was very audible. Helena and the officer looked out the window, retreated with a look of horror, then grasped each other in an embrace of mutual joy, and laughed hysterically.

Almost as one we moved towards the open window. Others opened the other two windows facing the street. Presented was a picture of utter confusion, as serious as it was comical.

The dye powder blowing out onto the street mixed with the flowing water along the curbs, produced a flowing orange-colored river. Vehicles caused the water to splash upon the sidewalks and spread onto the roadways. The unaware pedestrians tracking through the orange water produced orange footprints. It was this phenomenon that caused the near panic in the streets. The pedestrians running helter-skelter attempting to escape the following footsteps were hysterically funny to those who knew the reason.

Looking out the window made it easy to understand how the soldiers located the source of the dye. The wall of the building under our window was streaked with the brightest color orange.

Helena escorted the officer and his men to the door, pointing to the damage they caused.

"He will have the door repaired immediately," she said, then asked, "How did all this happen?"

The guard must have anticipated her question, because to our surprise, with verbal and demonstrative actions he replayed the scene in its entirety, with serious connotations. Then suddenly when the realization of his actions struck home, and the street scene emphasized his foolish reaction, he began to laugh and cry at the same time, truly becoming, "The Jolly Russian Giant."

CHAPTER 28 — LOVE ME

All of the confusion was put to rest, and we discussed the possibility of seeing the town under escort. We posed it as an option; some felt that there was still unseen danger lurking, and self preservation was still a priority.

"Hell," I said, "we wandered all over town. If you don't speak to anyone, just blend in with the other people, no one will even notice you."

"What the hell is there to see?" someone asked.

"I'm not talking about historical sights, or picturesque landscapes, just a change of scenery. To witness a country and its people, devastated just a few weeks ago, blend into a community of productive living, not yet free completely, but with prayerful hope, will be something to make this adventure worthwhile."

"Damn you," the Pilot countered, "stop pushing your luck! I just want to get the hell out of here in one piece, and believe it or not, I mean all of us, including you."

Novak suggested we not argue, but wait for Helena, to see what her thoughts were about roaming around town.

"I don't give a shit what she thinks. I'm in command here. I'm responsible for all of you. If something goes wrong I'll have to answer for it," was his retort.

Someone responded with (to my surprise), "How come you're only in command when it pertains to our actions? Why the fuck don't you exercise some command with the authority here, instead of passing the buck to Helena?"

The Pilot didn't respond to the questions. Either he didn't want to qualify the questions as being applicable, or to answer after his lack of command in past incidents would be embarrassing. It was hard to find compatibility in all issues that arose; each had his own degree of guts and mental know how. Even as a combat team, there were areas of insecurity, but somehow we survived. I prayed that despite our differences in areas of action and reaction, we would survive.

We spent the hours reminiscing about past missions, and of course the one that placed us in this situation. Someone brought up the kid from Brooklyn, who got sick and missed this piece of Air Force history.

"I told him to be waiting when we got back from Dresden. Shit, he's probably completed his missions by now," I said.

"Who knows? We're here alive. He could be dead," someone morbidly added.

Moans greeted that response, with guttural laughter that diminished the morbid intent of the statement.

Being cooped up and sheltered from any contact direct or indirect with the warring world led to the deterioration of the comradeship shared when we were cooped up in a B-17. There we shared all the contacts of the warring world, directly and indirectly. I hoped all the individual wants and desires would be shared collectively. Novak had emphasized the part of our travels through Russia without he or Helena would test our resources as an American team. There was the threat of be eaten alive by the Russian military or the desperate displaced persons we would encounter. Self preservation would be a must, for the people we would come in contact with were, for the most part, uneducated. Not only were they lacking in book learning, but there was little or no education in moral living. Life meant nothing to them; they had killed to avoid being killed. We would have to think with the same morbid, sick reasoning, or die. Novak had made this very clear in attempting to outline our future.

"I can't believe the shit he's telling us. I thought once we reached our allies, the danger was past," I stated, seeking some consolation.

Novak, in the hope of convincing us that the warnings were not "shit," as I described it, tried to vividly explain the situation as it truly was, and would be.

"You all seem to forget the way you expected to be treated if you were captured in Germany. You were prepared to defend yourself, anyway possible." Novak continued, and we listened intently. "In Germany, you were in a combat zone, under combat conditions, where in most instances military law prevailed. You had a chance for survival."

"But we'll be among allies. Why should we fear them?" someone asked.

"I can't believe you said that," Novak countered. "You have a short memory. Were you treated as an ally by the Russian military? Why would any civilian, or deserters, and there are many, show any respect towards you? We the Polish people know Russia is our enemy, and future history will show Russia is an American ally only out of necessity, for self preservation."

We wanted to take these warnings with a grain of salt, but his sincerity was apparent, and his concern for us heart warming. The American infantry sergeant and the English paratrooper suddenly came to mind. Would they be there when we started our trek through Russia? Being ground soldiers, they would have dealt with the public and the military and it would be comforting to have them with us. I reminded myself to ask Helena of their whereabouts, and the chance of her promise being fulfilled.

We attempted to make light of the picture Novak painted, but it was only wishful thinking. The brutality we had witnessed in the past could only magnify the possible events to follow. Our major concern was the fact wasn't physical, that everyone but me was unarmed. The rest of the crew had surrendered what little power and protection they had when they turned in their guns.

"I think after what Novak had spelled out you should insist our arms are returned before we go out on our own," I suggested to the Pilot.

"Who is going to know where they are?" was his cop out.

"So we don't get back our own pieces, just give us something to defend ourselves with," someone added.

Novak entered the discussion with constructive criticism, "You can't undo what has been done with arguments, I'll see what Sonia can accomplish with her lover friend when she gets home."

We all agreed with his suggestion, and also agreed to cut out the arguments, which only added to the mental anguish caused by the uncertainties that prevailed.

Sonia arrived as darkness was setting in; she looked drained, said something to Novak, who translated it as, "I'll get the food ready."

"Ask her about some weapons, the first chance you get," I whispered.

"Damn, you are not leaving this minute. Give her a chance to settle down. She looks like she had a tough day," Novak lectured.

"I'll give her a hand," the Navigator volunteered, as he followed her into the kitchen.

"Make sure that's all you give her," was chorused by all.

At that moment, the guard was rapped in the back by the door he was was leaning against, as Sonia's kid and his companion burst into the room. The man's casual posture caused his monstrous body to be catapulted across the room, arms and legs flying in all directions.

His embarrassment was multiplied by the two kids falling on top of him and using the techniques he had taught them to pin him down. His first reaction was to roughly throw them off, but he caught himself, and playfully staged a struggling act, to no avail, speaking to them in Russian.

"He's telling them that he gives up," said Novak. This brought a round of laughter and a big smile from the guard.

"You guys have made a friend. I am going to ask Helena if it is possible to have this Mongolian escort you on your journey," Novak suggested.

The footsteps ascending the stairs were Helena's, who as usual arrived unannounced, with her usual air of authority.

The guard was still sitting on the floor, and his position as such stopped Helena in her tracks. "What the hell are you doing? You'll get shot for assaulting him. Novak, how could you let this happen?"

Her face was livid, her voice stuttered with rage. "I just finished making plans for your travels to Odessa, where you will catch a ship on your first step to England. This episode will certainly cause some unwelcome changes," she screamed.

Her loud chastising voice brought Sonia and the Navigator bursting into the room. Not having been a witness to the incident between the guard and the kids, the Navigator demanded, "Who the fuck are you yelling at?"

The Pilot restrained the Navigator's forward motion by placing his open palm on his chest. It was becoming apparent that this close confinement with foreign authority was becoming untenable.

Helena was taken back by the rude action of the Navigator, but with her shrewd, cunning mind, realized the scene she encountered was not the scene as she had pictured.

"Don't get excited," she charged the Navigator. "Are you angry because my yelling disrupted your erection?"

"No, you bitch. What the hell do you know about an erection? Just your attitude and presence would have the same effect!" he responded.

"Come on, this isn't the way to act. We're all getting a little testy," Novak injected. "We'll be parting before long, We should part as friends, without losing respect for each other."

The guard, sensing the uncomfortable situation, laughingly hoisted the two kids above his head, then clasped them to his chest in a loving bear hug, which brought giggling snickers from the kids, and broke the tension.

The remaining hours of the evening were spent with idle chatter, with most of the conversation related to translating questions and answers from the guard. Sonia's son and his friend participated, and the antics they employed to relay the translations were quite entertaining.

Bedtime came earlier for some than others. I always attempted to ascertain Helena's intentions. Recently she had been excusing herself, and leaving before curfew, but curfew had long passed. I knew a bout with abstinence was on my agenda, and the request "love me" was on Helena's agenda.

CHAPTER 29 — LOVER'S DISAPPOINTMENTS

The double blanket and sleeping in my heated suit remained my primary seduction deterrent. I used any topic of conversation to change the mood she was in.

"Love me, love me, why can't you make love to me, as your Navigator does to Sonia?" she boldly asked.

"If you need loving, why don't you take up with the Navigator?" I responded.

She caught me by surprise with her answer, and I felt embarrassed.

"I am not in the need of loving, as you put it. I have always had my share. There is no one that has reached my heart as you, my heaven boy. I believe God has sent you to me. I give my love to you only," she shamelessly confessed.

What the fuck have I done to deserve this? I thought to myself. I'd been married just a few months, with self imposed promises to change my promiscuous ways. I could, I thought, use the overseas bullshit that rationalized any action.

As if reading my mind, Helena voiced the rationale I'd been considering. "You may die to-morrow. Who would ever know?"

Desperately I attempted to change the subject. "We were wondering if it were possible to tour the town to break the monotony?"

"We will discuss it to-morrow." She attempted to remove the blanket barrier that separated us, stopping abruptly when she heard a foreign sound. The noise of a crashing object, followed by curses in American, Polish, and Mongolian Russian, had resulted from too many degenerate eyes belonging to too many degenerate bodies bushwhacking two hopefully degenerate bed companions. Unfortunately for the views, their vantage point at the connecting door transom was insecure.

The noise, and the realization of its source, stemmed Helena's amorous intent, and the retreating footfalls blended in with the simultaneous, "Good nights". My honor was preserved.

I awakened to find that Helena was not in bed. Entering the sitting room, Novak informed me that she had departed, not only from our bed, but from the building .

"What kind of mood was she in?" I asked.

"It is hard to say. She left in quite a hurry," Novak answered.

"Damn, I hope I didn't jeopardize her aiding us, because I wouldn't give her a fuck." I hoped that Novak would have some idea of her reaction to rejection.

"It is none of my business," Novak stated. "She told me you were lovers, and you promised to help her to get to America when the war ended."

"Lovers? Shit, I haven't laid a hand on her, not that she would have stopped me," I answered.

"Well, believe it or not, everyone of your crew think you have been screwing her ass off. That is why no one else has even thought of approaching her. She made it clear from the first night we met, that she was to be your private stock, and I was to convey her choice to your entire crew."

It may sound trite, to use weak excuses for my lack of desire for sexual encounters. My desire was to get out of the war as clean as I came in. There were so many occasions during my short military life when I personally witnessed close associates who for a few moments of sexual gratification became embarrassed, sick individuals with a permanent mark, not only on their military records, but a permanent mark on their conscience. It always appeared to me that after any mission, when men get together, the conversation that broke the tension was always girl talk. Most of it was bullshit, but it served as an introduction to one's manhood and manly conquest.

The city slickers always had the most vivid descriptions of sex, and were always at their best when they had country bumpkins as an audience. Invariably, they were referred to as sheep fuckers who were suckers for any bullshit story.

When we sat down for breakfast, I made it clear that their actions the previous night weren't appreciated at all.

"You're nothing but a bunch of peeping toms and masturbators," I lectured. This statement brought not a humble response, but a response of hilarity that needed no explanation when as one they offered, "Join the club."

It brought to mind my doing a little "Peeping Tom" on my own, watching on Sonia and the Navigator. We all laughed.

Novak told us that Sonia was instructed not to make breakfast, just coffee. We were going out to eat. She also told her that she was seeking permission to walk about town.

We patiently awaited her return, hopefully with permission to move about. Actually, only the Engineer joined me in that aspiration. The remainder of the group denied any desire to see the town..

Helena arrived within an hour, with a smile that told me what I wanted to hear. I wasn't concerned about the rest.

"We have permission, with reservations. The guard will accompany us. Sonia, her son and his friend may come also," Helena instructed.

Her statement caused a strange reversal of acceptance which wasn't immediately explained. Novak cleared the mystery when he divulged the scenario planned by those not accepting the tour. Novak also pointed out the disappointment etched in the face of the guard. His being assigned as escort killed his long desired fantasy: a piece of Sonia. Sonia had promised to do a Gypsy dance, with sexual overtones, including sexual encounters with all those who desired same. This she said was her going away gesture of love and respect to all Americans.

"What the fuck," I said to myself, "she must have been gang-banged so many times, what's one more? This is probably the only time where she had a choice."

Helena sided up to me and whispered, "I realize you are embarrassed by the presence of your friends. We won't have too many more opportunities."

"Opportunities for what?" I interrupted. "You tied into the wrong guy. Forget it." I wasn't whispering, and heads turned. It was embarrassing to say the least.

My outburst didn't cause one iota of difference in her demeanor. She squeezed my hand in a punishing manner, as a mother squeezes a child's hand in a discreet action, where only the child understands its true intent. It had the connotation of, "wait until I get you home." I felt like punching her smug face, but we were genuinely dependent on her, so I made up my mind to play her game so long as she was useful to us.

This little scenario ended with a final whispered admonishment, "You proved to your friends that we are not lovers by your embarrassing outburst, but I know you do not mean it, I forgive you." She then in her usual authoritative voice, "Dress warmly, we leave in a few minutes."

Sonia's son and his friend, sensing a good meal, made a mad dash for the door. It was a sight to see the guard clothesline them to a sudden stop, with his arms outstretched across the doorway. It was apparent that his intent was not vicious, as it would have been a few days before; now it was a gentle reminder to behave. Everyone left to get their outer garments. I made for my room. As I started to get into my jacket, the door was slammed shut. I was almost yanked off my feet, by a sudden unexpected pull of my collar from behind.

"Don't dress, you don't have to go, please stay with me, I have permission from Sonia's Russian friend," she pleaded.

She unashamedly placed herself against the door to bar my leaving. I gently tried to remove her, but getting close to her in the attempt proved a bad move. She wrapped her arms around me as she planted kiss after kiss upon my face, whenever she could penetrate my hands and arms defense. She grabbed both my wrists firmly, pressed my hands caressingly to her breasts, and by her rotating movement attempted to motivate a reaction. It was hard not to respond, and "hard" was my bodily response. She must have sensed a conquest, as she pressed her body firmly to my erection. She released my hands, and caressed my body slowly in a downward direction. As she reached my hips, she retreated suddenly with a look of surprise. Geez, I thought, have I got bad breath. Her reaction broke the spell. I went limp. She was looking inquisitively at her left hand from every angle. I automatically reached for my right side where I felt a tug when she yanked her hand away. She had caught her hand in the looped wire attached to my electric heating suit. By whatever means, I was saved again.

Realizing I was free from her grasp, I opened the door, saying, "I'm ready, lets go." As we made our exit Helena was standing in the bedroom doorway, hands on her hips, with a "what the hell?" look on her face. I satisfied her questioning look by grasping the electric wire and twirling it as you would a watch fob. Her face was livid; with pursed lips she was mouthing words without sound. She was calling me "a non-fucking bastard."

CHAPTER 30 — GUIDED TOUR

It was crispy cold as we exited the building. There was a fresh coating of snow along with the cold, as one would expect. I was thinking how could we be inconspicuous, this motley group wandering through town under escort. I posed the question to Novak, who responded with, "We will travel together when going to eat, after we will travel in small groups, with Helena. The guard and I will escort one groups. Sonia and the kids will return to the apartment."

"Is the Russian going with her?" asked the Navigator.

"Of course not. I told you before, to knowingly be associated with a Gypsy, let alone one who bore the child of a German, would be a disgrace."

"Well, his loss is my gain. I don't want to go on this fucking tour. It's too cold, and I don't think Sonia and the kids should be left alone," he volunteered.

The conversation reached all those within earshot. All but the Engineer and I agreed that Sonia (fuck the kids) needed protection.

The sudden change in plans didn't escape the ears of Helena, whose response was not of a conciliatory nature.

"After we eat, all those who want to return to the apartment, will return with the guard. Novak and I will guide the rest," she ordered.

I really believed Helena felt the presence of the guard negated any pleasures with Sonia. I wasn't sure if Helena knew the guard was included, since his demeanor changed towards Sonia's son. I began to have reservations when I realized the scenario was formulating: two guides, two tourists. I had to somehow get Novak as my guide. I tried my damnedest to keep out of reach of Helena during our meal, wishing she would honor my wishes.

The meal was interrupted on occasion by friendly, inquisitive soldiers, mostly Polish. The few Russians who ate during our stay nodded politely, but remained aloof as always. The format remained the same as Turek; if it were so, we would be moving out in a few days. The food was genuinely American, as it was in Turek and outside Warsaw. Why look a gift horse in the mouth? However, the feeling still prevailed that this might be one's "last meal."

The Russian officer arrived. Helena greeted him in such a cordial manner, it was apparent she expected him. She introduced him with no fanfare. He responded with a salutatory wave of his hand. It was no surprise to any of us when he ignored Sonia completely, and she played her part as a good little Gypsy. It was apparent that Sonia's son was well schooled, or had no knowledge of his mother's association with the Russian officer, for he too displayed no recognition. I hoped the Russian, who was playing a lot of attention to Helena, would join us on our guided tour, and keep Helena occupied.

The breakfast was delicious, as American as American can be: fresh eggs, ham, bacon, fruit, even orange juice. There were Kellog's corn flakes, as big as life, powdered milk! The crowning glory was the Lucky Strike cigarettes offered with what almost tasted like real coffee.

As usual the conversation was a mixture of questions asked by the Russian through Helena or Novak, and we reversing the procedure, by answering and questioning through the same interlocutors.

It was warm and cheerful in this mess hall. I suggested we linger as long as possible to Novak.

"It is impossible," Novak explained. "They fed us first. The regular military personnel will not enter until we leave. They don't want them to associate with you Americans. As a matter of fact most if not all don't even know you are here."

"What the fuck, are we Lepers?" I asked.

"Do as you are told," the Pilot injected.

Which is what I expected from him, but his order was compounded by Helena's reiteration, in no uncertain terms. We remained a few more minutes. When the Russian spoke to Helena, it was as if he spoke to us directly; his words and Helena's were connected as one: "Get ready to move out." The bubble of contentment was broken. The order placed us right back into the military, and our status was made clear.

As we exited the building, what appeared to be platoons of soldiers, both Russian and Polish, were entering the mess hall. We had expected that, but they appeared to be escorting American soldiers and displaced persons. It was obvious that this meeting was not planned. The Russian officer bellowed a command. The guard, Helena, and some of the escorting platoon surrounded us, and with raised rifles hurried our exit. Some of the American soldiers made our identity, and shouted hello's, but they too were hustled along. Not fast enough for me not to spot the American sergeant and his English friend. Their presence brought to mind Helena's statement that they would be spirited to Lodtz, and be placed on the train with us. It was a sure sign of our being moved, and a sure sign that Helena's awareness of the forthcoming orders was what she meant when she said we didn't have much time.

Once we were in the street, the demeanor of the Russian and Helena changed. I suddenly realized Novak wasn't present during the disturbance, but was present now.

"Where the hell were you?" I asked.

"I located a cousin of mine who works in the kitchen. You will like her, I invited her to visit us at the apartment," he explained.

"Does Helena know about this?" I inquired.

"Oh yes. At one time they were lovers, when the Germans had them locked up. When Helena was chosen by the Germans to be the go-between for the townspeople and the German command, she went straight." Novak concluded, "Helena will not mind."

"How the hell do you know all this?" I asked. "Don't give me the shit that Helena told you. From what I have seen I wouldn't believe a fucking word of hers again."

"I do not understand your thinking. She has done so much for you and your friends, especially you," Novak countered. "I am indebted to her, she got me this assignment."

"What I tell you is true. Helena, my cousin and I grew up together. We had many an orgy in our youth. We used to watch each other making love. It was only when Helena gained the high echelon of the governing body in command, did she pick and choose only the ones who could advance her cause."

"What cause is she pursuing making up to me?" I asked.

"Because you are from New York City. The others to her are farmers. The word is, New Yorkers rule the United States." Novak almost sounded as if he wanted confirmation.

"Shit, man, I better tell her the truth. I'm no 'Wall Streeter,' just a hard working yokel from a place called Staten Island." Then I rationalized, what a crazy thought. I'll soon be rid of this convertible bitch, why make waves?

I softened my criticism of Helena, thinking I had no assurance Novak didn't tell tales out of school. He sure as hell wasn't shy relating revealing shit about himself and Helena.

It was about this time that Helena in her usual authoritative attitude dictated her orders.

"All you who wish to return to the apartment, do so immediately. I am ordering the guard to lead you directly to your quarters," and with emphasis, "I mean directly."

She followed her orders with a barrage of Russian directed at the guard, which certainly were her instructions as related to us. His response was almost a curtsy, which diminished his mammoth size.

There was a private conversation between Helena and the Russian, as they casually moved away. He did most of the talking, she did most of the affirmative head nodding. He shook her hand, and lovingly stroked her cheek. She withdrew with a reluctant look at the Russian, and a look of reaffirmation toward me. His eyes followed her glance. I thought, this cunt is going to cause me problems.

I tried my damnedest to attach myself to Novak, but Helena never gave me a chance. She directed Novak to take the Engineer under his wing, with the directive, "Keep from any military installations, mingle with the crowds, be home before dark." She concluded with, "I will see you at the apartment."

It was cold as we started to walk up what appeared to be the same street Novak and I had walked in our journey through town. We hadn't walked but a few blocks when Helena grabbed my arm and turned me into a doorway of a building.

"What gives?" I asked.

"It is much too cold to wander about. Besides, Novak has shown you most of the town worth seeing," she explained.

How do I get out of this bitch's clutches without alienating her? I thought. My mind was a blank as we passed through what appeared to be the lobby of a hotel. Helena gently took my arm and led me to an alcove where there was a stairway. A door adjacent to the stairway caught my eye. As it opened and closed, men and women entered and left. It must be the way to the shit house. Could I use this discovery to separate myself from this scheming nymphomaniac?

"I have to go," I declared.

"Oh, you recognized the rest room. I will go too," she volunteered.

I not only recognized the rest room, I recognized where we were as we walked. We were not far from our quarters. I'd ditch her when she's in the shit house, I planned. As we walked through the door, I said, "I'll wait for you, or you wait for me after we're finished."

She looked at me with a questioning glance, and its connotation was translated by the sight and sounds that greeted me. There were both men and women seated in little stalls, not unlike the stalls in shoe repair stores in the States. They had the double swinging doors in front, and sides that were waist high, and a bench. When seated only your private parts were concealed from view by passerby. Your neighbor, male or female, had a complete awareness of your actions, both visually and phonetically, not meaning speech. They responded to passing salutations with a wave of their hand in acknowledgement, despite the odor punctuated by sounds of gastric emissions, in varying degrees of decibels.

Not really wanting to go, I did an about face, but not before Helena entered a stall and asked if I had changed my mind as she pulled up her skirt, and lowered her drawers.

I knew then, if I had any idea of lovemaking with her, this scene killed it completely. The only result of any value from this scene was the opportunity to retreat quickly from the building, and escape once more from temptation. I could hear Helena, yelling, "Wait,

wait, don't go," as I tried to minimize her embarrassment by pretending it wasn't me she was calling to.

When I arrived at the apartment, Novak and the Engineer were already there. I asked the Engineer if he liked the tour.

"You must be kidding-we came right back here. You missed some show," he continued. "Sonia is teaching us Gypsy love making, and Novak's cousin is some piece of ass, so the replacement waist gunner told us. He was the only one who chanced this unknown quantity, and bragged about her prowess as a blow job."

"The best part of the whole show was the guard and the two women doing a threesome, fucking, sucking, the whole bit," added the Navigator. "How did you make out? Did she finally get you alone?"

"I got the guided tour. What a tour, I got to see the inside of a shit house, and I got to see Helena pull up her skirt and drop her drawers. I didn't wait around to find out which, shit or piss," I answered.

I thought Helena would come storming back with a chip on her shoulder, looking for some kind of apology. She returned just before curfew, with some wine and cigarettes. Her actions were questionable in my mind. She never mentioned the scene at the rest room to anyone, but she cornered Novak, away from earshot, and Novak's nodding head in the affirmative convinced me she was issuing orders.

Helena noticed Novak's cousin for the first time, and appeared taken back, genuinely surprised to say the least.

"What the hell are you doing here?" she asked, and not in a friendly tone.

Novak answered for her. "I did not think you would mind."

"How could you do this?" Then reflexively added, "I am sorry, Novak. I remember now, I never told you about her. Get rid of her immediately."

My God, I thought, what could have happened to change the feelings Novak had portrayed to me between the two? Novak said something to his cousin; she dressed as he escorted her to the door. She turned towards Helena, and the gesture she used had the connotation of the Italian sign for "up yours."

Helena dismissed any thought of retaliation by asking in a subtle questioning tone, "What kind of day did we have?"

Her sideward glance in my direction, with a curled lip, had an earnest request: "Please do not embarrass me by divulging today's incident."

I nodded affirmatively, hoping she would never find out the story was already told.

CHAPTER 31 — THANKS FOR NOTHING

The rest of the day and evening was spent not relating the incidents of the day. Everyone but I was of the opinion Helena would raise holy hell if she had any idea of the things that took place. I felt the nymphomaniac would be the star attraction, and more so if she could perform with me.

Since Helena was here after curfew, I realized I had to prepare another barrier of defense. Remembering her words, "We do not have much time," I delayed going to bed with any excuse possible. The rest of the crew, sensing my dilemma, made the best of the situation by retiring early. They always had in mind the possibility of catching Helena with her guard down, which included catching her with her drawers down.

The Navigator said, "I'd like to fuck her just once, to make her angry, the conceited bitch."

Someone suggested that, before I cut her off completely, a little foreplay would help us find out why she turned on Novak's cousin so vehemently. Novak, when asked, was as uninformed as we. I didn't think it would be a great task to get that information, unless it was so personal it would cause Helena embarrassment.

With my commitment to try, I declared, "I will use any persuasive means to extract the information you desire, short of fornication or the many other degenerate acts of perversion, you use to satisfy your fantasies."

This utterance brought a chorus of boos and verbal abuse that bordered on being sacrilegious by using the name of God in vain.

"What are you, a fucking saint?".

"Were you sent here by God, to protect the world from sin?"

"You must think you are God's gift to woman. We will agree, where Helena is concerned, so don't bullshit us. Her drawers are open to you. So is her mouth, for more than talking!"

This conversation ended when Helena, Novak, Sonia, and the guard appeared from the kitchen. I believed Helena must have satisfied their curiosity concerning her behavior to Novak's cousin. Hopefully Novak would relay the information to us. If so, my chancy commitment would, I prayed, be negated.

The Pilot asked Helena if there was any confirmation about our moving on. She replied that from what she was told by the Russian earlier in the day, "If everything goes right, and the transportation is available, tomorrow is the day."

This declaration was pleasant to all concerned, but somehow I got the feeling the emphasis she placed on "sometime tomorrow" was a definite threat to my abstinence.

"By the way," Helena said, "the food that disappeared from that truck before it got to you was located, I learned from the Russian officer. He told me the culprits concerned are now dead, and the food will be aboard the train for your travels."

Good God! She mentioned the "culprits" like they were some inanimate objects! What a fickle cunt, I thought. Then again if you rationalize what she has gone through and survived, a morbid situation that would be unthinkable to us, is just a passing acceptable incident to her. Given her reactions to any situation, be it casual, domineering, authoritative, and sometimes downright arrogant, how could she feel real love? Especially to an American, whose respect towards woman was enhanced by just the opposite behavior? If Helena's behavior was normal, the old story of European woman always walking behind their men was a lot of shit.

Someone asked Sonia where her son was, he wasn't seen since breakfast. The question was picked up by Novak, after an exchange of a few words. Novak laughingly repeated what Sonia had answered.

"Her son for his age knows too much already. His sex education is strictly European. I did not wish him spoiled by American love making." He then added, "She says from what she has witnessed, both seeing and physical, Americans need more teaching, her son could teach them."

Helena couldn't pass up this opportunity to gloat, and declare, "I agree. A solid example is my 'heaven boy,'" and without one iota of embarrassment, "He thinks it is only to piss out of."

Of course this brought laughter, but it was received jokingly, and led to other cliches, and more laughter. I had to get even with Helena, but I wanted her to lead into a conversation where I could really stick it to her. I used her remark about the only use for it was to piss, as a lead in.

"You know Helena, you are absolutely right about my lack of sexual knowledge. I confess, I was a virgin when I got married but the war deprived me of my sex education."

"Well it shows. Your experience is without a doubt for a man your age inexcusable. We know more at grade school age."

"Well thank God for your blessings," I responded. "If all the pricks were sticking out of you, that were stuck in you, you would look like a porcupine."

A hush was the response to that statement, but Helena took it stolidly with the remark, "Yours will not be sticking out, because you have never stuck it in, and never will."

Of course that remark dispelled all the ideas that I was screwing her ass off. I could only believe, or made myself believe, her statement meant I had nothing to worry about. I excused myself, and went to bed.

I still used the double blanket protective device, and bedded down with my heated suit to offset the cold. I lay there wondering if Helena would punish us because of my attitude. She seemed to have the clout to have any desire she wished. My repeated denials to make love to her were beginning to affect her behavior.

I must have dozed off, with my mind continuing to focus on the eventual events Helena could control. Would she, in feeling that she played the wrong card in choosing me as a passport to America, and my complete disregard for all she had done for me personally, perpetuate a complete hatred for us as representatives of all Americans? I was unqualified for the position I found myself, where my decision, seemingly so irrelevant, could possibly endanger the lives of my crew.

The whispered, "I love you so much, why do you deny me?" jogged my mind to reality.

The kisses enveloping my face, and the hand caressing my penis to a complete arousal, proved I wasn't having a wet dream. She was desperately trying to remove the blanket I was rolled up in.

"Please, Helena!" I was almost pleading. "Don't say you love me! I'm a married man, and there is no way we could ever be together! That is why I always try to discourage you.

"You must believe I am very grateful for all you have done for me and the rest of my crew, and will always respect you for the dangers you faced by helping us.

"Please let me thank you from the bottom of my heart. I love you as a wonderful friend, I'm forever grateful, but I'm not the love you wanted," I concluded.

"This may be our last night together. All I can say, is thanks for nothing," she responded, as her advances ended.

She turned her back to me. I would swear I heard her sobbing. I really felt a sadness, as I attempted to return to sleep.

I would also swear I heard someone say, "What a fucking jerk." In what you call twilight sleep, I recall thinking, "Those degenerate pricks were privy to our whole conversation. I hoped they realized that it wasn't all funny."

The next morning, after Helena left, we were told by Novak we would go to breakfast as yesterday, and when we returned Helena would have the final word as to our status. The fact that our status wasn't set as yet, brought confirmation of my belief the crew had listened in the night before. The Pilot confirmed it when he said, "I hope your puritan attitude last night doesn't cause us any change in plans."

"I'm sorry you feel that way. I didn't want to believe, and still don't, that fucking that cunt has any bearing on our situation." I added,"She wanted us to feel she had control over our welfare, and you guys are buying her bullshit."

"You'll see. We'll move out regardless of how she feels. She wanted us to believe she had control over us. Her actions were self serving at best, and now believe me, she has run out her string," I explained.

"We hope you are right," was chorused by all.

"By the way Novak," someone asked, "did you find out what caused Helena's reaction to your cousin's presence here?"

"It is a sad story, but Helena made it clear I could tell you, just to redeem her actions."

We all agreed she must have had a sound reason for her actions. We voiced our beliefs to encourage Novak to relate the story, who by his tone seemed reluctant to tell.

"I myself," Novak commenced, "do not feel Helena owes you an explanation. It is really none of your concern."

"Shit, man," someone said "don't make this a big thing. It's only our curiosity. We can't change what's history."

Novak insisted she did not want her actions to negate her love and respect for Americans and what they had done for Poland, and their great sacrifices.

"It appears to me if the explanation will make her feel better personally, tell it. It will certainly won't effect our lives in any way," I declared.

"I personally find the story hard to believe, but I also have great trust in Helena, and a love for my cousin," Novak stated, as he related Helena's disclosure.

It all started after Helena was released from confinement, and was appointed the liaison between the German command in Turek and the townspeople. Her most important function was to choose people who were willing to be quislings, and in so doing, became an outcast to all true Poles, including his cousin. He explained how Helena used her connections with the high command to help the Polish underground. She was fortunate that the Germans weren't barbarians. She had to sleep with them, but she was never forced or raped.

All the woman who were not interned enjoyed their freedom. They were in demand, but were approached with a form of dignity, and responded in kind. He went on to explain the actions of his cousin that angered Helena.

Helena was attempting to get his cousin released from confinement, but his cousin wanted no part of Helena, as a collaborator. Helena tried to get word to her, to explain how she was working with the Polish underground, to no avail. Helena did find out that his cousin had a new lover, which hurt her badly. His cousin remained in custody throughout the German occupation. Helena helped the advancement of the Russian occupation forces, and remained in good stead with the Russian high command. Helena escaped the pillage and rape by the Russian hordes, because of her status.

The final touch of hatred towards his cousin was the information that she had contracted a venereal disease, and kept it a secret, hoping to exact revenge for the Russian savagery perpetrated on the men woman, and children, regardless of age. Helena would have forgiven her actions, but when she was apprehended and placed in a military hospital, she tried to discredit Helena by revealing Helena's collaboration with the Germans. Of course the charges were easily discounted. The true facts were a matter of record: Helena was a Polish hero.

Novak concluded, "Even with the short-comings of my cousin, Helena spoke out for her, got her released. To this very day, my cousin does not know Helena was responsible."

We had listened quietly, and intently. The facts placed Helena in a different light, a hero in their way of thinking. The results proved it so. I being the focal point of her intentions, and being privy to her personal desires, I disagreed. I still thought she was nothing but a self serving, surviving cunt, fucking her way to the end she desired.

Novak had just about concluded, and we were placing a credibility stamp of approval on the story, when Helena made her appearance. It was obvious that the nod by Novak made it known that her story was told. If she expected any affirmation from us, negative or positive, it was not forth coming. She was visually despondent, but shed her feelings by giving us a disappointing bit of news.

It was short and sweet: "You will not go today. At least one more night," with no explanation.

All eyes looked directly at me. Was I the reason for the change?

Helena's toss of her shoulder in my direction had two possible interpretations. Was she saying, "Fuck me or else," or was it a more hopeful, "We have one more chance."

CHAPTER 32 — PARTING IS SUCH SWEET SORROW

The next morning was a repeat of the day before. We were awakened at daybreak. For some reason, the apartment was colder than usual. Someone asked Novak, who in turn asked Sonia. The negative shrug of her shoulders made it clear she had no explanation.

We moved out into the street; the cold outside was a match for the cold inside the apartment. Sonia, the guard, and her son led the parade. They quickened their gait, and we followed, thinking they were as eager as we to absorb some of the mess hall heat.

The mess hall was dimly lit, and only a few men were sitting at the table to which we were led. I wondered about the lack of activity and asked Novak if he had any idea of what was going on.

"I really do not know. Maybe Helena will be able to explain. She will arrive momentarily," he responded.

As if on cue Helena arrived, and immediately volunteered the information we all wanted.

"The displaced persons and freed prisoners of war you witnessed yesterday have been moved to the railroad marshaling yard. That makes it almost a certainty you will move out tomorrow. I await final confirmation from our Russian friend," she related.

The food wasn't as appetizing as the day before; it appeared to be what was left over. But the food wasn't our immediate concern. I believed that, at that very moment, each of us felt a nausea of gratification in the pit of our stomachs. Food would have an adverse effect.

We were able to linger, with no time table set for arriving personnel as the day before. We casually went through the motions of eating.

"We can remain as long as we care," Helena said. "I will have to leave for a spell, to check our status for tomorrow. I will probably see you at the apartment," she concluded.

"Before you leave, see if you can use your clout to get some real smokes," I asked.

She had to get in a parting shot. She answered, "As usual my Heaven Boy likes to receiveth, but never giveth."

In my mind I would have liked to counter with "Fuck you," but she would have construed it to be an invitation.

After an hour or so we left to return to the apartment. The streets were beginning to come alive, but not with the volume level as in the past.

"What is it, some kind of holiday?" I asked Novak. "All the stores appear closed."

"You have lost track of time. Today is Sunday," he replied.

"Is it possible to go to church?" I asked.

I was thinking to myself, this trip we were about to make had all the earmarks of another mission, and a little Godly sojourn wouldn't be out of order.

"After we are settled at the apartment, I will take whoever wants to go to church with me. I was going myself," Novak suggested.

"Does Helena go to church?" I chided Novak.

"I know what you are thinking, all of you. She is very religious, and we will probably find her there if we go," he said emphatically, and added, "Sonia goes also."

"I know their type. They pray, 'Forgive me Lord, I know I am doing wrong, but I love it,' then walk away feeling righteous."

Novak didn't join the snickering laughter, and was adamant in his defense of Helena.

"You will miss her in your travels, when they start treating you like the other American released prisoners of war and the displaced scum you will encounter," Novak lectured.

"Hell, man, we're only kidding," chorused the crew, "these are American forms of jokes."

"We do not accept slander of a personal nature," Novak advised us all. "Remember, most of the people you will meet are uneducated and hostile, and will kill you without any remorse."

The streets were sparsely populated as we walked towards the apartment. Most people were bent into the cold wind, and showed no recognition or concern as we passed each other. As we neared the apartment, two figures bundled in oversized outer garments were standing at the entrance. They made no move towards us but, as we reached within earshot, they uncovered their faces, and said, "You'll get yours," and moved quickly away.

Their words surprised us, but a moment's thought brought the realization that the two scum bags had reached Lodtz, and still remained a threat to be reckoned with. Novak's head snapped to attention, and turned towards the threat's place of origin.

"My warnings to you were real. You have to be concerned even with the radical Americans, who are no better than the hoards of Russians, roaming the country sides like wild beasts. They too think that pillaging, rape, even murder is part of the spoils of war, owed to them as a reward. You must accept it as fact," Novak stated.

He then added, "I will inform Helena of the threat by those two. She will know how to handle it."

"We better be serious about getting some weapons for our travels. The one I have isn't enough fire power," I suggested.

"You may not realize the situation you are in. You are trained airmen. You never face your enemy one on one. You are now ground soldiers. Combat on the ground is not only with the enemy, but with anyone who can use you, or what you have," Novak warned.

We spent the better part of the day discussing the situation Novak pointed out to us. He was too right about the difference between air war and ground war. We were like fish out of water.

The pilot said, "We'll have to play it by ear. We won't know our position until we are released from Helena and Novak. I don't think they will turn us loose on our own, like the other released prisoners of war, American or otherwise."

It was a fact. They had never placed us in the same category, either for safety or for information they hoped to obtain. The reason for the separation at the outset was plausible, but now I believe our status, encouraged by Helena, placed us above the lowly prisoners of war.

Helena arrived, and with an air of authoritative success, physically threw a carton of Lucky Strike cigarettes, not to me, but at me, then smiled as I caught it on the fly.

"Nice catch," she said. "I know about your American baseball, and I have good news: you definitely move tomorrow."

There were guttural sounds and incoherent mumblings, and I found hard to distinguish between "yeah man" or "oh shit."

Novak grasped the opportunity to apprise Helena of the verbal threats by the two men from Warsaw. She had not been made privy to the situation at that time, and was a little miffed, making no attempt to hide her irritation.

"You have placed me in a compromising position. If these men caused you harm, I would have to answer for it. And you, Novak, if you knew about these incidents, you placed both of us in serious jeopardy."

"He didn't know," we chorused.

The simultaneous response was a dead give away as a defense for Novak, but Helena made no reference to its validity as being acceptable or not. Case closed.

Helena went on to tell us the time schedule for the next day was not yet set, but would arrive by courier before bedtime. Whenever she mentioned bedtime, I would swear a gleam appeared in her eyes that caused me to blink. I was beginning to wonder if the love war with Helena was more acceptable than the toils of war facing us in our travels. I found it amazing that in my mind going home could ever be challenged by anything or anybody, yet some of the conversation discussing the option did exactly that.

"Why the hell don't we sweat it out here?" was qualified with, "Who the fuck wants to get killed by some screw loose idiot?" We used this kind of rhetoric to camouflage our fear of returning to the flying war. Some felt the odds of surviving were better here. I supposed it was their choice. Not all felt as I did, "It's God's will, so be it, come what may."

Helena explained the lack of heat before being questioned about it. "The oil is running out. They do not want to refill the tanks, so they consolidate what is left to heat the main room and Sonia's quarters. We will have to bundle up in the sleeping quarters," she concluded.

When she mentioned "bundle," she looked at me. I think she was thinking of "bundling," a New England custom of lying in bed with one's sweetheart without undressing. Hell, we've been doing that all along, that kind of "bundle" was OK with me. All I could think of was one more night, if all went well, to protect my abstinence.

Helena brought up the subject of the two threatening Americans.

"I will convey the situation to the Russian officer. I know from what he has told me you will be separated from the rest of the people traveling with you. I suggested the possibility of your guard here escorting you in your travels. He told me it was out of question: a wounded hero is usually assigned to such a task. It is considered a reward."

"Then we will have an armed escort?" I asked

Her confirmation brought audible sighs of relief, but her qualification of armed escort, as one man, prompted another question.

"How about returning our weapons if possible, or replacing them with others?" requested the Pilot.

"I will see what can be done, but do not place too much hope that your request will be honored."

"Goddammit, we don't want to be honored, we just want to be treated like an ally, not a fucking prisoner of war," I retorted.

I expected some back lash from the Pilot or other members of the crew, but to my surprise, there was complete agreement, which strengthened my faith we were a team again.

Helena, with what appeared to be true sincerity, said, "I know that the outward treatment towards you at times was out of character as far as allies are concerned. I want to assure you it was the Russians, who in the attempt to build their own importance in the eyes of the Russian people, used any means to belittle and embarrass you. That is the reason for the isolation process. To know you is to love you Americans. We Polish people were informed by the Polish and Slovak officers that the American entry into the war would end Hitler's war, and not only free the allies, but free the German, and Italian people also. The Russians will never admit the American importance. They have the

Russian people believing your equipment, which is everywhere, comes from America, but is made by Russian workers sent to America."

"Can the Russian people be so gullible?" someone asked.

"The multitude of fighting men are peasant farmers, Mongolian Cossacks, led by Slovak officers. The Russian elite soldiers and officers are used as home guards, and for parades," Helena confessed. "I hope and pray your country recognizes them for what they truly are. I know in my heart Poland and other countries in this part of the world, will be enslaved if your country deserts us," she concluded.

Novak added, "You must wonder why Helena tells you all this. It is because you are leaving us, and the danger of this information effecting each of us, if its source were known, will be remote. We pray this information, through you, will alert America that the enemy of the future world is Russia."

As we heard all this, I wondered if we could shepherd such vital information to the right echelon of authority. We realized this clandestine meeting, spoken in English only and not understood by Sonia or the guard, posed no threat to Novak or Helena. We agreed that the information we possessed was vital, and we must forget it, until we reached the proper authorities. The information was given to us and us only, and even Americans or allies we meet in our travels including our two friends, should not be privy to it.

"But they are witnesses to what we were told," I said.

"Let them reveal the atrocities if they want to, but if it were known that was their intent, I do not believe they would reach home," Helena warned.

"You must understand," Novak added, "they are part of the same group, and there is the belief of honor among thieves, even if they did not participate."

"You have been isolated from the past degenerate acts of these animals. That is why you must be protective of each other in your future travels. When it is obvious that you are witness to these acts, and not part of them, that is when your asses are on the line," Novak concluded.

Novak's last words of wisdom seemed to put a lid on the topic. Not another word was uttered pertaining to the information entrusted to us.

The Navigator was beckoned by Sonia to her bedroom, and Helena retired in the direction of our room. Someone suggested that this was farewell night, and if I was going to react as before to Helena's advances, I should ask Helena to partake of a more receptive individual.

"Hell," I responded, "if you can persuade her, be my guest."

"You don't mind?" someone asked.

Before I could reassure him he made a beeline to my room. I heard the sound of an object bouncing off the bedroom door, and the enraged voice of Helena, "Get out, you pig, you treat me like a whore, you should know by now where my love is,"

Her response frightened me. This bitch is serious, what the hell am I in for? Everyone was taken aback by Helena's retort, but Sonia came to the rescue when she appeared and spoke to Novak, with a broad smile on her face.

"What makes her so giddy?" Novak was asked.

The Navigator laughingly replied, "This beautiful person will allow all you of you to watch us perform, if you promise to masturbate in silence, and most of all, by Helena's request, refrain from bothering her and her 'Heaven Boy' on their last night together."

Suddenly there were footsteps approaching the door. A knock ensued. The door, opened by the guard, framed a uniformed person.

"The courier," the Pilot guessed, and called to Helena.

118

"Novak, you take the message," came from the bedroom.

Novak accepted the sealed document, and thanked the messenger. The soldier bowed at the waist in response, clicked his heels, did a military about face and departed. From the sanctum she created, Helena asked Novak to read the message aloud. As I had mentioned before, to leave or not to leave could effect each of us in our personal desires.

"You leave tomorrow, definitely, early in the morning," Novak related.

Helena's voice from the bedroom confirmed the message, then emphasized early morning with, "Let's all get to bed as soon as possible. We can not miss the transportation in the morning."

At that moment the fact that we were about to head for home was secondary in my mind. I sure as hell would rather watch Sonia and the Navigator than wrestle with Helena. The fact she didn't exit from the room when the messenger arrived painted a picture of a seductive, nymphomaniac bent on tempting me beyond human resistance.

The first glaring change was the warmth of the room as I entered. The second was the absence of the hallway light through the over-door transom. The third and most provocative was Helena's dress. She usually wore flannel pajamas and a bed jacket. In all the occasions when she tried to seduce me, it was mostly verbal. Her body was silhouetted through the light, flowing night gown she wore. She glided across to the door, and locked it. I had envisioned a cold room, so I was dressed for the outdoors. Helena climbed into bed, and made no attempt to shield the loveliness of her body.

"Come," she beckoned,"remove your clothing. Join me in this fine warm bed."

I turned to leave the room. It was then I noticed the blanket covering the glass transom. She really meant business.

I didn't want to embarrass her, by saying or doing anything that would cheapen her intentions.

"Please, Helena," I pleaded, "you don't have to do this to show your love for me."

"You fool," she said,"I want you to make love to me to show your love for me, not for thanks, not for my people, just me.

"Please," she said,"come sit beside me, give me a chance to entice you," as she brazenly, seductively parted her gown, and exposed her womanhood.

Even a priest would have found it difficult to control his bodily response. She realized the bodily response was available, and proceeded to attempt to release it from captivity, but the layers of clothing prevailed. I gave her no assistance. She kissed me about my face, caressed my penis, revealed her bare breasts, begged me to kiss them. Then without one overt response from me, she unashamedly begged, "Please leave with me your baby, that is all I ask."

She actually swooned limply, trembled a little, kissed me passionately, I think she had an orgasm. I had already had mine.

CHAPTER 33 — SEEING IS BELIEVING

I sort of drifted into and out of a sleep punctuated by the sounds of throttled sobbing. I should have felt remorse, but in my heart I knew I had never encouraged an affair. The fact we had knowledge of our going home tomorrow was a blessing to me, but at this very moment I had other thoughts. It may sound out of character, but going home had its merits, and going home at this very instant meant freeing myself from a situation that had become a very serious one-sided problem. I would probably laugh about this, if I lived to tell it, but if Helena was professing true love and not using me as a means to get to the U.S.A., it was no laughing matter to Helena.

We were awakened by the guard. Sonia had prepared some coffee and black bread toast. I awoke to find Helena missing from bed. Novak had also departed.

"Gee," I said, "were the hell are Helena and Novak? I hope we get a chance to thank them, and say good-bye," I added.

They all agreed, but we had no way of obtaining an answer from Sonia or the guard. Then by a stroke of luck Sonia's son appeared. He was asked if he had any information concerning Novak or Helena. In his limited English, he informed us. "They are in the street, waiting for you," he answered. He went on to tell us to eat and dress warmly, as it was very cold. Helena and Novak were waiting for our transportation, and wanted to make sure it arrived on time.

"What the hell difference does it make, as long as it gets here," someone said.

"Hey, don't start making waves. Who gives a shit what the reason, let's just get the fuck out of here," I responded.

"Maybe some of you guys would rather sweat it out here. If you have the balls, ask Helena, I know she would help you," I added, "especially if you would knock her up, which she thinks will give her a passport to the U.S.A."

"What are you talking about?" asked the Pilot.

"Are you making this shit up? Why are you condemning her after she treated you more personally then us?" added the Navigator.

"I don't have to defend myself to you guys. I tried to play the part Helena wanted me to play, not to jeopardize our reliance in her, and always found a way to stalemate the situation," I replied. "I always felt her actions were self serving, but there were times she seemed so sincere. The times she stuck her neck out would alter my thoughts, and I would figure, what the fuck, whatever her motives, it could be worse."

"Did you pay her back with a little loving last night?" the Navigator asked.

"Last night? Last night," I responded, "was the crowning glory of her desires. She wanted me to knock her up. Would you believe, she didn't just want to get laid, 'Leave me with your baby,' she pleaded. What a parting shot."

"All kidding aside, is what you are saying the truth?" someone asked.

Before I could answer, Sonia's son said something to her. She nodded her head, and answered him in a rapid torrent of words, making explanatory gestures with her hands.

"What the hell is she saying?" I requested.

It took a little time for him to formulate the right words, but slowly he made understandable utterances. He explained how his mother knew of Helena's plan at the outset, but the plan became untenable because I had not responded as desired. She knew I was married, but hoped if I conceded to her desires, she would see to it that I impregnated her. Being newly married, it would cause my wife great embarrassment, a divorce would follow, and Helena would gain entrance to the U.S.A., which was her goal.

Almost as one they all agreed, "And we were almost forcing you into a situation we thought was a big joke." "Whatever her plans, I feel she has made it a lot easier for all of us, who knows where we would be if we weren't placed under her wing. We owe her some respect," I concluded.

"By the way, my friends, I haven't heard any true confessions from you degenerates. How about a little pictorial review of your sex orgy last night?"

"We had a good time. This Gypsy knows how to please a man. She excited each of those who wished it with a little foreplay. Everyone but the new waist gunner joined in the action-he didn't feel too good," the Navigator related.

He went on to add that he was kidding about performing in front of everyone. Sonia agreed to perform physically with everyone who wanted to say goodbye, with an action of love, privately, in her warm bedroom.

"Well at least we weren't asked to knock her up," some smart ass stated.

"You had to remind me, you prick. I wish one of you were the target. Not one of you could have resisted as I, especially last night," I argued, then added, "you farmboy sheep fuckers think a self-imposed hand job is the epitome of success."

There were the usual retorts of defense, which were always a denial of sheep fucking.

"We had girls, even on the farms," was one of the escapes used by the sheep herders.

"We in the big city are led to believe that the girls on the farms, either played stoop tag in the asparagus patches, or used corn cobs, rather than one of you yokels," I answered.

It turned into kidding rhetoric. We bantered back and forth. As we did so, Sonia's son laughed occasionally when he picked up some of the descriptive cliches. We continued to gather our belongings. Some of us still had our parachutes, which were retrieved and returned by our Polish rescuers.

Novak suddenly appeared at the doorway. "There will be a slight delay. One of your crew is very sick. Helena has used your truck to take him to the Hospital."

It was then we realized he was missing. The Navigator had mentioned he wasn't feeling well the night before. We sort of dismissed his absence as being by choice, resting in the dorm.

The Pilot asked Novak why he wasn't notified. Novak reminded him that it happened suddenly, and he was instructed by Helena to inform us, which he did.

"What the hell do we do now?" the Pilot thought aloud. "We can't leave him here alone."

"He will not be alone. Helena and I will look after him," Novak volunteered.

I would never say what I was thinking in the presence of Novak. This guy we hardly knew would be easy prey for Helena's designs. He fucked Novak's cousin, who was a victim of a venereal disease; Helena would be a conquest.

Two of our war heroes blatantly declared, "We'll remain with him, until he can travel."

"Not on your life," responded the Pilot. "I'll chance one man, not three."

That issue was resolved, not to everybody's satisfaction, but put to rest.

We made our way to the street. The cold greeted us, but Helena didn't. There was no truck, only the guard and Novak. For some unknown reason, there were some civilians standing about, just gawking, and talking amongst themselves.

"What are they doing here?" I asked Novak.

"When your crew member collapsed on the street and was put into the truck, a crowd collected. Some offered to help. I think they knew he was an American," Novak related.

"I think we should go back into the apartment. We'll freeze our balls waiting here," the Pilot suggested.

"You're right, we have no idea how long the ride is to the train, and you can bet the truck is an open body one," I reminded them.

As we returned to the apartment, Novak remained on the street to await Helena's return. It was beginning to snow. Sonia and her son followed us, Novak followed suit as the wind began to swirl the falling snow. The sudden change in the weather dispersed the civilian onlookers. Then an amazing thing happened: they retreated a few steps, lined up in a military platoon formation at rigid attention, and smartly saluted us. They said something in Polish, and Novak's interpretation was as I had suspected, "Thank you and,God bless you."

Helena not returning for more than an hour caused us great concern as to the condition of the waist gunner. When she returned she brought information relative to both the sick crew member, and us.

"Your friend is very sick, has a high fever, and will not be able to travel. It has been diagnosed as Scarlet Fever," Helena revealed.

"Scarlet Fever?" I asked. "Must be a new name for Gonorrhea, or Syphilis," I declared.

"Do you not ever give anyone one iota of compassion, must you always suspect a deception?" Helena asked, with a reflective tone towards my response to her advances.

She was unaware of Sonia's revelations through her son, concerning her plan towards me. If she knew, she would never had made her last criticism about me. It was getting to the point where the more she attempted to defend her actions and degrade mine, the more the whole crew believing me and opinion of Helena.

"We will have to wait for further instructions. I believe you have missed the train intended for your departure," Helena related.

It suddenly struck me, "maybe those two scum bags made that train. Good riddance," I practically screamed.

"I will check on their whereabouts as soon as I can contact the Russian officer. He put them under surveillance the instant I explained their threatening position," Helena promised.

It was this kind of cooperation from Helena that minimized her self serving deceit, to be forgiven, tolerated, and understood.

We sat around fully clothed, as the apartment was as cold as outdoors. The heaters had been turned off, because of our intended departure, in every room but Sonia's. We were forbidden by acclamation to even think of entering her room, when Sonia and the Navigator retreated there.

"Shit on this scenario," I stated,"we outnumber the fuckers, let their actions keep them warm."

Helena was the first to agree, and the rest cheered her decision. We moved as one, and burst into Sonia's room with a boisterous, "Here we come, ready or not."

Novak asked, "What does that mean, here we come, ready or not?"

I explained that it meant, "If you are doing what we think you are doing, we'll be coming because of what you're doing, and we will come, if you're ready or not."

Novak had a look of utter confusion, and Helena, questioned my sincerity by stating, "If what you say is true, all will be coming, but you will be going."

The sight that greeted us as we entered the room wasn't photographed by any camera, but you can bet it was a picture forever indelibly imprinted in our minds. There was the Navigator, sitting on the end of the bed, Sonia's son opposite him. Sonia, was sitting in a chair, cuddled next to the oil heater, watching intently, as the Navigator was scratching X's and O's on a piece of paper. He was teaching the kid how to play Tic Tac Toe.

Imagining a sexual encounter, then being greeted by a platonic scene of reverence, stopped us in our tracks.

"How could you leave us out in that cold room, you, you, bastard?" the Pilot stuttered through chattering teeth.

"Come on, don't get your dander up. I had my intentions curtailed by mother nature. Before the kid showed up, I had a beautiful blow job," the Navigator, proudly declared.

Believe me, picturing what he had revealed, then looking at that beautiful person, instantly caused mind and body to involuntarily react.

Helena broke the spell with, "You decide between yourselves what is your preference, teasing yourselves with imaginary fornication, or just sitting together in warmth.

"I will leave to check if you are to move today, and will attempt to acquire some food, while we are waiting," she added as she departed.

We spread ourselves about the room. Some retrieved chairs from the other room, removed our outer garments, and soaked up some of the warm but oily-smelling heat. The conversation was sporadic, and usually without substance. Someone suggested a Tic Tac Toe contest to kill time.

"What will the winning prize be?" had to be asked by some idiot, as if it really mattered.

Everyone answered his question by looking directly at Sonia.

Sonia's kid said something to his mother in Polish. It didn't need Novak's interpretation. She sort of retreated, with hands raised, palms faced outward in an international, "No way."

The sudden change in her sexual demeanor was not expected; a sort of estranged atmosphere prevailed. Sonia must have sensed the situation, and responded with her usual showing of her personal love towards us. She went to a closet, returned with a guitar, and immediately began strumming and singing, "Roll Out the Barrel."

I for one felt embarrassed, and I think every one else had a feeling we imposed on Sonia. It was obvious that we took her for granted, and when nature dimmed her sexual desires, we were out of line. We followed her resolve of the atmosphere that prevailed by joining in. Her face lit up with a loving smile. She said something to Novak, and he nodded in the affirmative.

"Sonia is very sad that you are leaving, but was more sad because she is sick bodily, and she had lost your love. She is now happy again, because you show your love, by forgiving her," Novak translated.

God, I thought to myself, how one's values and priorities are altered to your personal wants, with utter disregard to another's feelings, especially under unfamiliar circumstances.

We sang and joked the time away. The Pilot, who could play the piano, knew enough about music to strum the guitar. We sang all the songs we knew, and had Novak, Sonia, the guard, and Sonia's kid humming along. We were proudly rendering, with loud exuberance, the Air Force song, when Helena made her entrance. It may have been a subconscious reaction. but I would swear, tears formed in her eyes, as she joined in our song.

Helena asked the guard and Novak to retrieve the box of food that was left by truck at the doorway downstairs. "I made sure this food did not disappear. I rode with it right from the commissary. They promised to transport what is leftover to the train for your travels," she concluded.

The food was a welcome sight, but the blackberry brandy and the potato whisky were received as potential body anti-freeze. Sonia set a table in her bedroom, poured a little brandy for each of us, and toasted us in Polish. We responded in English.

"Amerikanski, forever," was clearly understood.

"Popolski, forever," we responded.

"Popolski, forever, only if you Amerikanskis do not desert us," Helena whispered into my ear.

It was on occasions such as this, that the seriousness of our position was more than one of personal survival. The information conveyed to us in trust changed our status as mere American airmen to non-elected, non-appointed representatives. The information we possessed could be instrumental in changing the political structure of the world. I wondered if the rest of my crew realized the dangerous circumstance we were in.

We just started to enjoy the fruits of Helena's efforts when we received word our transportation had arrived. It was a moment of mixed emotions, and the uneasy feeling of death do us part was present. The fact that there was still a war going on, and there was no guarantee of survival for any of us, meant this goodbye could be permanent.

We snapped up what remnants of food we could stuff into our mouths, chug a lugged the savory remaining liquid in our glasses, gathered up our belongings, and made ready to depart.

A tug on my sleeve stopped me in my tracks. "Please remain a few moments, I want a favor from you," pleaded Helena.

We certainly haven't time to knock her up, I thought. She can't be that desperate.

Producing a piece of paper and a pencil, she relieved even my most outlandish thoughts.

"Please give me your address in the United States," she requested.

I gave her my address. She thanked me, and said,"I do not want to say goodbye in the street, please kiss me as you would someone you loved, then go. God be with you," she concluded.

I honored her request. I kissed her for the first time. I had never returned one of her kisses. She realized this, and responded hysterically, "I love you, I love you, please say you love me too, just once, it will remain with me forever."

"Helena, I can't say it the way you want me to. I do love you, as we all do, with respect and gratefulness for all you have done. Please don't make me lie, it would have no meaning."

I turned to leave, as I descended the stairs, her sobs trailed me to the street. I boarded the truck. Its engine roared us into motion, but the engine's roar didn't obliterate the sound of Helena's sobs, which I could hear with every beat of my heart.

The ride to the marshalling yard was cold, the swirling snow impeding the visibility of the driver, which caused many a moment of anxiety as he involuntarily skidded into three hundred and sixty degree turns. One time he became so confused after one of these turns that he headed in the wrong direction, and had to be corrected by Novak, who was riding up front.

We finally arrived at a point in our travels where the buildings that confronted us had all the earmarks of a railroad. They were no different than those at home, or in England. As a matter of fact they appeared no different than the ones I had seen from the air when we bombed Frankfort, on one of my first missions. I remember that target, because of Brooklyn's heroic results toggling our bomb load late and scoring a direct hit on the MPI.

The sight that greeted us as we entered the main elements of the yard brought back vivid memories of the chaos in Turek, when Helena caught a train to Gydenia. There were thousands of people, who seemed to be herded at the edge of a wooded area. There was a formidable line of military at parade rest, with stacked rifles at the ready. It was hard to distinguish the civilian population from the military personal, all raggedly dressed, cuddled around hundreds of fires to defend against the bitter cold.

There were about six track lines. Two appeared to be main lines, the other four were spur lines, apparently used for side tracking, or loading and unloading. The track adjacent to the wooded area had a line of what appeared to be empty cars, of the four and eight type, with no engine attached. All the doors were closed but one. Our truck made for it. There was a short bow- egged Russian peasant soldier standing at the car. I say Russian peasant, because he was ill-fittingly dressed, fur hat, bulky insulated jacket and pants, rag wrapped boots, with the ever present burp gun. I would venture a bet his canteen housed potato whisky.

We disembarked from the truck and tossed our gear into the car as directed by Novak. A surprise visitor appeared: our Russian officer friend. He shook hands with each of us, and through Novak, wished us well.

"Where is the food we were to get?" I asked Novak.

Novak addressed the question to the Russian. An exchange of words produced an answer from Novak, "It is aboard the car already."

An automobile drove up. The Russian entered, throwing a salute in our direction, which appeared to me as a good riddance wave off.

I was the first aboard the car. The interior was dark; my eyes needed adjustment from the white snow outside. I heard muffled laughter before seeing the source. Just as I was acclimating to the darkness, a bear hug from two sides revealed our two friends, the American Sergeant and the English soldier. Again Helena's goodness was shown by her loving deeds. I called out to the others of my find. They too were elated, and remarked as I had thought, that Helena's word was her bond.

I thought to myself the whole trip would be punctuated with reminders of Helena and Novak, because of their warnings, and incidents we would encounter. It wasn't long before the forewarned incidents occurred.

While the Pilot was attempting to assign sleeping positions to the eleven of us, it struck me that these cars were designed for four horses and eight men, or was it eight horses and four men? It was about this time that our car was surrounded by armed guards. I tried to open the door that was closed on one side of the car, and found it securely locked. The door that we entered by, was now blocked by a heavy plank placed there by our assigned guard, standing at the ready, gun poised. The line of soldiers holding the multitude at bay at the wood's edge had now retreated to stand at a position between our string of cars and the main tracks. Their weapons were not stacked at this juncture, they were poised and in a firing line position.

There was no semblance of order or direction. We gazed in amazement as somehow, somewhere a signal was given, that turned these poor wretched people into screaming, clawing animals, with no resemblance to human beings. The only action taken by the military was to fire shots into the air if someone crossed into the protective zone, which thank God, we were part of.

"Is this like what you related to us when you and Novak got Helena aboard a train in Turek?" the Pilot asked.

Just as I was about to confirm his question, shots rang out. What we saw right before our eyes was the answer I was about to give. As the people were fighting to board cars in our train, a train pulled up on the main line, going east away from the front. Those who were not able to find room on our train, and there were thousands, without thinking crashed through the guard line. It was as if they wanted to commit suicide. They were shot down like the enemy. Our guard, and the soldiers surrounding our car, laughed hysterically, as the blood of dead and wounded stained the virgin snow.

CHAPTER 34 — MEN? NO, HORSES

Being a witness to this carnage substantiated all our two friends, and Helena and Novak, had divulged to us. The utter disregard for fellow men, and the frivolity that prevailed as blood was let out, was hard to comprehend as human behavior. We watched the survivors crumble upon their apparent friends or relatives, hoping for life to be restored. The worst of all was watching, as did the soldiers, the scavengers actually stripping the belongings from the dead and dying, and waving them on high as you would a trophy.

The guard in our car was approached by a Russian officer, and words were exchanged. It was apparent we had seen too much, and the door was slammed shut, but not before I caught a glimpse of the two pricks from Warsaw, dragging some knapsacks away from a dead body. I had no way of knowing if they knew we were on the same train, and I didn't know if our guard was made aware of the possible threat of these two. We were isolated from any source of interpretation.

The jolt of our car as the engine was being attached was accompanied by the grinding of the wheels, defying friction, suddenly meshing with the tracks in a rolling motion. This action not only jolted us like ten pins, scattering us in all directions, but jolted me into the realization, that as Helena and Novak had predicted, "You will be on your own."

We regained our balance, and the train developed a smooth rolling motion, accompanied by the click, clicking sound of the wheels passing over the butts between the track sections. We settled into a reasonable air of normalcy. This was the first opportunity to inspect our home on wheels. The single oil lamp produced a dim view of our surroundings, but the door was thrown open to afford us a vivid picture of our home away from home.

The first item of prominence was the pot belly stove, set right between the two side doors. Its presence was most dominant because of its ominous, black, cold appearance, which accentuated the swirling snow and the cold snow-covered countryside that served as a backdrop through the open door.

There were three tier-like shelves at one end. The first was about six inches off the floor. The two above were about twenty inches apart, and about eight feet deep. These were our bunks, with bedding of straw filled burlap mattresses. These bunks did not afford room to turn over. If you were broad shouldered, your choice of sleeping positions was on your belly or on your back. They certainly were not designed to cure a person with claustrophobia. It took but one entrance into these bunks to offset the feeling of being trapped, by sliding in feet first. You may have felt like cords of wood, but having your head exposed relieved that blind helpless feeling.

The assignment of bunks was voluntary: officers in the lower bunks, non-coms in the upper. The other end of the car was clear, probably for equipment, and probably at one time, stalls for horses. We used this area to store our gear, but not for long. After the first night it was found to be more comfortable to spread your mattress on the deck. Since we had very little gear, there was plenty of room for all.

It was at this time that each of us who possessed one realized the absence of our collection of parachutes. It was an instant realization, and the instant hilarity that prevailed relieved the tension at that moment, as we looked questioningly at each other.

"Where the hell did all your parachutes disappear to?" asked the Pilot. "Six of you had them," he added.

Each of us sheepishly confessed to having Novak deposit them in Sonia's custody, without it being known to each other. They were to be shared equally between Helena and Sonia after we departed. Each of us had retained our pilot chutes as a souvenir.

"Don't you know you are to safeguard your equipment?" the Pilot injected.

"Cut the shit, you should have thought of that when you gave up your guns. It was the least we could do to show our appreciation. I'm happy we all shared the same feeling of gratitude," I responded.

Really incensed by his remarks, I added,"I'll give you a real case of not safeguarding Government property. I gave my hack watch to the first guy who saved my ass. I could think of no other way to thank him, not only for myself, but for my parents, my brother, sisters, and most of all my brand new bride, whose bed I meagerly shared, fuck you."

Quiet filled the car, as we awaited his usual retort. His answer broke the tension. "I don't know what I was thinking of. Shit, I gave mine away too, to the guard at the apartment."

"He got two watches," revealed the ball gunner,"I gave him a Mickey Mouse watch for that beautiful stiletto he had."

What appeared to be a serious problem, by the Pilot's idiotic statement, was dismissed by his own revelation. Someone mentioned the food that was to be placed in our car. "Drag it out, I'm starving."

"Is this what you are referring to?" asked the Englishman, pointing to a foreign bundle stored in one of the upper bunks. It was pulled down by the Engineer, who was closest to it. Then came the first surprise of our trip into destiny. The bundle was a burlap bag with the open end tied with a piece of rope. The first thought that entered my mind was, "What the fuck could be in that bag, that resembled the food served to us at the mess hall?"

The mystery of the bag was soon shared by all, as the tie string was removed.

"Don't dump the contents," someone jokingly suggested, "you might break the eggs."

Without one reason to believe the contents were breakable, they were dumped in an unguarded manner. The contents were so unbelievable, our response boarded on hysteria, not knowing if we should laugh or cry.

"Who do we blame for this fucking joke?" I asked.

As we sorted out the bag's contents, the Russian guard, who more or less had kept his distance, surprised us by speaking to us in a very understandable broken English.

"I will help you with food and water along the way," he volunteered. "We must get wood for stove, at first stop, water from the steam engine up front," he added.

The question of whom to blame was never answered. The contents were the same crap usually served us: black bread, with the usual lard or apple butter spreads, those same unidentifiable greens, and beets. The added attraction was a bag within the bag, of what was finally identified as brown sugar.

The quantity of everything combined signified a very short trip, or a very hungry one. Without a fire in the stove, and the lack of water, our immediate consumption of food was the black bread with the lard or apple butter spread. Most chose the lard; judging from past diarrhetic experiences, the apple butter was a no-no.

The guard produced two buckets. He explained their function by holding one in front of his body, for pissing. The other he placed on top of the stove, for cooking.

"What do we do for shitting?" someone inquired. The guard took the piss pot, placed it under his ass, feigned taking a crap, walked to the open door, and dumped it. He explained in a slow vivid manner the importance of dumping it towards the rear of the car, in a downward direction. Here he again feigned the action of throwing a bucket full of shit out the door, but in a straight outward direction. To emphasize the result of such an action. he waved his hands in a shielding posture, in front of his face.

It was apparent that the furniture in our traveling car afforded only the choices of standing, laying in the bunks, sitting on the floor, or sitting on the bench across the locked door. The bench across the opened door was the guard's private domain; we discovered later on that it was also his bunk.

We soon settled into a reasonable state of acceptance, and collectively discussed our present situation, and a probable developing situation in the future. We were just idly making conversation, mostly by the Sergeant and the Englishman telling of their experiences and reiterating the horrors they had witnessed. They reminded us that we were now witnesses to the same atrocities, and our response to these actions must be one of indifference. Their words returned Novak and Helena's presence to our minds, as their words of warning were repeated.

I was storing the bag of food away, when I noticed another small bag, which had been overlooked. I retrieved it from the shelf. As I did so, the smell of tobacco reached my nostrils.

"What have we here?" I exclaimed.

All heads turned in my direction, as I opened the bag and exposed the contents. It was the same shredded horseshit and splinter form of tobacco, with paper-towel-thick paper to roll cigarettes. Right to the last our fucking Russian friend stuck it up our ass. He never punished anyone for stealing our food, because it was never stolen except by himself. He was going to make sure his black market activities weren't short changed by giving food away for nothing. Again the evidence solidified the accusations of betrayal and deceit Helena asked us to convey to the American government, to prepare them for future negotiations. It kept entering my mind, there we were trying to survive a situation caused by a war not of our making, and we kept finding ourselves armed with information that could change the diplomatic relations of two great powers.

Suddenly the train slowed. Looking out the open door I could see we were being switched off the main line onto a siding. The guard stepped over the plank bench across the door, and as the train with squeaking brakes and grinding wheels came to a full stop, jumped to the ground. We all went to the door for a look-see. The sight that greeted us was unexpected, yet in our hearts it came as no surprise. We soon discovered that there were cars strategically intersected by armed soldiers, who dismounted with arms at the ready, all along the train line. There was language in a tone of commands. The raising of the arms with the motion of "back up" in our direction, certainly needed no interpretation - we were being told not to disembark.

Our personal guard appeared with another soldier. They were pushing a two-wheeled cart with what appeared to be buckets of water and cords of wood. They proceeded to load it aboard our car, when our guard said, "Handle easily."

"Handle what easily?" the Pilot asked.

"You ask too many fucking questions," the Navigator injected. "Do as you're told for a change," he added.

"Store wood carefully, I will start fire after we are on the move," he instructed.

The guy with the cart took off, and our guard remained on the ground at our open door. Without warning the line of soldiers moved back, adjacent to the main line, about twenty yards away. A command came from out of a loud speaker in an authoritative tone. The line of soldiers assumed what we know as parade rest. Our guard with a wave of his hand signaled that we could leave the car.

"You may relieve yourselves," is what we understood him to say.

We dropped to the snow covered ground. Where we were to relieve ourselves didn't remain a mystery too long. It seemed anywhere you could squat to defecate, or stand to urinate, was acceptable. Skirts were raised, drawers dropped, pants dropped, flies opened everywhere. The soldiers were pointing, and talking amongst themselves. They appeared to single out the younger women, for future targets to rape. At this juncture, we made up our minds to hold mother nature at bay. It may sound facetious, but we felt we were the focal point, that everyone who knew we were Americans wondered if we shit and pissed, like the rest of the world. We kept them guessing, this time around. Even at a time like that we maintained our dignity.

Being outside the car gave us an opportunity to check the train. There were about forty cars, with three steam engines, two up front, one in the rear. What was most prevalent was the armed guards' cars. Each had a manned gun turret on top, with three hundred and sixty degree visible coverage.

A train whistle broke the air. A train was entering the main line going west. As it passed our view, it was easily identified as a troop train with flat cars carrying armed equipment. The tanks and planes were recognizable even though covered with tarpaulins. The cheers and waves from the guard line and the return from the soldiers aboard the troop train, dispelled any attempt to conceal the train heading towards the front lines, which appeared to be the intent of the military guard, as they fired shots into the air, causing our guard to order us aboard. It was a comical to watch those caught between shitting, pissing, with their clothes in an entangling position, attempt to disengage themselves from mother nature's call, when mother nature was in her first stage.

The whistle on our train blew the signal to embark. Our guard boarded our car, as the military guards boarded theirs. We could see the straggling ones caught short. As the train started to move, it was obvious that some were not going to make it. Those who got close enough to an open door were encouraged to throw their belongings into the open door, as hands were offered to help them aboard. The moment their belongings were safely aboard, a foot in their faces disengaged them from the train and their belongings. As we watched these unbelievable events, people aboard the train began to throw there belongings out of the cars, then jump after them. We conjectured that they apparently were relatives or friends separated from those left behind. Shots rang out as we picked up speed, and the human devastation faded from view. I wondered, "Were these human animals worth the sacrifices by those gone, or those in the future?" It was this thought that encouraged my survival, come what may.

The fate of those left behind was an unsolved mystery to us. To ask our guard a question of that nature, resulted in periods of utter silence and non-compliance. In other words he became no better than any of the other Russian pricks we had met. He did start a fire in the stove, and it was then we were made aware of the reason for the careful handling of the wood. Carefully secreted between the cords of wood were bottles of potato whisky. He removed them and stored them in his burlap mattress. The son of a bitch made no indication of sharing his treasure with us; he didn't so much as look us in the eye during the transfer. Our having knowledge of his secret horde only emphasized his estrangement towards us. If we requested water, he could climb over the other cars to the engine, but he would wait until we made a stop, which could be hours. This meant a constant diet of lard and black bread. As the lard was disappearing, the apple butter became a must. With water we could cook up some of the greens and beets. The brown sugar tasted like sweet sand, but added to the greens and beets enhanced their flavor.

The heat of the stove at least relieved one source of discontent, the cold. We could remove some outer clothing, and still be comfortable. Our two companions, feeling as outsiders, said very little, nor did they enter in our discussions that centered on decisions. They did agree when I stated, "We have one thing in our favor: if we are not being bullshitted, we are on the way home. We appear to be isolated, and safeguarded from problems that befall the other travelers, displaced persons, or released prisoners of war."

We really had no concept of the traveling time to Odessa. The Navigator figured, as the crow flies it was about one hundred and seventy five to two hundred miles. If we averaged thirty miles per hour, it would take about six or seven hours. What a miscalculation. The stops and lay-overs could never be anticipated. It seemed every time we started to roll with any consistency, we were shunted into a siding. There we would sit for hours, until a troop train headed for the front would pass us. It was at these frequent stops that the rapes and pillaging would occur. During daylight, it was amazing that the indecencies perpetrated before thousands of witnesses went unchecked. If by chance someone attempted to interfere, he or she was shot down in cold blood. Screams were muffled by shots, and when the train started to move, the right of way was littered with dead or dying bodies. There were times when a front line train was shunted along side our train. It was then the rapes and assaults were at their worst. Men, women, young boys and girls were subjected to the vilest forms of degenerate acts of sexual perversion. Here were people who survived the tyranny of the Germans, years of captivity, only to be subjugated to the depravity of those who were their saviors. We did very little movement at night, and the long dark hours were filled with the screams of those being violated.

When we were stranded for hours, day after day, the call of mother nature superseded dignity or even morality. In the mornings when nature called, it called each and every person on the train. At first we would attempt to seclude ourselves under the car behind a wheel. There were just so many wheels. If we had been at the same siding more than one day, the right of way was strewn with waste of all descriptions and sizes. You just made your way to any clear space, and disregarded the eyes that searched your backside. This was probably the only time I thanked God for the cold weather: the odor was minimized, and the frozen waste covered with snow didn't stick to our boots.

The craziest scenario was the sudden appearance of a peasant woman in the car next to ours. A script writer could not have conjured this scene up; it literally set the morning in motion, each and every morning. If we were stopped or came to a stop at a siding in the morning, and disembarked to relieve ourselves, no one made a move until this elderly woman hoisted her skirt and exposed the brightest green bloomers I had ever seen. The moment she commenced to lower them was a signal for all the multitude of humans to join in the relieving revelry, with a chain reaction right down the entire train, in each direction.

It became obvious that our presence on the train was becoming common knowledge. After a few days of travel, each time we stopped brought a group of people to our car. At first the guards discouraged them, but their insistent behavior, and apparent interest, caused leniency. They were mostly displaced persons at first, who regarded us as their benefactors and just wanted to see we Americans, and in their humble way thank us, with cheers of "Amerikanski, victory."

Once in a while. a few American ex-prisoners of war would show up. They would attempt to mingle in with the displaced persons. Even with the civilian clothing they wore, we could spot them. We had agreed between us, coached by the Sergeant and the Englishman, to show no signs of recognition, in any manner.

"What they think you don't know, will never hurt you," explained the Sergeant.

Then one morning the inevitable happened. In the midst of a pleasant cheering crowd were the two pricks from Warsaw. They were dressed in civilian clothing, easily blending in with the displaced persons. We kept our cool. I went to my gear and retrieved my forty-five; the Sergeant eased me into a corner away from the door.

"Don't. Now is not the time. We have friends close to them - they just want you to do something foolish, to embarrass you."

The words out of their mouths, as they moved up close to the door, proved the Sergeant's words.

"Well,well, we were told there were some men in one of the cars. These cars carried four horses and eight men at one time I don't see any men, so you must be horses," one said, as they turned and walked away.

CHAPTER 35 — SIDE SHOW

The next morning was clear, sunny and crisp. The snow had stopped falling, but the day began as usual, with the green drawers initiating the massive bowel and bladder emptying action. It had become common place, so the embarrassed feeling was displaced by the natural feeling of relief. A new problem arose when the few toilet tissues in our escape kit were used up. The next to serve the need was the miniature bible, also part of the escape kit. If we hadn't used the escape money, that would have been next. The cigarette paper was coarse, and the choice was a rough ass, and no smoke, or smoke, and an itchy ass. If you had a pocket handkerchief, it was use and wash. We tore bits off our long johns or any piece of material at our disposal, which didn't offset its designed purpose. This was one of the "American ingenuities" that won the war.

These little annoyances only made for conversation, and time killing factors. The real hazard was the lack of movement, causing an uneasy feeling among the traveling populace. We became the focal point of attention, and the crowds that gathered in front of our car created the atmosphere of a circus side show. When the crowds became too large to handle, our guard would close the door. If this didn't disperse them, the military guard would use violent and deadly force to effect a dispersement. Witnessing such unnecessary mayhem, we decided to sweat out the side show atmosphere, and accept the attention as that of not only curious, but grateful people. We had to create some sort of response to the gathering throngs that would convey some meaningful gesture of friendship.

At first I would stand in the doorway, with a big smile. Then through smiling clenched teeth, I would in English say, "What the fuck do you sons of bitches expect us to do, a fan dance?"

Believe it or not, this approach separated the disguised, disgruntled prisoners of war, and the true displaced people. The real civilian would smile and wave, shout Amerikanski, Popolski, or Russki, Amerikanski. The Polish people always prefaced their salutation with Amerikanski, the Russians would always start their salutations with Russki. The disguised bastards would look at us with disdain, and would slowly disperse to shield their identity. We hadn't had the pleasure of our two Warsaw pricks, and we wondered why. Our two friends must have read my mind, and volunteered, "You won"t have any trouble from them during our travels to Odessa. Our friends informed them of the consequences if they stepped out of line."

After a few days of using the approach of ridicule as a means of entertainment, it became not only stale, but in my heart I felt they deserved better. The next day I created a character that displayed both respect and gratefulness to the people before us, both physically and demonstratively, being impartial to their ethnic origin. I would come to the door bareheaded, bow at the waist, raise my arms in a V, with my fingers making a V for victory sign. This usually brought a vocal cheer, which after a few days, was interpreted by our guard as a good morning in both Polish and Russian. Each of our contingent would come to the door, and wave some sort of salutation, with a smile of endearment. This simple yet genuine action received a positive response in return. I had dug up the Polish medallion and Russian star from my gear. I attached one on the front, and one on back of my Russian fur hat.

Going to the door I would shout in a questioning tone, "Popolski?". I would have the Polish medallion displayed on the front of my hat. Hands would shoot skyward.

"Amerikanski, Popolski," would be the response, apparently from the Polish. What sounded like jeers would accompany the cheers, apparently the Russians. I would then reverse my hat with the Russian red star displayed. The hands withdrawn before would shoot skyward. "Russki, Amerikanski," was the response, and again what sounded like jeers were mixed in. There were discussions among the viewers which by their tone appeared to border on altercations. I felt now was the time for a diplomatic maneuver, American ingenuity. I gathered all of our people at the door, and instructed them to shout in unison, "Amerikanski, Popolski, Russki," with the V sign of victory.

As they complied, I put my hat on sideways, the Polish medallion on one side, the Russian star on the other. I proceeded to turn my head from side to side, exposing one and then the other. This action was received with humor and compassion, and a semblance of unity. Even the guards within hearing cheered.

"You're a crazy son of a bitch," someone said, but in an endearing tone.

The side show atmosphere continued, but each appearance made it easier to perform. The rest of the crew participated with some little skit. The acting urge surfaced, and was received warmly. Whenever a troop train heading to the front was shunted into a siding near our train, the people were forbidden to visit with us. The soldiers were brought in groups of about twenty to see the "Americans." We didn't know what they expected to see, or what they were told to expect. We felt like freaks. After a few of these sojourns by the visiting troops, a distinct characterization of the visitors was established. The Russian soldiers appeared ignorant as to the purpose of their visit. The officer in charge would order a vocal salutation that bordered on blasphemy. When that was obvious, I would respond with the old Italian salute, extending my right arm with clenched fist, and striking my right bicep with my left hand. The rest of the crew would close their hand into a fist, with the middle finger extended in a upward angle, with a chorus of, "Up your ass with a piece of glass, up your nose with a rubber hose."

The Englishman had a unique response. He would cup his hands around his crotch, and shout, "Eat this, you Russian cock suckers!"

They would have a sullen look, accompanied with shrugging shoulders, and some wry smirks or smiles.

When the gatherers were Polish or Lithuanians the atmosphere was casual, and friendly. They would insist on shaking our hands. I believe if they could have gotten close enough to us, we would have been kissed. There were times when someone in the group could speak English, most times the Lithuanian officers. They would whisper endearing words of gratitude about our entry into the war. When out of earshot of our guard would almost plead, "Remember what you see here. Tell America, Russia is your enemy."

It was very cold that morning. The fire was out, and the guard was also "out." He had a personal party with one of the military escorts during the night, and didn't feed the fire. Since we weren't to visit the wood supply where he had his whisky cached, we would just bundle up the best way available, and curse the prick. He awoke in a half-stupor, shivering from the cold, and without so much as a "how do you do?" went to the wood supply. It appeared that the old remedy for a hang over, as we know it, was the same in Russia: "A little bit of the dog that bit you."

He retrieved a bottle, gave us a sideward glance, turned his back to us, and gulped a quantity of its contents. The effect was visible as his body responded to the ingestion of the whisky. The trembling presented two connotations: one, that the cold was being shaken from his body; or, he was being shaken into the world of reality. He proceeded to start a fire, and as it burst into full flame, the results were welcomed.

Appearing satisfied with the results, he gathered some wood, placed it where we could retrieve it, and ordering, "Keep fire going," flopped in a corner as if he were dead.

The train suddenly blew its whistle and jerked slightly in a forward motion, but didn't continue. Looking out the door we could see the morning contingent of relief seekers boarding the train.

"Damn. Between this drunken idiot and the fire, no crap," I muttered.

Just then a military guard approached our car, raised ten fingers, pointed to his crotch, bent at the waist in a shitting posture. We got the message, "Ten minutes to defecate and/or urinate." We exited with an anticipation of gratification.

We had missed the usual green bloomer go ahead signal, but at this juncture, I needed no urging. The train whistle blew two short blasts, and the escape of steam with its hissing sound gave notice, ten minutes were up. We boarded the car, and the sight of the prone drunk, gave vent to a series of foul adjectives which did little to salve our feelings. The fire was at the stage of doing justice to the cold, but the realization that the drunken bastard had gotten no water for cooking prevented any true appreciation. There was very little of anything left to eat; even the apple butter was consumed entirely. What greens were left needed water to cook-they didn't taste well uncooked.

"When that prick comes to, I'll remind him of his promise to get food along the way," I volunteered.

"He won't even talk to you, he's no different than the rest of the Russian goons," the Pilot offered.

"Why don't we throw him off the train while it's moving? Who the hell would ever know?" was the first suggestion, from the Englishman.

"Now wait a second," said the Pilot, "I hope you're not serious."

"What the hell, he's no good to us. If we don't get some food, we won't be worth a shit by the time we get to Odessa," he added.

"Right now he's the only authoritative contact we have. With no authority to make demands of, we're up shit creek. Let dead dogs lie," I suggested.

Everyone agreed, and the Englishman apologized for his suggestion and interference. The Pilot surprised us when in a sense he relinquished his authority to make or even suggest an action of any sort by anyone but him by saying, "At this point and time, we all must share in the burden of survival. At any and all times when an important decision must be made, rank has no bearing, we must agree. Finally, any action of immediate response must be supported by all."

This act of comradeship dispelled any ideas of individual responsibility, which made for a more unified existence.

We were rolling along at a moderate rate of speed, and the only concern was that we keep moving. We kept the fire going, and hoped the drunken sot would awaken before we ran out of wood.

"Do you think the prick would miss a few slugs of his whisky?" someone asked.

"I wouldn't chance it," said the Pilot, "he isn't too friendly now."

The train began to pick up speed. The rolling motion caused the guard to stir, but he only groaned without awakening. We closed the door about half way to conserve the heat, but we were aware that ventilation was a must. The pot bellied stove was white hot, and we appreciated the warmth, but not being able to cook for lack of water reduced our appreciation and increased our hatred for the guard.

The guard suddenly awoke, struggled to his feet, and stretched and shook himself into a semblance of alertness, which wasn't very convincing. He took one step. When his equilibrium didn't serve him well, he went into a Leon Erroll dance step, one forward two backward, but not in a straight line. Before he could check himself, or before anyone of us volunteered, he was embracing the white hot pot bellied stove. We stared in wonder as the burning flesh of his face gave off an aroma of a barbecuing meat. I think it was the aroma and thought of steak and absence of steak that dulled our minds and reactions. In his stupor his reflexes were nil, he just couldn't disengage himself from the stove. I placed a boot into his shoulder, and physically kicked him away from the stove. His face on one side had taken the brunt of damage. He just lay there, slightly groaning, never fully regaining consciousness in his plight. I suppose we Americans can only hold hate for so long; suddenly this was not a Russian, but a human being needing help. I went to my gear, and retrieved the zinc salve Helena had given me. I proceeded to coat his burns, now blistered and ugly. He slowly opened his eyes, but never moved, as tears began to flow down his cheeks. A blink of his eyes projected a gleam of gratefulness. We all nodded in acceptance. I believed we had made a friend.

By the end of the day, he regained a reasonable attitude of soberness. We were shunted into a very large marshalling yard, and tracked on the outermost spur. It was dusk, and the number of tracks off the main line were easily visible.

"This is one of the main collection areas for those going to the front. The rest go to their homes, or hospitals for the sick and injured," the guard explained.

"The traffic here is great. I have no idea how long we will be here," he added.

"How about some of the food you promised?" I asked.

As if he needed a reminder, only momentarily, he touched the burn on his face, and came away with a smudge of the zinc salve.

"We will wait until darkness falls. I will take you to one of the military guard officers," he suggested. "If he meets you personally, it may make a difference," he said without too much conviction.

"Take us to a Polish or Lithuanian officer, if possible," I asked.

"They have no control over materials, only fighting men up front," he said, killing the thought of a friendly response.

We laid around killing time by exchanging stories of past missions, since we had two strange members we hadn't flown with before. The toggelier explained how he had gotten sick, missed a few missions when hospitalized, and was reluctant to accept this mission because of its duration and purpose. He was looking for some easy milk runs to catch up with his crew.

"Don't complain, your crew could be wiped out, you're still alive, and a page of Air Force history," I encouraged.

Of course there was no one to speak for the waist gunner sent to replace Brooklyn. We just assumed he was either a pool gunner with no crew assignment, or in the same category as the toggelier. The American sergeant and the Englishman had many experiences to tell about. The more they described their combat and POW situations, the more we appreciated being airmen.

It was during the story telling that our humanitarian response to our guard's hurts paid dividends. His first response was to produce a couple of bottles of his cached whisky, offered to us with, "Drink, make warm, thank you."

The next surprise was his involvement in the story telling. He explained his participation at the defenses of Leningrad, with physical proof by displaying the wounds on his legs, arms and back.

"My reward is my assignment to you. Which at first I refused. I educated in Poland, learn English. Polish people like America, in Russia, America is enemy. America is using Russia to fight America's war," he explained.

No one wasted any time attempting to explain that Russia was an ally of Germany and an acclaimed enemy of America, and that the attack on Russia by Germany brought the aid of America to fight Russia's war. It was amazing: as we were thinking the truth, he was already reiterating our thoughts.

"We who lived and educated in big cities, know truth. We are kept close to home, for fear of defection. Polish and Slovak soldiers also kept under close watch," he related.

"What a fucking army. We're here to help them, and they treat us like shit. Well, fuck them. Let's find the prick with the food, Comrade," I requested.

"Wait," the Pilot asked, "let's check out the dangers of this kind of an approach."

"Sitting here like a bunch of pansies makes us look like a bunch of side show freaks. We're going to have to establish some area of respect," I insisted.

"With some of the enemy out there, even American POW's, whomever goes is taking some hell of a chance," warned the Pilot.

"Chance? What is chance? We're here by chance. What the fuck has chance to do with it? I'm not asking for volunteers, I'm going because I see a need for survival!"

"We will wait for darkness, and remember, we must stay close to our train line. To cross into military track will get us shot. Even soldiers never cross military track without permission," the guard instructed.

We left the car dressed warmly. The snow had ceased, and the warmth of the stove faded with every step. The guard walked slowly carrying a lantern. I followed closely in his wake. The multitude of languages mixed in all measures of decibels, some in anger, some in anguish, some pleading, some in fear, and there were times when you knew they were sounds of impending death. Every time I would hesitate as if to investigate, the guard would yank me into reality physically, and quietly advise, "Mind own business."

We had passed about ten cars, when the guard paused. We had reached one attached to one of the military guard trains. It was easily identified as an officer's car: red star, hammer, and sickle emblazoned the side. The two armed guards were so intent on peeking into the inner confines, we were upon them before they could react. Our guard whispered in Russian, and the response was an agreeable smile. What ever was discussed, resulted in a hand being extended, not only as a salutation, but an assist to pull me up on the car's rear platform. My guard was at the invitation of the train guard peering in the window at the action inside. It didn't take long to understand the lack of military alertness when we approached, when they offered me a look inside.

The three women present were young, well groomed, and attractive. It was apparent they were not being forced into the acts of perversion on display. Their utterances weren't the screams of anguish and despair of women being raped. Theirs were those of pleasure, satisfaction, and complete voluntary compliance. It was amazing how as I watched Helena came to mind. These women were of the same ilk, collaboration with subordination, for survival.

The officer was certainly unaware of the viewing audience. If he were, he either didn't care or wanted proof of his sexual prowess. They say position is everything in life.

To view the positions of the participating bodies, gleaming in their complete nudity, within the confines of a dimly lit car...How the hell could I think of food?

Through all this I thought, "I could have had all this voluntary love making, if I conceded to Helena's wishes."

"We had better wait until later," our guard suggested. "Why don't we just have his guards knock on the door, as if we just arrived?" I asked.

Our guard whispered my request, and the response appeared in the affirmative. We dropped to the ground from the platform, backed off a few yards, and approached with less than a quiet request in Russian, "Can we see the officer?"

The officer's guards responded as planned: "Who goes there," in Russian of course, loud enough to be heard inside.

Our guard went through the format of requesting an audience with the officer. I could tell by the tone of questions and answers that the train guards were playing a reluctant attitude, not wanting to bother the "fucking" officer.

We hoped the officer, hearing the confrontation outside, would make a voluntary appearance out of curiosity. He did.

He appeared at the doorway wrapped in a blanket. His language needed no interpretation. I began to feel like an unwelcome guest. I sort of hid behind our guard, hoping his introduction of an American presence would ease the obvious tension. You could have knocked me over with a feather when a smile crossed his face as our guard was talking to him.

"We are OK to enter his car," said the guard.

The three women were still present. They were now clothed, but still very appealing. The officer sort of introduced them, by waving his hand in the direction of each, and mumbling a name. The only name I recognized with was "Helena," believe it or not. Somehow the name of Helena or a Helena situation kept popping up.

The guard was in what appeared to be a cordial dialogue in Russian, with the officer. His constant gestures at me assured me I was the topic of conversation. The officer was very hard to decipher. He was nodding in the affirmative, and saying *nyet at the same time. Nyet was one Russian word I understood.*

"What gives?" I asked of the guard. "The only word these pricks know is nyet. Don't they know da?" I inquired.

"Please don't use bad talk. Some officers, and many of these women, talk English," the guard warned.

I suddenly realized he wasn't talking through his hat. One of the women was pursing her lips, with her index finger positioned in the keep quiet mode. Since the officer made no comment as to the name I blessed him with, I felt no loss of a possible conquest.

The conversation evolved to the point where the officer was showing us the food stores he possessed. Through the guard he informed us he was on short rations. He had to feed his personal guards, and of course, the playthings traveling with him. He finally agreed to some black bread, lard, and a few greens. He threw in some Russian tailored made cigarettes. As a final gesture of friendship, he offered the three women for our pleasure, at the next layover. When the guard presented his offer to us, he closed with, "Me too, OK?"

CHAPTER 36 — PERSONAL WAR

As the guard and I returned to our car, although we were feeling no great accomplishment in acquiring some substantial food, I felt that at least we had made a connection with someone in authority. Our guard assured me that the two pricks from Warsaw were under close scrutiny, as were the other released POW's, using their new found freedom to fulfill their degenerate and greedy wants. It is hard to describe the repetition of activity so inhuman, so cannibalistic, as we returned to our car. The guards compounded the felonies by laughing and encouraging the sadistic behavior. It was hard to understand why the present situation, when the war seemed to be coming to an end, didn't have the feelings of happiness and comradeship I had naively expected.

No matter the conditions, the disappointments, I felt we were all heading in the same direction: home. It now appeared that a personal war between allies was in the making, and the enemy were greedy, corrupt pricks who probably raised their hands in surrender, at first opportunity.

Our appearance at our car brought a sigh of relief from the rest of the crew.

"What the hell took so long? Did you score with some food?" was the unanimous question.

"Give us a chance to regroup. The question of food is a simple response, some of the same old shit, with some tailor-made Russian cigarettes. The guy in charge had the same crap as us, just a little more of it. He gave what he could spare," I responded.

I went on to explain the scenes of unbelievable carnage perpetrated around us, and the fact that American POW's and the Russian military were actually banding in groups to rob, rape, and even kill the poor defenseless displaced persons. The American renegades protected their ill gotten proceeds by attempting to disguise themselves as refugees, and collectively remaining in close proximity to each other. There were times when a group of Russian renegades, drunk beyond responsibility, would attack an American group, with mayhem in mind, hoping to relieve them of their ill gotten booty. The results were just so many casualties attributed to the war. The next of kin were so notified, and the sins of their misbehavior were forgiven, not by God, but by a stroke of a pen, not to tarnish their image to a loving parent, or the American people.

Our guard, when asked, substantiated the story I had related. He emphasized the hatred of the Russians towards Americans. They believed the Americans were interlopers, and had no right to exploit their advantage of being free in their country.

"What a fucking analogy," I retorted, "like the kettle calling the frying pan black."

"All our results were not negative. After the guard gets some water, we'll cook up some of these goodies. Then I'll relate the type of news you unfulfilled lovers will appreciate," I promised.

The pot puree prepared wasn't a gourmet's meal, but it served its intent, by filling the void in one's stomach. To finalize this contentment with a tailored made cigarette, prepared the eager degenerates for my belated story of a positive nature.

Attempting to relate the orgy we witnessed without instilling involuntary arousal was hard to accomplish. The vivid details had the guard nodding affirmatively, and practically salivating with every word. Fantasies are usually reserved for the virgins. Their minds are easily misled to acts of perversion, cunnilingus, and fellatio. Straight fornication is child's play, with no impact on their wishful fantasies.

After all the gees, wows, and no kiddings had relieved their tensions, I hit them with the promise made by the Russian whore master.

"The Russian pimp," before I could continue, the guard injected, "What is pimp?"

"Pimp is short for pimpernel, a starlike flower, very nice," I explained.

He shrugged his shoulders in an accepting attitude. I said to myself, "Where the hell did I dig that shit up?"

I continued to relate the promise made by the Russian officer, leaving out the colloquialism "Pimp."

"The officer who we befriended offered to place his three beauties at our disposal at the next layover," I explained.

"What does he expect from us, for his generosity?" the Pilot asked.

"He just wants to be friend," the guard injected.

"Friend, my ass, he has something in mind. These Russian pricks don't give anything for nothing," the Pilot added.

"I don't give a fuck what he has on his mind. Let's worry about his intentions after we fuck the ass off these beauties he offered!" Of course these words of wisdom came from lover boy himself, the Navigator.

The guard stoked the fire, set the damper, and loaded it with enough wood to last the night. He closed the door, leaving an opening for ventilation. He wrapped himself in a blanket, spread his body on the plank bed across the door, and said, "Good sleep." We all bedded down, each in his own world of thoughts.

"What if we don't move to another layover," asked the Navigator, "do you think his offer could be consummated here?"

"What's this consummation horse shit?" the Pilot asked. "Let go of your prick, and get some sleep."

There was laughter and snickering during this impromptu conversation. It relieved the tension, and blotted out the screams accompanied by gunfire that penetrated the night's concealing darkness.

The quiet of sleep was shattered by rapid staccato bursts of automatic gunfire. The close proximity caused all to dive for any area of cover. I reached for my forty five, which I kept under my burlap pillow. The only light was the glowing pot belly stove, which cast its meager light on the back of our guard, standing in the now fully opened doorway. His burp gun was at the ready, spewing lead in a fanning mode. What he was shooting at was an invisible target. The blackness outside wasn't at all reduced by the glow of the stove; the door framed our guard against a black void. What was immediately obvious was the lack of return fire. What was immediately identifiable was the screams of anguish in English, "You son of a bitch, I'm hit, help me," and the collective grunts, groans, and cursing in English of scattering men.

"What the hell is going on?" was the unanimous question.

"Stay back, out of door, away from light," he ordered.

"Band of rebels, looking for loot, try to enter car. They don't know you are here with guard. Big surprise, we see how many I shoot, tomorrow in daylight," he related.

"Listen, I hear moaning outside," someone said.

"Stay inside, may be armed, go sleep, I watch," the guard suggested.

"Did you hear the pricks, they were American," I said. "What a sick world, with such sick people."

It was a restless night. Sleep was only a casual nap with my mind acting as a portfolio of pictures, flashing a vivid repeat of the incidents I had encountered during the night.

It was as if I had slept, but didn't sleep, as I was awakened by voices outside our car. Everyone was awake, and standing in the doorway.

I made my way to the door, asking, "What's going on?"

"Some officer is talking to our guard, apparently about the two bodies laying in the snow," the Pilot guessed.

"Whatever our guard said, must have satisfied the officer. He shook his hand, with an assenting smile," suggested the Navigator.

As the sleep left my eyes, and I got a closer look at the officer, I realized it was the "fucking Russian." To our surprise, he gestured in our direction, whispered something to our guard, and waved a salutation jauntily with a smile.

The guard related the officer's whispered words, "His promise still good, will tell when OK."

"Shit, I can't believe he was serious," I said, "just an idle bullshit promise."

"He must want something from us, we must be careful not to become involved in any of his schemes." advised the Pilot.

"Like I said before, let's fuck them, then leave them, we have nothing to lose," the Navigator offered.

"That degenerate mind of yours is going to get us in trouble, you can't be lucky all the time,"I replied.

"Hell, you know, most of the time I'm kidding, I wouldn't do anything to hurt us, I'm just making conversation,"he pleaded.

"The best way to avoid any confrontation with the guy would be to not ask him for anything," suggested the Englishman.

We all agreed with his suggestion, but the Navigator agreed with reservations. The guard surprised us when he injected himself into our conversation. "You not worry about that Officer, he good friend of your friend, Helena."

We looked at each other with utter amazement, indirectly she was still looking out for our asses. I wondered if I hadn't misjudged her, but then I figured, she was nothing but one of the same ilk as the three with him now, and my conscience was spared.

They had thrown the two bodies in a wagon, and the crowd that gathered was being dispersed. We were never told the nationality of the dead men. We wondered if they were part of the band shot up by our guard. Again we realized the importance of befriending the Officer. His protection was probably contracted by Helena, with a personal sacrifice.

The guard explained the action of the Russian officer in reference to the two dead men. "He was just doing what he was assigned to do, protect you Americans, from any and all threatening situations."

"But we think the men you shot were American POW's," I stated.

"You do not know for sure, so forget what you think," he suggested.

"Don't give me that crap, we heard them speak English, we're not deaf," I replied.

"You forget, do as I say, other people speak English, besides Americans," the guard repeated with an authoritative and conclusive tone.

The rest of the day was spent discussing the happenings of the past few days. How in God's name could we not honor the requests of Helena and Novak to reveal the atrocities which were not just hearsay, but to which we were now witnesses?

"We must not speak of what we have seen, as Helena, and Novak warned. We must either join the renegades, or be absolutely oblivious to their actions. The proper time and place will come to speak out," I volunteered.

"I don't know if I want to be a part of such revelations. We're including Americans, if we tell the truth," the Pilot said.

"You may have a point, let's hope they are caught up in their own follies before we reach Odessa," I concurred.

The guard left to get some fresh water, to drink and cook. He returned with the water, but also some bad news. He told us the Russian officer informed him, there will be no movement this day.

"Wow," the Navigator bellowed, "let's hold the prick to his promise. If we're going to be stuck here, let's do a little sticking ourselves," he continued.

"I can't believe you're serious," the Pilot responded. "You're sick, and don't shit us that you're only kidding."

"I don't know about you guys, but the way things are progressing, we're still at war. Who knows about to-morrow? We may all be dead," he stated, attempting to make a case for his remarks.

"I'd rather remain here in the protective custody of our guard, than be caught in the saddle with some collaborating bitch," I confessed.

The Navigator's reply made light of the situation, when he said, "What a way to die."

The guard's response to this conversation was a bombshell of hilarity: "We make love three at a time, others keep watch, to protect each other. I give gun when I go."

This idiot really meant it, but we didn't embarrass him by responding, so we just let it slip by. Of course the Navigator thought it was a great idea. "I'll go first. No sloppy seconds for me."

"I can't believe you are serious, you treat this dangerous situation like child's play, people being killed all around us, and you worrying about a piece of ass," I reminded him.

"We agreed to vote on all our actions that effect us as a group, this appears to be one of those situations," the Pilot added.

We all agreed not to place ourselves in any compromising situation, and if anyone personally did so, he was on his own. We have sweated out many threatening and even inviting offerings, but managed to survive by keeping our cool. Still being together except for the waist gunner, was in my mind, under the prevailing conditions, a God send, an achievement.

The day progressed without incident. We managed to survive with the food at hand, and the potato whisky shared by the guard repelled the cold by dimming the mind into relaxing naps. It was about dusk when commanding voices filled the air. The armed guards were ordering the people outside their cars to retrain. The guards were stationing themselves in a cordon of a protective line between our train and the adjoining track. Our guard jumped to the ground in hopes of ascertaining what was going on. It was as if he were some strange alien, as he was thrown bodily back into our car, with the aid of a rifle butt to the side of his head. We automatically went to his aid. This action brought a rifle shot into the air. The door was slammed closed and locked.

The guard, though stunned, never lost consciousness, and shook off our assistance, as though embarrassed. He reached for his burp gun and made for the door with a vengeful look in his face. Whatever his intent, it was never fulfilled. The door burst open, and there was our "fucking Russian officer." He boarded the car, closed the door, then spoke to our guard. Our Guard continuously nodded his head in the affirmative, accompanied with, "Da, da." The conversation ended with a hand shake and a pat on the back, and the officer departed the car.

"What gives?" the Pilot asked.

"We have to be very careful, next few days," the guard replied."An advance group of Russian elite troops have arrived to isolate all of us from a train due tomorrow."

He went on to explain that a troop train heading for the front would arrive by morning. It was loaded with elite Russian troops, but most of all it would be carrying the most modern Russian armament, to be used to drive the remaining German forces to their knees and complete annihilation. He explained that we will not be able to move on, until the train is resupplied and serviced.

He ended his explanation in his own broken English, but the picture he painted was sickeningly effective. This elite corp of Russian troops were the most deadly, used primarily for clean up action. They felt impervious to human dignity, he continued, and placed themselves above any law or order. They were, he concluded, hated and despised by other branches of the Russian military. No one challenged their authority.

"It is best they not know you Americans are here," was his final warning.

"Are you trying to tell us they would have no respect for we Americans?" I asked.

"From what I see and hear, you would be treated no better than the rifle butt I got, that you saw," he said.

The incidents we had witnessed, and the tales told to us by Helena, Novak, and our guard, certainly seemed truthful, yet still unbelievable. In the name of God, and justice, we must somehow survive, to relate these inhuman happenings.

The background of memories focusing on the stories of the German atrocities perpetrated on their own citizens, and the people of conquered nations, was the motivation instilled in the hearts of most Americans to engage the enemy. To witness the same cold-blooded treatment between allies, makes one wonder,"Why are we here?"

As we discussed our situation, we all agreed to be as inconspicuous as possible. We would remain secluded in our car, and leave only when permitted. Our bodily necessities would be achieved in the buckets provided, and disposed of by the guard, who was agreeable. We were thankful that the orders to remain entrained applied to everyone. The constant arrival of trains going to the front, or trains going east, always brought visits of those who heard Americans were nearby. We adopted a wait and see attitude which irked our Navigator.

"Since there is very little activity going on, why can't I at first opportunity sneak over to the pimp's car? I could share his benefits, and remain there until things return to normal," suggested the Navigator.

"I don't know about the rest of you guys, but the insistence of loverboy to perform sexually at every opportunity makes me believe he's all talk," the Pilot replied.

"Come to think of it, even with Sonia, some of us know we scored. He always told us about his achievements," added the Co-Pilot.

The guard listened with a wry smile on his face, then with a stern authoritative command ordered, "You will remain as others. Very dangerous what you say. I will shoot you if you attempt what you say. We are all in danger, must obey."

"Come on you guys, I'm only kidding, be reasonable, I'm no jerk," he pleaded.

"Then cut out your so called kidding. The guard must understand we all act as one, and he is in charge," the Pilot requested.

We placed that conversation on the back burner, and turned to the events we anticipated. Our two friends kept themselves more or less in the background, when we had what appeared to be conversations of a personal nature. Now that we were discussing events that would effect the well being of all, they became an integral part of the group, and not only innocent bystanders.

The Englishman, being a long time professional soldier, spoke with experience, and conviction.

"The next days of movement, when they occur, will be the most vital, and most dangerous," he explained.

He went on to explain, "The closer we get to Odessa, and a semblance of authority, the more important it will be for the renegades to attempt to circumvent body searches and use you airmen to assist them.

"You must understand, you not being POW's, and being under protective custody at all times, relieves you from the scrutiny of the POW's traveling on their own," he continued. "Your vouching for us, has them thinking your word will clear them also."

"But your presence with us was cleared in advance," the Pilot answered.

"They don't know that, and feel equally deserving of your help, as fellow Americans," the Sergeant added.

"Americans? The dirty miserable cock suckers will get help from me over my dead body," I challenged.

"From what I have seen the things they are capable of, your dead body would afford no deterrent to their goals," someone emphasized.

All this conversation was conjecture built around facts we had witnessed, or told to us. We found ourselves thinking the worst, which I felt prepared us for the worst. The night passed quietly for the first time, the usual sounds of despair and gunfire magnified by their absence.

The welcome quiet provided a background for the undisturbed sleep that blotted out the miseries surrounding us. It was a strange feeling to awaken with a composed mind, gently prodded by the sound of steel against steel, as a train braked to a stop on the adjoining track.

CHAPTER 37 — MADE IN U.S.A.

The guard opened the door a slight crack, and peered into the dim light of a new dawn. We all gathered close to him awaiting his revelation of what confronted us. He opened the door a little more to afford him greater peripheral vision. A few seconds later, after scanning right and left, he closed the door gently.

"What's out there?" the Pilot asked.

"This special train next to us, right outside door, with armed guard on car, has covered airplane," he reported. "I see no people outside train. All must be confined. This not good," he concluded.

"Is it possible to open the other door, away from the view of the guard?" I asked. "Now that you know we will not leave without your permission, what prevents you from opening the other door?"

"Good, will get key for lock," he responded.

He retrieved the key from his knapsack, unlocked the door gingerly, and surveyed the area before reporting the situation.

"We on outer rail, near wooded area, can if careful enter woods for relief, not being seen," he reported.

"What a blessing, not to have to use the bucket," I said.

The blessing was not restricted to us. As we exited our private domain for bodily relief, we found green drawers enjoying the same blessing, and signaling the blessing to all in a chain reaction throughout the train. Apparently, American ingenuity isn't confined to Americans.

Of course we knew the massive exodus could not evade the scrutiny of the Russians, and we wondered what their reaction would be. Whatever their intentions, it wasn't forthcoming immediately. As a matter of fact, it was as if they were oblivious to the whole situation.

Under this new found freedom, some ventured to approach the special train and converse with the guards. Between our two trains, one venturous fool attempted to cross over the special train to the other side. He was lucky, as one guard placed a rifle to his head, but another mercifully rifle-butted him off the car. With the ground rules established the hard way, we all obeyed without question.

We weren't sure if the Russian contingent were aware of the American presence. If they were, they didn't show any discernible signs. Being as discreet as humanly possible, I casually walked down the tracks, along the wooded area, keeping out of sight of the train guards. On my return, I walked between our train and the armed train. I attempted to refrain from looking directly at the contents of the special train. Although all the armament was covered with tarpaulins, field pieces, tanks, and airplanes were clearly defined. Remembering the words of the officer, relating to the secret weapons of importance aboard this train, aroused my curiosity. I first asked our guard if he knew, or could find out any information. His response was in his own lingo, but I could read "mind your fucking business" in his tone.

The cliche "God acts in strange ways" came to mind the next day. When we awoke the next morning, a raging snow storm was in progress. It was unexpected, but this unforeseen occurrence solved the mystery of the secret weapons. The tarpaulins on many of the cars were either blown from their covered armament or dislodged enough to expose the armament beneath. The first revelation was the car alongside ours. It was obvious before the gale winds that an airplane was the cargo. Now it was doubly apparent. However, the type of aircraft was the real revelation. It was an American P-39, since discarded as an obsolete fighter plane, unique in the fact its armament included a twenty millimeter nose cannon. Its sole function was relegated to ground support. I imagined the Russians had that function in mind, for their advancing ground forces.

The swirling snow and the biting wind caused the speedy consummation of one's bodily relief. The special train guards were hurriedly re-covering the exposed armament.

"The phony creeps. Did you notice every piece of secret weaponry was American made?" I revealed.

"They are still bullshitting the people that they are fighting our war," the Pilot added.

"We should have let the Germans kick their ass. We could have rid the world of two enemies, Hitler and Stalin, and the misled Italians would have taken care of Mussolini," I countered.

It was a strange circumstance. There we were actually fighting to survive in an area which should afford us safety, with gratification. With all that had developed since our trip to Odessa commenced, it was hard to believe, as the Englishman posed, it could get any worse.

By early afternoon, the snow ceased, and the ugly remnants of human defecation and urination were obliterated by a white, beauteous accumulation of snow flakes. This white, cleansing blanket made a futile effort to completely remove the irresponsible acts of depredation that were perpetrated by one human to another. There were mounds of snow, scattered throughout this vast expanse of cleansed ground, that defied nature's intent. An exposed hand of death, a red stain of blood, marked these mounds as God's reminder you can not conceal man's sinful acts.

We hoped that the next day would see the special train move out, or by some quirk of fate, we would move out. The next day was cold and crisp, without a semblance of a breeze. We were surprised at the friendliness of this elite, so-called hated contingent of the Russian military. They arrived in groups, and usually accompanied by English speaking Lithuanian officers. It was conveyed to us by these same officers that in the higher echelons of the Russian order of command, American airmen were revered. Those with first hand knowledge of the caravan of equipment flown over the so-called "hump," bringing supplies to Russia, instilled this reverence. It appeared that here, as in the United States, the people who were in the position to receive the news of the war lived with the heroic and picturesque reports, and not the vile, inhuman realities. The convoys plying the submarine infested waters, from the United States to Vladivostok, were as heroic as the defenders of Leningrad.

Since the restrictions related to us appeared relaxed, we ventured to ask our guard if there was a possibility of obtaining some decent food from the special train. He without hesitation suggested a visit to our "fucking Russian," to intercede on our behalf.

"You're putting us in a compromising position, asking him for favors," the Pilot injected.

"Geez, we're running out of food. God only knows when we'll get to Odessa, or any place where we'll be supplied," I pleaded .

"If you visit the Russian, check to see if his word is any good," the Navigator requested.

"I don't know your despicable, irrelevant utterances are an attempt to relieve tensions, or if you are hopelessly insane," the Pilot suggested

"I want to remind you Christian zealots that the scriptures unquestionably state, 'Man cannot live on bread alone,'" the Navigator retaliated.

"I suppose your answer to man not living on bread alone would be, 'No bread, give him pussy,'" I added.

This response brought a touch of humor to the situation as the guard left to inquire about our request.

We were attempting to entertain some visiting soldiers from the special train. The language barrier made it hard to communicate with true understanding. No matter what we said or did, we smiled constantly. There were times when our smiles apparently didn't jive with the answers to the questions asked. The blank questioning looks at each other, and the accompanying shrugs, usually initiated a mass exodus.

The guard returned with a real tale of woe: the "fucking Russian" had been replaced. He explained how a high ranking bemedaled officer was in his car. The guard was told that our guardian was placed under arrest, because of the women he had smuggled along with him.

"What happened to the women?" the Navigator asked.

"Strange, they still with new officer," our Guard answered.

"As always, rank has its privileges," was chorused.

It suddenly dawned on us that our guardian connection, set up by Helena, was gone. We wondered what our situation for the remainder of the trip would be. When we questioned our guard, he convinced us the if we remained together where he could watch us, we would be safe.

The Pilot reminded the lot of us, especially the Navigator, that he would tolerate no breeches of security. "This situation is getting hairy, and we have no idea where we stand under the new command. Until we do, we play our hand close to our vests. This is an order," he concluded.

Everyone felt the seriousness of our position, and we accepted his order as such.

We had hoped that the departing officer passed on the word of Helena's contract. The friendliness of the so-called tough contingent towards us as airmen gave us the impression that they separated us from the other travelers.

Although we felt a blanket of protection existed, there was always their reputation that behooved us not to relax our vigil. We had witnessed their immediate reaction to a breech of conduct. They gave me the impression that as long as they were in command, and the format they dictated was obeyed, all was well. Their reaction to any violation that impugned their authority was never dispensed in a half-way measure. Any and all such encroachments were punished with violent acts of mayhem, with no regard to human dignity. Retaining these facts of their reputation, we attempted to refrain from any direct confrontation, except in a cordial response to their visits.

Another day arrived with no news of departure, cold as usual, and the food practically gone.

"We have to make some kind of move to obtain some grub," I suggested.

"What do you suggest?" the Pilot asked.

"Damn, you're in command, you always insist, why can't you pull a little rank?" I retorted.

"You know damn well my rank don't mean a shit here," he responded.

"How the fuck do you know? You never tried!" someone injected.

"How about me giving it a go?" the Englishman volunteered. "Lend me your flying jacket with your rank insignia."

"One word out of you, he'll know you're not an American," the Pilot said.

"You're not thinking clearly. The only voice he'll hear is the guard's - it's your rank that will be noted to him by the guard," the Englishman defined.

"If you want to chance it, you're on your own," the Pilot stated.

"Wait a fucking minute," I injected, "we had a commitment that we would vote on any action suggested, and we all must agree to back such action unanimously."

"You'll not get my vote, how about the rest of you?" the Pilot asked, as he looked towards the other officers for support. He was surprised when he found himself the only dissenter.

"We'll just have to abide by the Constitution, majority rules," I challenged. "All in favor, say aye."

The aye's had it. The one nay never made an entrance.

We probably should have expected it, but it did come at a serious time, and was received as a tension relaxer. As the Englishman was donning the Pilot's jacket, the Navigator posed a question to the Englishman.

"If the Russian officer is congenial, find out if he will share his good fortune, as the other officer promised."

"We'll make believe we didn't hear a word you said," the Pilot responded. "We'll all laugh, like it was some kind of joke, coming from a 'jerkster' like you."

The Englishman left with the guard. We waited with bated breath, I with a prayer on my lips.

About an hour later the guard returned. His face wore a broad smile, disenchanted by broken and missing teeth.

"Geez, I never saw this guy with anything that resembled a smile. I guess the condition of his teeth was a secret he wanted to keep," I laughingly declared.

"What happened to make you so happy?" the Pilot asked.

"Me sorry you all miss boat," he responded.

"Fuck the boat, where is the Englishman?" I asked.

"He in boat, very happy," he slurred

"This son of a Russian bitch is stoned," the Navigator guessed.

Although I felt no immediate danger to the Englishman, we were unable to get any coherent response out of the guard, so I volunteered to check it out. The sergeant agreed to accompany me, and we started to detrain. My feet had just touched ground and the sergeant was about to follow when our mission was completed before it began. The Englishman, was returning, escorted by a large bemedaled Russian officer. It was hard to determine who was assisting who, as they slipped and stumbled on the snow covered ground.

The Englishman was too drunk to climb aboard the car. The Russian, after a couple of unassisted attempts and a few pratfalls, accepted our assistance. The Englishman flopped on the floor like a sack of potatoes, giggling gibberish accompanied his giddy manner. The Russian escort did an about face, and tossed a hand-waving goodnight as he flopped face down, without so much as a hand to break his fall. We jumped from the car to assist him, as he was out cold.

"I'll go to his car, and get some help," I volunteered. "I'll go with you," the Navigator said.

"You'll stay right here," the Pilot ordered, "one of you guys go with him," he suggested.

The response was deafening silence, to the Pilot's chagrin. We detrained from the outer door and made our way to the officer's car. We had expected to find his personal guards available to assist in returning the officer to his quarters.

There were no guards present on the outside of the car, but we could hear sounds emitting from within. When we mounted the rear platform of the car, the sight that greeted us was right out of the cartoon pornography books of sexual fantasies.

The scenes I had witnessed with the other officer were of action. The condition of those present was the aftermath of what must have been an abundance of reciprocal perverted acts of sexual desires.

Even the Navigator's usual utterances of sexual conquest were stilled by the sight before us. The bodies were entwined in grotesque positions with perverted intentions, which, if alive, would have furnished sexual desires. The sounds we heard on approaching must have been the last sounds of life from one of these poor souls.

"What the hell gives," I asked aloud.

"Let's get the fuck out of here," the Navigator suggested as he grabbed my arm.

I assumed by their lifeless appearances and the amount of blood there was no way we could help them. We jumped from the platform, hoping we were not seen by anyone, and returned to our car. Since we traveled to the rear of train along the wooded area, we hadn't passed the fallen Russian officer.

We arrived at our car to find anxious faces awaiting us. The Englishman and the guard were still unconscious. Their condition prevented us from discovering the beginning, but it didn't prevent us from revealing the end.

As I started to describe the havoc we had witnessed, all hell broke loose. The area next to the control car was illuminated by large anti-aircraft searchlights, mounted on Dodge trucks. They swept the areas up and down the tracks, revealing that the perimeter between the special train and ours was cordoned off with armed elite troops. Near-hysterical commands filled the night air. As one light swept towards our car, it revealed the absence of the fallen Russian.

"Where the hell is that drunken bastard?" the Pilot asked.

"Thank God, he wasn't found near our car. Close the door, we don't want a connection between the Russian and our two drunken sots," I suggested.

I continued to describe the scene at the control car, the story giving rise to various degrees of conjecture and an equal variety of conclusions. It was apparent to all that the dead guards had taken advantage of the drunken condition that practically incapacitated our friends and the Russian officer.

I don't believe it was apropos at the time, but I couldn't pass up the opportunity to stick one to the Navigator. "See what an uncontrolable prick can get you?" I directed to him.

There was a momentary quiet, then a wait for response. None was forthcoming. The Pilot broke the silence.

"What you witnessed must have happened after the guard, the Englishman and the Russian left the car," surmised the Pilot, "at least I hope so," he added.

"They certainly were surprised, and slaughtered in cold blood. They were in the midst of sexual endeavors," described the Navigator.

"You degenerate bastard! Only you would notice something like that, instead of the bloody carnage perpetrated there!" I screamed.

"The thing that bothers me is the fact that these were armed guards caught with their pants down, and whomever did this must have had a motive of premeditated revenge," I declared.

The only person fitting the description of such a person was the dismissed officer.

We decided to keep our solutions to ourselves. We thanked God the son of a bitch didn't realize who he was shooting. He could have just as well killed the Englishman, if he hadn't left earlier. There was little information available from the guard or the Englishman, while laying in a drunken stupor. We would wait until morning.

The final discussion was to collectively pray that the Russian officer would forget, either intentionally or by drunkenness, the happenings that included our guard or the Englishman. We knew, without a shadow of a doubt, an incident such as this could place us as the prime actors in a deadly scene. We are not immune, was a unanimous agreement, as we fitfully attempted sleep. My forty five was clenched in my hand. The guard's burp gun was cradled in the Navigator's lap.

"I'll stay awake for the first two hours. We'll take turns at guard duty," he volunteered.

The others declared their services as next, and so forth, until the night time hours were covered. We felt a little less anxious about our safety, at least for this night.

CHAPTER 38 — SURVIVAL

A sober awakening of our two drunks would, we hoped, shed some light on the previous night's happenings. Realistically, the only first hand knowledge they could possibly possess was the scenario they left. The guard arrived before the Englishman and the Russian. From what he said to us when he arrived, even in a drunken stupor, the gathering had been gleeful; there was nothing to hint of the slaughter to come. The Englishman and the Russian could not in their condition have perpetrated such a heinous crime. The most important issue was that we not be connected to the crime, even in the smallest detail. Because Russian soldiers were the victims, we had to believe the investigation would be intense, not like the daily killings that were largely ignored.

I slowly opened the front door. The cordon of elite troops still remained, separating our train from the special train. The intensity that permeated the area was dangerously explosive. I believed at that moment, by the penetrating stares of the guards in our direction, any indiscretion on our part would give them cause to blow us away. With no sign of acknowledgement, I gently closed the door. I slowly opened the rear door to find old green drawers, idly looking our way, like she was waiting for our appearance.

"What the fuck do you want?" I asked, knowing she understood no English. I hadn't noticed the young girl beside her, and the girl's answer to my vulgar question took me by surprise.

"We do not want, what you say 'fuck.' We want you to talk to your American friends. Stop stealing our belongings, and give us too much 'fuck,'" she pleaded.

"I'm sorry," I sheepishly apologized, "I didn't believe anyone within earshot understood English."

"Bad language is not our problem, the war has made us used to it. Surviving, being close to home, only to be raped and robbed by our allies, is worse than war. German prison or occupation was more acceptable," she sobbingly related.

This confession only supported the stories we had heard and what we had witnessed ourselves. We were not in the position to do anything for these poor souls. Our personal survival was our first priority.

She concluded with, "After what happened last night, they have excuse to question everyone and visit our cars. What they force us to do cannot be denied, under threat of implication."

We lied and told them we would look into their problem, not wanting to have them lose hope, or respect for all Americans.

The guard and Englishman awoke almost as one; their waking was announced with a simultaneous groan from drunken hangovers.

"Who punched out my lights?" the Englishman asked, grasping his head in a vise like grip, violently shaking it from side to side in an attempt to unscramble his disoriented memory.

The guard's return to reality was less demonstrative. He just staggered about from bulkhead to bulkhead, his desire to fall prevented by each of us as we passed him about like a basketball. They resisted our belaboring questions, and it was many hours before they were actually aware of the enormity of then situation the questions related to.

When asked if they were aware of what happened last night, they drew a blank. The

Englishman admitted he had a ball, and remembered very little after the guard left to inform us of the congenial offerings of the replacement Russian officer.

"Blimey, we had all the bloody loving we could handle, and this guy had all the best of whiskeys, but no food," the Englishman reported. "I think he made mention he would try to help us out, the guard told me," he added.

The guard mumbled something that sounded affirmative, but with the situation as it was, all was hopeful wishing. We all felt the further we remained from the Russian, the better off we were. The Pilot instructed the guard in no uncertain terms our position concerning the Russian. When I and the Navigator described the scene we witnessed, the guard was visibly shaken.

He proceeded to provide an alibi for his participation. "I leave, there was no trouble, ask him," he said, pointing to the Englishman.

"Likewise. When I left with the Russian, who escorted me so I wouldn't be challenged on my return here," he recalled, "I vaguely remember the Russian ordering the guards to enjoy themselves. I think he said something about having to get rid of the women, that they could be trouble."

"All of a sudden you understand Russian? Who are you kidding?" I asked.

"Believe me. I didn't mean to make you think I could understand Russian. I only interpreted their conversation from their gestures and from what the guard told me."

I remembered the first encounter with these same women, and remembered the one girl who by her signal to me to refrain from criticizing the first officer, understood English.

"Did one of the girls speak to you in English?" I asked.

"Blimey, now that you mention it, it was she who told me they were being taken to testify against the officer who was arrested for having them with him" he revealed. As his head cleared during the day, he could remember more clearly the happenings of the night before, and he admitted his position was very scary. He remembered how our guard told him the Officer gave his guards orders to be on the alert, while they partied. He went on to say that before he became involved in the sexual orgy, and the drinks took their toll, our guard had a conversation with the Russian officer. He assumed it was about getting some food for us, but when our guard had the opportunity to speak to him in confidence, what he revealed surprised the shit out of him: The officer who was arrested had escaped, and his whereabouts were unknown.

"There's your fucking killer," I declared.

Everyone agreed, and the consensus was to keep our suspicions to ourselves, and pray we weren't suspects. We were afraid the Russian officer, who apparently was assigned to protect the girls, had a lot of explaining to do. We couldn't see in what manner, but we were afraid he might implicate the Englishman to save his own ass.

"He high ranking officer, many decorations. I think all will be forgotten," the guard injected.

"Bullshit," I retaliated, "somebody will take a fall, you can bet on that."

"It will not be any of us, he knows of contract for your safety," the guard assured us.

It was a comforting feeling to know we weren't completely on our own. The day passed without any incident relating to the atrocity of the night before. Since we were confined to our car, any action or reaction wasn't made known to us. Our guard attempted to engage the guard on the flat car in conversation. The guard's response was to point his burp gun in a threatening manner in our direction. Our guard took offense, and a shouting match ensued. The train guard let go a burst of gun fire into the ground, then raised his weapon in a direct line towards our guard. I grabbed our guard, and pulled him back in as the Englishman slammed the door shut.

"Are you trying to get us all killed, you idiot?" I screamed as I wrestled him to the floor.

He was very strong, and pulled away, making for his own weapon. We all pounced on him, and held him down as we tried to calm him.

"Do you really think that prick would have shot you, just for asking a question?" I queried.

"I'm a hero, real soldier wounded in combat. I told him of my assignment. He told me I am nothing to him, he would shoot me," he said. "When I told him to do so, he fired into ground. He then say next shot my head," the guard explained. "I will kill him first chance I get."

"Good God, we don't have enough problems, we have a personal vendetta in our midst," announced the Pilot.

We spent the next few hours trying to calm the guard and appease his hurt feelings. All efforts appeared to be wasted, and only the train's sudden movement changed the atmosphere of dread.

The metallic sound of the couplings between cars and the air brakes whistling as they released the wheels from captivity was a welcome symphony. We were on the move, we hoped to any place away from this malaise of both physical and mental discomfort.

We never reached any headway speed; the train sort of humped its way down the track. We would move a few yards, come to an abrupt stop, then proceed a few more feet, in the same herky-jerky manner. It made me remember the shuttling of trains into a siding at home in Behan's coal yard, for car positioning was being duplicated here.

"We're not going anywhere, they are just repositioning the train," I explained.

We opened the door to confirm my reasoning. The one happy result was the absence of the flat car with the belligerent, belittling adversary of our guard. We were parked at the extreme end of the marshaling yard. The tow engine was departing, which left us immobile, and caused a sick feeling of disappointment. It was also apparent that our train had been shortened to about half of the original car count. The officer's car was still present, and the special train appeared to be getting ready to move out.

Our guess was wrong, as they just moved to an adjacent spur, and another military loaded train was shuttled alongside ours.

The readjusting of the trains appeared to minimize the intensity of the situation. There was a more casual atmosphere between the military assigned to the newly arrived train than the so-called "secret," laden train. The cargo on the new arrival was not covered, and therefore easily identified as solely Russian weaponry. Our guard explained that the planes and other Russian equipment was only used to back up the so-called secret weapons, that were manufactured in the United States by Russians. He smiled apologetically, exposing his broken and missing teeth.

The birth of a new day reminded us of the fact we had no food, and the availability of some appeared unlikely. The lines of people tracking to the command car in quest of food caused the first confrontation between the displaced persons and the newly arrived military personnel. Luckily they were not the elite separatist troops. These were ordinary peasants conscripted into service, whose authority was more humanely enforced. The only occasions they resorted to the belligerent "obey or else attitude" were when the sovereignty of their train was violated. As with the secret train you dare not cross over it at any point. You may crawl under it at any point, or walk around it to get to the other side, and this dictate applied to anyone, including the military.

From our position on the siding, the presence of a flat car alongside afforded a clear view across the snow covered terrain to the adjacent countryside.

"Blimey, am I seeing things? Aren't those bloody chickens in that yard across the tracks?" the Englishman said.

We all gathered at the door opening, as if the sight of any kind of food would ease the pangs of hunger. It's funny how one's memory reacts to particular incidents. We all involuntarily blurted out the menu of chicken we most desired. From chicken soup with rice, chicken fricassee with dumplings, Southern fried, or whatever, never entered my hungry mind. It was other types I thought of: my mother's stuffed chicken, with her Italian dressing, chicken cacciatore, chicken parmigiana, caused my mouth to water in memory of her cooking.

"Now wait a minute," the Pilot said as the Englishman leaped to the snow covered ground. He stopped in his tracks, but not because of the Pilot's order. The guard aboard the adjacent car fired a round into the ground at the feet of the Englishman, as he attempted to cross the flat car. It wasn't done as a malicious or threatening gesture, but as a gentle reminder to pass under if he wanted to get to the other side. The shot drew the attention of all within earshot, and in so doing drew attention to the antics of the bolting Englishman. He had to pass under about four tracks of train, and his crawling and running caused everyone within sight to stop in their tracks. Guards on the military trains stood in bewilderment, hands on hips, following the crazy actions of the Englishman.

He finally reached the fence surrounding the farm house. Without hesitation, he hurdled the fence, without even trying the gate in front of him. Now the spectacle of all spectacles developed before our eyes. I wish I could have charged admission. "Truth is stranger than fiction" is no idle cliche. No scenario could have been written with the same impact as this adlibbed scene.

Here was this crazy Englishman, slipping and sliding on the snow covered terrain, chasing some bewildered, frightened, cackling chickens. The scene, although serious in intent, seemed like a comedy act. When the door of the farm house flew open, a man emerged carrying what from this distance appeared to be a rifle. Now the true meaning the improvised scene developed.

The shots he threw into the air produced a staccato burst of sound that caused the inattentive to join the arena of spectators. Their voices were muffled by the distance; the volume of sound, though not intelligible, was in the violent category. The farmer continued to point his weapon in the direction of the Englishman, at a safe distance. It appeared the Englishman was moving forward a step at a time, in an almost pleading manner. His gestures with his hands were almost comical, as he pointed to his mouth, to his stomach, then to the poor non-understanding chickens. For some unknown reason the spectators began to cheer what appeared to be encouragement, not to the farmer, but to the Englishman.

"Geez," I said, "I hope they haven't the idea we"re going to share our food with them."

"If that guy don't get the hell out of there, we'll share a funeral together," the Co-Pilot added.

Suddenly without warning the Englishman took one quick step towards the farmer. His unexpected action caused the farmer to withdraw defensively. The suddenness caused the farmer to slip on the snow covered ground, his rifle moving from the ready position to an upright angle. This gave the Englishman the opportunity to snatch the rifle.

The sudden reflexive action of the farmer caused a shot to discharge into the air. The Englishman came away with the rifle, and he backed off with his palm of his hand in a "stay where you are" attitude.

The farmer walked towards the Englishman, screaming threats in what was certainly Polish. Without warning he was brandishing a hunting knife, and charging our friend. His action was so unexpected the Englishman, who was carrying the rifle by the barrel, had no chance to raise it to a firing position. He grabbed the barrel with two hands like a baseball bat. It appeared from our distance he was attempting to knock the knife from the farmer's hand. The farmer drew his knife hand aside, which exposed his head, and that was where contact was made. The blow was devastating; the stock separated from the barrel, and the farmer collapsed to the snow covered ground, his blood framing his motionless body.

All hell broke loose. The comical scene became one of tragedy. The Englishman finally corralled three chickens, then made his way back to our car. With the farmer lying motionless, the foodless multitudes broke ranks and charged the military guard. The Englishman had to fight off those who attempted to wrestle the chickens from him. His success in escaping to our car was helped by the military guards firing shots into the air. The guards of the secret train used this situation to inflict mayhem and even deadly force on these poor wretched souls.

During the confusion, our guard disappeared. He suddenly appeared with the wildest, silliest smile he could muster.

"You look like the cat that ate the canary," I exclaimed. "He no canary," he replied. "He respect real hero from now on," as he patted his burp gun.

The screams of uncontrolled, rioting people stilled any further questioning of our guard. Shots every now and then cut short screams into guttural gurgling sounds of life into death. The Englishman was snaking his way over and around the trains blocking his return.

Without warning the so called secret train began to roll out of the marshaling yard. This action eliminated the only thing blocking the people from moving beyond the marshaling yard to the now-inviting chickens. As soon as the track was cleared, they moved as animals towards the farm house.

They fought each other, walking over the prone farmer with no concern if he were dead or alive. We had no way of knowing, and we hadn't had a chance to question the Englishman. Almost in an instant the chickens were torn apart savagely in a animalistic act of sharing the spoils. The parting shot of this unbelievable carnage was the one fired into the head of the farmer as he lay there. They then went through his pockets, removing whatever he possessed of value. A group of men entered his home, with no restraint from the military.

It was about this time that the Englishman reached our car breathless. He threw the chickens into the car, and climbed aboard with the help he needed.

The men who entered the farm house emerged about an hour later, waving whatever trophies they possessed. The last to exit was dragging a naked woman by the hair; he laughingly threw her body upon the prone body of the farmer. As they approached close enough to be readily identified, there was no doubt they were Americans. Two made it a point to crawl under the train adjacent to hours.

They were the two bastards from Warsaw.

CHAPTER 39 — CONTINUED
SURVIVAL

"Son of a bitch!" I screamed. "Why couldn't those two pricks have caught a couple of stray bullets!?"

"It would have been just as well if they were dispatched with the trains they cut loose from ours," someone added. Our guard, realizing our concern about the two renegades, very simply and with little or no emotion suggested an option of remedial action to solve our dilemma: a direct confrontation, even killing them if necessary. He would assist us, even to the point of pulling the trigger.

"You're out of your potato-whisky-picking mind," the Pilot responded.

"I know you not accept suggestion, but must offer to you." He went on to explain the reason such a choice was not really feasible, since the officer in command was aware of our personal grievances with these two scum bags. If they met their deaths by accident, or by the hands of other than Russian military, it could be written off. As before he explained their actions were being recorded, as were all other renegades, and a personal watch was constantly in force in our behalf. If we took personal action, suspicion would immediately fall on us.

"They will receive just punishment when they attempt to clear search teams in Odessa." The guard concluded with, "Patience and alertness, is only option at this time".

Feeling a little more secure, our minds focused on the chickens, the cause of the tragic scenario. We had witnessed so much death and inhumanity perpetrated without any semblance of remorse, that we had become steeled to personal feelings. Our aim in the present situation was to continually remind ourselves of the importance of continued survival at any cost.

We closed the doors of our car, more or less slamming them in the faces of the gathering of pleading, hungry, desperate people. Shots could be heard; an investigating peek by our guard stilled our fears of mass slaughter.

"They have dispersed the people around our car, shots are only in air," he explained.

"We need some hot water to defeather the chickens," I suggested. "I'll gut the birds," the Englishman, volunteered.

"Save the heart, liver, gizzard, and neck-they will add to the flavor of the soup," I directed.

"Can we fry some of the parts?" someone asked.

"We have to make what will last the longest. Chicken soup with what greens we have will sustain us the longest," the Pilot advised.

"Let's not consume all the birds at one sitting," the Englishman suggested. "I'll clean them all; with the natural cold and snow we can keep them reasonably fresh," he added.

It suddenly dawned on me how easy it is to forget how tragedy can be wiped from your mind, when you are the victor and not the victim.

The guard returned with a couple of pots filled with water. We first had to get the water to a boil, to dunk the chickens to loosen their feathers.

"You farm boys are natural chicken fuckers- I'm sorry, I meant chicken *pluckers*. That job is yours," I recommended jokingly.

They were pretty good size birds, and we hoped to ration them with some intelligence. It's amazing how, under virtually any circumstance, "some idiot" will make an utterly inappropriate comment.

"It's too bad you couldn't have gotten a few more chickens," the idiot (our Navigator, of course) said. He acted like the Englishman had gone to the butcher shop and, was too cheap to buy the quantity we needed.

The water came to a boil, and it became apparent the Englishman knew his chickens. He had cut the head off one of the chickens, hung it from a lock on the door neck down, draining the blood into the "lavatory" bucket. My expertise in chicken plucking came to the fore. My education in chicken plucking had commenced at an early age. Although not Jewish, my mother would buy no other than a fresh, Kosher, Rabbi-killed chicken. My mother would turn away when the ritual killing took place. I was brought along to witness every bloody step, from the throat slitting, defeathering, gutting, right to the bird entering the sack to carry it home. The instructions from my mother as she turned away, had been, "Make sure they don't swith chickens from the ones I selected."

I dunked one of the birds into the boiling water, after I had tied a piece of string to its legs. As I would hold it out of the scorching hot water, the Englishman would pluck whatever loose feathers were presented. After a few dunkings, the chicken was as naked as a jay bird, ready for dismembering. Fresh water had to be set upon the pot belly stove, using a clean pot. The water was heated just short of a boil, and the greens we had were portioned out to furnish three cookings, one for each chicken. We all made suggestions as to the rationing portions, not to eat it all at one sitting. I couldn't help but remember the times in my life I refused to eat certain dishes my mother prepared, and the quantities of good food thrown into the garbage cans. As a matter of fact, one didn't have to go back that far to remember the waste of food right in the military. Oh for that slice of bread, the mashed potatoes, the pat of butter, that extra piece of cake you scraped off your tray into the garbage can in the mess hall. Collectively, one day's waste by each of us would satisfy so many of these poor unfortunates, but our survival nullified any concern or compassion for "total strangers," or so we made ourselves believe.

The aroma from the simmering pot belied its true contents, and offered false relief to a hungry stomach. All the anguish of the farmer's sacrifice, and the furor that resulted, gave way to self-serving beliefs: "better him than me."

The results of the pot puree were savored by all with the first true activation of our taste buds since the favorable meals in Lodtz. The guard produced some potato whisky and black bread, which added to the festivities. The aroma must have leaked from its confinement into the outside area. We became the focus of attention, which dulled our contented attitude into one of remorse.

The screams of anguish, enlarged by hunger pains, caused actions unfitting for civilized humans. Those who were fortunate enough to obtain a chicken after the farmer's demise found themselves in a very precarious position. They didn't have the military to protect them. It was declared war of riotous behavior. They clawed and punched at each other in an attempt to share in the chickens in a ravished frenzy. The chickens were torn apart as they passed from one agonized hand to another, with bloody, ugly results. The parts obtained by the fortunate combatants were quickly consumed in their natural state, feathers and all. The white virgin snow was stained by both chicken and human blood.

A long period of time passed after the carnage had subsided before the simmering pot became a focal point. It appeared to me to be a symbol of the degeneracy we so greatly abhorred, but of which we had become a part.

The simmering contents had reached their edible tenderness, verified by a sampling taste by the Englishman. His declaration of such immediately caused an involuntary salivation usually reserved for mad dogs. The Englishman warned of consuming too much too fast. He shredded the chicken into minute silvers of meat, stirred them into the now softened greens. This procedure assured the equalization of chicken portions. The warmth of the broth, and the solid substance of the chicken and greens, was savored with contentment. The appreciation of this life enhancing banquet selfishly ignored the deadly efforts required to obtain it.

We slept soundly through the night, the empty feeling of prolonged hunger satisfied. The morning brought no change in our status, or the status of the miserable peasants. It was easily established that the renegades had acquired food during the carnage. They were seen in groups, gathered around fires, enjoying the fruits of their murderous actions.

I felt such a growing hate for these perpetrators of inhuman atrocities, intensified because some were Americans. Knowing the reputation of the Russians from stories furnished by Helena, Novak, our two companions, and eye witness accounts, allowed no surprises. It was the cowardly actions of the Americans that instilled a feeling of complete disgust in my usually forgiving heart. My desire for survival became intense, not just for my personal sake, but also survival to report the savagery of these renegade scum bags.

I knew in my heart that all my companions had the same intense feelings, but I also knew from past experiences they didn't possess the same feeling of self involvement. Maybe, I prayed, in the environment of complete authority, they would support my accusations, if necessary even in military courts. I made up my mind, regardless of any consequences, these pricks would be punished.

The day was grey and a foreboding atmosphere permeated the surrounding area. The unusual quiet caused concern, like the "calm before the storm." The military personnel appeared less visible by their inaction towards the traveling civilians, but their sudden attention to their military cargo suggested a possible move, or the arrival of ranking authority.

The guessing game was settled, and both answers were right. A hospital train, heading east away from the front, arrived, grinding to a halt on the outermost spur, at the water tower.

"Maybe we can get some first hand information about the status of the war," someone suggested.

"Don't any of you get any ideas about approaching that train, and that's an order," the Pilot directed.

"I will see if I can find out something," the guard volunteered.

"You'll do no such thing," the Pilot warned. "We don't want any unnecessary attention drawn towards us."

"You can be of service, if you can find out our chances of getting the hell out of here," I directed to the guard.

"You first tell me, no talk to train officer, who I ask?" he responded, with an air of bewilderment.

The sudden military behavior of the train personnel was explained to our guard by the guard aboard the adjacent train. Our guard conveyed to us that a high ranking Russian General was aboard the hospital train.

"I am told, he not too seriously wounded, will inspect all trains, and make investigation about killings," the guard explained.

"I knew we hadn't heard the last of that fiasco. I hope that train officer keeps the Englishman out of it," the Pilot wished aloud.

"Don't forget the chicken episode," I added. "Let's be as inconspicuous as possible. Keep the door closed-no shows today," the Pilot related as he looked directly at me and the Navigator.

"We'll have no control over the actions of this visiting officer. Just don't panic. The truth from the train officer should eliminate any connection or suspicion of us in regard to the atrocious murders," I wishfully declared.

The day passed slowly. We kept the remains in the pot simmering slowly, adding water at intervals to keep it from scorching. About noon we dealt out small portions, which we hoped would sustain us until late evening. The presence of the hospital train had a calming effect over the marshaling yard. It was the first time we had witnessed any respect for another human being. I thought the consciences of the sick renegades finally were being affected. Reality dictated that they were doing their best to minimize attention from the investigating officer.

It was dusk when the investigating officer approached our car, with the train officer in tow.

"Now remember, we stick together, no matter what. No cop outs," I said. "If that shit-head train officer attempts to use any of us to cover his folly, we accuse him as witnesses of his part in the murders, and swear to it."

The only ones to readily agree were the Englishman and the infantry sergeant. The others didn't flatly disagree, but in defending their minimal support, said as one, "We hope it doesn't come to having to lie to survive with the blood of an innocent person on our consciences."

"Guts up, men. After what you have witnessed, you would rather have our blood on their consciences? You seem to forget: we're at war, and right now, our so called ally is our worst enemy!" I added with heartfelt conviction.

My words must have had some effect, as they all mumbled, with raised, clenched fists, what sounded like "we're with you."

As the investigating officer approached, the strangest thing happened. The two officers were walking directly towards our car. The only obstacle was the troop train, next to ours. Our guard had opened the door, and had popped to a rigid attention, awaiting the officer's arrival. The train guard had assumed a "present arms" attitude in military respect to the officers, then just as quickly dropped his weapon into a "desist or else" attitude, which stopped the officers in their tracks.

Geez, I thought, now the fur flies-this guard is in for some grief. Without so much as a retaliatory word or gesture of redress, they made a right flank turn and walked about twenty yards to the end of the train, did a three sixty around the military train, and proceeded in our direction.

"I'll be damned, do you really think that lowly train guard would have shot the officers, if they attempted to cross over that train?" I asked.

The answer came as a surprise, both in substance and with conviction.

"We will never know what the guard would have done, but for sure he would have been shot by the officer, if he failed to stop the officers," our guard answered.

"American friends," the visiting officer said, and put our guard at ease.

He extended his hand to our guard for assistance in boarding our car. He turned to the train officer who was about to enter our car and said something in Russian, which caused a look of utter astonishment to appear on his face. He stepped down from the train stirrup in such a frenzied haste that he slipped on the snow covered ground in an unceremonious pratfall. To further compound his actions towards a brother officer, he had our guard close the door in his face. I could only think this bastard was serious about something. We were caught with our pants down: this prick spoke English, so we had no way to set up answers. We would have to play it by ear.

"A serious incident has occurred, and an answer of truth must be obtained," he stated.

"I will state the information I have received in its entirety, with no interruptions. Then I will ask for your pros and cons, if you have any," he concluded.

He had used the words "serious incident"- singular. I thought to myself, and the quizzical looks exchanged between my companions indicated they wondered the same thing: which "serious incident"?

"We are pretty sure we have the culprits in mind. We hope to find creditable witnesses to substantiate our case, when we charge them in Odessa," he went on.

My curiosity got the better of me; before I realized what I was saying. I asked, "What incident? Charge who?"

He snickered. He did not answer my questions, but continued with a wave of his hand in my direction, "The act was dastardly, without provocation, and must not go unpunished."

Since the train officer was left outside, my first thought was he was a suspect in the killing of the women and the Russian guards. The investigating officer must have read my mind: his next statement cleared the air, and the release of pent up emotions was noticeable.

"I have received complaints of many misgivings, but the killing of the farmer and the raping of his wife is the most serious. Stealing his chickens is no crime during war; the military has the right to confiscate any property in order to survive"," he coldly explained.

I was now in a cold sweat, thinking how the Englishman cold-cocked the farmer. Was he about to accuse him of killing the farmer? By the looks on the faces of my companions, I knew they were all thinking the same thing. The agonizing looks were transformed into surprise and relief by the next statements uttered by the investigating officer.

"Raping his wife as he lay in the snow after being knocked there by these barbarians, and then dumping his naked wife on top of him is unthinkable, but to shoot him dead for no reason is the most abominable act of depravity by one human to another," he related.

"If any or all of you can identify the killers, it would be most appreciated," he asked almost pleadingly.

"Now that you know my mission, I will explain the reason I left the officer out of our conversations. He told me what he had seen, and if you agree with what I have related to you, your stories are the same, now I know how to proceed," he concluded.

The son of a bitch covered for us. I thought how easy it was to condemn a person without really knowing them.

The door was opened by our guard, anticipating the departure of the Russian. He extended his hand to each of us, and wished us luck.

"I will look you up in Odessa, when I charge these renegades. The American ones will have to be charged by you to the American authorities," he reminded us.

Just as he descended to the ground from the stirrup, aided by the train officer, he casually looked over his shoulder at the pot on the stove, like it was the first time he had seen it.

He subtly remarked, "Have a good meal." He returned a salute from the train guard. We could almost swear he was chuckling to himself.

CHAPTER 40 — REBELDOM

There appeared to be a relaxing atmosphere, apparently because of the presence of the investigating officer. We fell into that same mode, because we knew no suspicion of any wrong doing pointed in our direction. The rebellious rebels were on their best behavior. Little did they suspect their every move was monitored.

Because of the calm, the interested displaced persons began to visit our car. Most were Polish or Lithuanians. Their presence was always an exhibition of friendliness, and through the interpretation of our guard, poured volumes of gratitude for our entrance into "their war." Most didn't know we were fighting "our war," which was with the Japs to prevent them from invading the United States. Once Hitler started his move to conquer the world, sides were chosen, some because of mutual ideology, some because of power. Whatever the reason, there were good guys and bad guys. The God-fearing people were the good guys, I thought, but what I have witnessed established one fact: war isn't only war between nations, but war between God and the devil.

Slowly but surely, we returned to our casual showmanship, me with my ethnic two-way hat, all Slovak, all Russian, or half and half, depending on the majority in attendance. Of course those who had witnessed my favorite performance before, smiled a respectful, courteous smile. New arrivals laughed heartily. I realized it wasn't because my act was so funny, it was because we as Americans recognized their plight, and joined them openly, with deference.

With the sudden relaxing of tensions, due to the investigation, people moved about in a more secure atmosphere. The violations openly committed in broad daylight were at best committed with discretion, out of sight. The screams during the night by women being violated, and the wanton killing of their defenders, were obliterated by quiet.

One visible non-change was the strict rule of not crossing over any of the military-cargo-ladened trains. Another was the total non-activity of the personnel aboard the Hospital train, other than the investigating officer. I questioned our guard regarding this situation aboard the hospital train. His answer revealed startling reasons. The Russian wounded are never put on display, because they fear German spies or German collaborators left behind would have the opportunity to determine the casualty count. More important, the military going to the front would lose their indoctrinated fighting edge if they could see or talk to the returning wounded.

The day passed slowly, and would have been slower, but for the visiting people and some Lithuanian officers we had not seen before. Most Lithuanians we had met spoke some English, and they were willing to discuss the status of the war. To our surprise and good fortune, these officers were from the Hospital train. With subtle discretion they cleared the area of the displaced persons, which left us with the opportunity for one on one conversation. They told us the walking wounded aboard the Hospital train were interested in meeting the American airmen, when our presence was made known to them. They were seeking permission to bring small groups to our car, and if they were granted permission, they would do so. We asked about the status of the fighting, and how the war was proceeding. They reiterated what sparse information we were aware of, from the action we witnessed while on the front lines, and the information furnished by our two traveling companions. The war was winding down in Europe, against the Germans, but the war between allies was very much a focal point. The final bit of information they provided was one of concern, if true. The Americans were stopped in their progress through Germany; the Russians were moving without resistance, winning the war.

"Some shit," I said, "they'd never admit without us they were dead. As Helena and Novak said, the Russians are our future enemy."

"I wondered if it will be politically expedient to divulge the atrocities our Russian ally committed in our presence. Would it have any impact on the higher echelon of American authority?" the Pilot questioned.

"I don't give a shit what the outcome is, I couldn't live without revealing what we have encountered. Let the chips fall where they may-at least my conscience will be clear," I said.

In early evening we doled out portions of our chicken concoction. The warm broth, flavored with greens and slivers of chicken, was a reward well worth waiting for. It removed the cold dreary emptiness of not only your stomach, but the emptiness of heartfelt disappointment. We all agreed that our future, after surviving death in our mode of war, was very bleak at the present time. Openly there appeared to no real concern for our well being. We had to rely on the utterances of our guard, who would disappear for long periods of time. He would return crocked to the gills, and remain useless to us. We would stick him in a corner, cover him, and steal any of the potato whiskey he brought back with him.

"This is our reward for his incompetence," I said, as I passed our reward around.

The next day the Englishman dissected another chicken, and prepared it for cooking. We had about four feedings from the first chicken, and hoped to stretch the second one the same distance. We needed some fresh water, and only the guard could get it for us. No one was allowed near the water tower without permission from the train commander. When we were attached to a steam engine, water was furnished from the train operator, and easily obtained.

"Where is the fucking guard?" some one asked.

"Probably getting his load on," I answered.

"I suppose he is as bored as we, and probably as much in the dark as we, not knowing what the hell is going on," the Pilot stated.

"I think we have the right to ask that investigating officer what the situation is," I remarked.

"After he casually by-passed our participation in the chicken incident, I wouldn't even think of our right to anything," was the answer I received from the Pilot.

The guard suddenly appeared, staggering and drunken. He was being helped by an apparently sober Russian soldier, who held a bucket of water, and offered it to us with the connotation of, "I know you need this."

He helped us load our guard into the car, and remained aboard as we dumped the guard into his usual corner. We tried by gesture, a wave of the hand, a pat on his back, a nudge towards the door, bowing in a grateful thankful manner, to attempt to to rid ourselves of this person. All failed; we had an unwelcome guest for dinner.

Of course we weren't sure if this intruder was playing stupid, or was in fact not understanding our intentions. He sort of wended his way around us to the pot belly stove and peered inside. As a matter of fact, he actually took the ladle from the Englishman's hand, and stirred the contents in the pot.

I looked towards our guard hoping he was in a condition to intercede on our behalf, but he still looked out of it. I went over to him, planted a boot to his side in the hopes of awakening him to our plight. I had done this in a discreet manner, out of sight of our intruder. The gentle nudge caused the guard to grunt and scream out as if he had been shot. His response caused the intruder to whirl quickly, remove his sidearm from its holster. He pointed it in my direction. A shot rang out. I'd swear I heard the bullet whistle over my head. I was sure I heard it impact the bulkhead behind me.

"You fucking son of a bitch," I yelled, "who the hell do you think you are?"

Each of the others made a move towards him, causing him to retreat to the door, as he waved his gun in a menacing manner. The Englishman was closest to him as he reached the door opening. I was at this time contemplating retrieving my gun from my tote bag. Before I could act the Englishman, nudged the bastard out the door backwards. He landed hard on his back, his weapon went flying, and it was apparent he had the wind knocked out of him. As we closed the door behind him, our last view was him indignantly sprawled in the snow. The guard on the adjacent train was laughing hard and loud enough to minimize the seriousness of the situation. As we looked at each other, we giggled a little too.

Our guard was awakened to a pissed off Pilot. "What the hell are you thinking about, bringing a food stealing prick back with you?"

"He was from hospital train, wanted to meet with you Americans, make deal with you, for friend. Then he would get us food," he explained.

"How the fuck would you know all this, you were out of your drunken mind?" I challenged. "Some deal, throwing a shot at me. Who is the friend he's making deals for?"

"I not know, but he say, he is important officer," he answered, then added, "Can be big help to us."

"Forget this shit, we don't want to get mixed up in any Russian escapades," the Pilot retorted in no uncertain terms.

"Maybe his friend has the authority to hurt us, especially after the way we treated his emissary," I suggested.

"Why the fuck don't they just leave us alone? I think you should tell the train commander, and the investigating officer, what's going on. Let the Russians settle their own grievances," I directed to the Pilot.

"You're crazy. We don't want any more attention drawn to us. Let sleeping dogs lay," he answered.

"Why is it, when your rank can help us, you cop out with some weak excuse? There will be plenty of attention drawn to us if that embarrassed prick decides to repay our assault on him," I stated.

We all agreed that we were in a very precarious situation, and diligent observation of every thing around us was a must. We not only had the two Americans from Lodtz, but also a Russian deal maker to contend with. Our guard, who disappeared for hours on end, and usually in a drunken stupor when he returned, was of little consolation. Even our Navigator, who found something light hearted in every situation, admitted a real concern for our safety.

With the danger that prevailed, I decided to make my weapon readily accessible, giving us at the least a fighting chance. I removed it from its holster, cranked a round into the chamber, removed the safety, and placed it under the corner of my sleeping blanket.

"We can't just shoot the bastard if he comes back," the Pilot commented.

"If that prick pulls a weapon on me, he's dead," I responded.

"If it's just food he wants, fine, we'll share, but if he wants to throw his weight around, fuck him," I added.

"I don't think he was hinting for food. His observation of the cooking chicken was to advise us of his knowledge of the way we acquired it," explained the Englishman.

"The son of a bitch was blackmailing us! Can you top that?" I stated.

We had to be very observant of the people who visited us. We scrutinized them as if each of them was a death threat to us. When the crowds became too large to screen thoroughly, we cut our little show quickly, but with candor. The most embarrassing was when nature called, and we made our way to the wooded area, with an armed escort. It was a comical scenario to the uninformed witnesses.

We were sharing our fresh pot puree, when the door was opened unexpectedly there was our Russian dealing friend. Before we could respond, he boarded our car, waving a malicious looking burp gun. His gestures were easily interpreted, "Hands up, against the bulkhead." I backed against the bulkhead where my piece was. I could feel it at my heel, under my sleeping blanket. The next piece of action was the ultimate surprise, when a civilian appeared in the doorway. The gun toting Russian assisted him in boarding. As we watched in utter disbelief, he slammed the door shut.

"What gives?" the Pilot asked.

The civilian's answer was a wave of his hand for attention. It was then he removed the scarf hiding his face. We gasped simultaneously. There stood the escaped Russian train officer, wanted for those heinous murders of his trollop companions.

He spoke at great length in Russian to our guard, who only nodded his head in what appeared affirmative. It seemed our guard was agreeing to whatever the bastard was suggesting.

"Don't you make any deals for us you drunken bastard!" I screamed.

The volume of my voice was understood by the gun-carrying prick, causing a violent reaction in kind. He made his way towards me, with the butt of his weapon poised to strike at me. Our guard stepped between us, planting his hands into his chest, saying something in Russian, which stopped him in his tracks.

"Do not anger these men, hear what they ask. We will have time to decide, only if we remain alive," the guard suggested.

"Remember we have edge, they do not understand English, I must remain in their confidence, for them to trust me," he added.

"I can't believe we have to take shit from these scum bags," I retorted.

"I keep warning you, we are on their turf. Not getting home to American authority because we're dead would kill any chance of our reporting what we have witnessed," the Pilot related.

The guard in his clipped English related to us the deal proposed by the two interlopers. In essence, we were to conceal the murderous officer aboard our car, when we were surely going to move out. In the mean time, if we agree, food, water, cigarettes, and even whisky would be furnished us. All these goodies were available from the stores on the hospital train, of which the gun toting prick was in charge.

"They must have answer now to make plans. They are sure train will leave soon," our guard said. He added, "Food and other promises will be come, if you agree".

"Geez, lets play their fucking game, agree, stuff our coffers, and when we get our chance, fuck them where they breathe," I volunteered.

"It's a dangerous game you suggest, but if we realize we are at war, and to the victor go the spoils, let's do it," came from the Pilot. All agreed. We instructed the guard of our decision. He readily passed it on. A smirk of conquest appeared on the faces of our adversaries. A responding smile of "up yours" appeared on all our faces. The guard, in his impassive demeanor, smiled his broken toothy smile.

They kept their word: items of food arrived without notice, under unusual guises. Small quantities arrived with our fire wood, or with some medical supplies. The smaller items were actually carried in by the visiting audiences, soldiers in disguise. One day the dealing officer brought in cigarettes, and a bottle of whisky. To show our appreciation, we shared a drink with him, which I think gave him the confidence we intended.

We discussed the reality of the request asked of us. To be forced into a conspiracy to protect a murderer was not only breaking the law regardless of what country we're in, but every moral law of civilization, and God's law.

"Maybe we shouldn't goad them on. I think they really believe we intend to help them," the Pilot said.

"We shouldn't have any qualms for our actions. They would kill us all if it would serve their purpose," the Englishman responded, and the American sergeant concurred with emphasis.

"We should not forget what the Englishman says is very true. We are more or less witnesses to this bastard's crime. They may dispose of our potential danger to him, by disposing of us," I related with a real concern.

We all agreed that the best procedure to follow was one of compliance, until we somehow separated ourselves from them. The train's departure, if and when it occurred, would give us the first opportunity to formulate a new plan of action.

Rumors began to increase in intensity, and the movement of equipment within the marshalling yard gave the rumors credence. The real possibility of moving out was accepted with happiness by the multitude of persons involved. We accepted it with mixed emotions, which were visible when our dealer Russian appeared. He now was to ask repayment for the goodies he provided. Through the guard instructions he dictated were directed to us, and the importance of obedience was stressed, almost as a threat. The murderer would be secretly placed aboard our car just before departure. The reason was an expected car search for deserters, and known collaborators. A fresh supply of food would be provided before departure, which must be shared with our uninvited guest. The format was established; now was our opportunity to reestablish the format to our liking. Of course we readily agreed through our guard, and our dealer friend left, we hoped with a little more relaxed defensive posture.

"Geez," I said, "do you realize the prick is going to board our car in broad daylight, just as we move out, probably while the train is in motion? They really have faith in our helping him. What a fucking surprise they're in for," I concluded.

"What are you going to do, shoot the bastard?" someone asked.

"Use your fucking brains. What is the easiest way to keep prick the out of our car?" I questioned.

"Close the fucking door in his face," was the simultaneous response.

The next morning the coupling of the engine shook us awake. It was apparent the time to move out had arrived. People engaged in camp breaking activity throughout the area. Outside living quarters were being quickly dismantled, and possessions were being loaded aboard cars, but not without controversy. The rebels were using the confusion to intimidate and rob these poor souls. How I prayed to survive, just to indict these miserable creatures for their crimes.

Just thinking of moving in the direction of home eased some of the anxiety. We discussed, or I should say guessed at, places we would visit or ports we would hit on the way home. The Navigator plotted what he thought the route would be, from our starting point to the port of Odessa, which was simple, since the guard explained the direction of the tracks we were on.

"Some Navigator," the Pilot declared, "'somewhere in a cloud over Germany,' what a pin point fix!" he reiterated.

Through all the confusion, a small group of people began to arrive at our car, some with crutches, others with bandaged injuries.

"These from the hospital train given permission to visit," the guard explained.

Under these personal anxieties, we had no desire to entertain. We instructed the guard to make a reasonable excuse for our indifference, and apologize. These instructions were negated when we realized the physical torture they endured to get to our car. In their condition, few could manage the trek from four spurs away in a straight line, let alone ducking under train couplings, or walking great distances around the trains. Our indifference became respect, and humility.

It became a pleasant experience, not having to screen these people. They were escorted in small groups, with a military nurse or non-com officer in charge. Those who spoke English would interpret for those who couldn't. As always the questions were forever about America, and their desire to live there one day. It was getting dark. The departing group informed us that one more was on its way. To think that a whole day had almost passed with no unpleasant incidents, and with fond hopes. The last group could be seen rounding the adjacent train, proceeding with problems. Those with crutches were being helped by the nurses or soldiers as they slipped or fell because of the snow covered ground.

There was a sudden outburst. "Hey, yanks, remember me from Lodtz, at the mess hall?"

At the sound of his voice, we collectively turned our heads. I didn't know about the others, but I immediately recognized him. The turban covered head didn't alter my memory of his laughing attitude when he explained in Lodtz how he wound up in the Polish army.

Asking him what happened was a silly question. It was obvious he had some sort of a head wound.

"I caught a head shot the first day in combat. As a matter of fact, I'm pretty sure one of these fucking drunken Russians did the job on me. Wait until I get over to you, I'll tell you the whole story," he concluded.

He placed his foot in the boarding stirrup of the adjacent military train, and reached for the hand rail to pull himself aboard. The train guard struck his hand with his rifle butt, causing him to fall backwards onto the ground.

"You cossack prick," he yelled as he made for the guard.

"Don't!" I screamed. My scream was obliterated by the sound of the shot directly into the advancing Pole.

Good God, could this really happen right before our eyes? For no good reason, a man was shot in cold blood. I jumped from our car, crawled under the coupling to his side. He was still alive, but from his chest wound his life was ebbing away. I cradled his turbaned head into my arms; to chastise his actions at this time was futile.

Mixed with the blood now beginning to gush from his mouth came an almost happy utterance, "I'm on my way back to the states, probably on the same ship as you, from Odessa." He breathed his last.

The advancing people from the hospital train knelt in prayer. The show they were to see had been closed down by a critic with a gun.

CHAPTER 41 — EXPRESSLESS EXPRESS

The body was removed without fanfare, as just another statistic. The praying visitors were herded back to the hospital train the long way around. I was almost tempted to challenge the murderous guard, but common sense won out over senseless action. It was just incomprehensible that wanton killings, without remorse, could go unpunished. I hoped the look I gave the guard could kill, as I crawled under the coupling to get to our car.

As I boarded our train, someone asked, "Did you know that poor bastard?"

"Don't you remember? He was the Polish soldier going into the mess hall in Lodtz as we were leaving. I think he said he was a tailor in Queens, or somewhere in New York. Caught up when visiting relatives in Poland, and drafted into their Army," I explained.

"I felt he was one of us, an American. I didn't even know his name. Maybe we can get his name from that dealing prick, so his relatives back home can be notified," I suggested.

"What a case you have. He's dead, murdered. He never existed as far as they are concerned, and for the present, he never existed as far as we are concerned," instructed the Englishman.

So be it, we all agreed. Just one other incident to report, if and when we were afforded the opportunity.

The only sign of any possible good fortune was the quantity of goodies arriving systematically, with the utmost discretion. Our cupboard was no longer bare, and food was no longer one of our problems. The arrival of our dealing Russian, bearing gifts, was our most predominant problem. When he presented the bottles of whisky and the carton of Lucky Strike cigarettes, it was a foregone conclusion the day of reckoning was at hand. Although his presence was unwelcome because of the demands he was to make on us, the words that he spoke through our guard were critical.

"We are moving out tomorrow," interpreted the guard. "He will make arrangements to have a group of hospital train visitors brought to your car tomorrow. You are to put on your act to relax surveillance by the guards in the area. At that time his friend will be among your audience. You will invite a few of the visitors to visit aboard your car, as participants in one of your acts. Friend will board with them. Make arrangement to hide him when other visitors leave car." It appeared he had given considerable thought to his escape.

The conditions as presented caused us great concern. He would be aboard the train before we moved, negating the plan to close the door in his face as we started to roll.

"He will probably be armed, but he has no idea that we have a weapon," I remarked, then added, "He knows our guard is armed, but expects no challenge from him, which is in our favor."

"When we reach a decent rate of speed in an open countryside, we'll kick him off the train - good bye, good luck."

"Where the fuck do you get your hare-brained schemes?" the Pilot questioned.

"At the present time, it seems like a good idea...if the situation remains the same," the Englishman volunteered.

"Any other idea will have to be spontaneous, when and if it presents itself. Until then, if he's in, we have to get him out," I concluded.

It was a mystery how the news of our moving out reached the multitudes that appeared through the night. The fighting and clamoring to get aboard the train by the newcomers was the ultimate in animalistic, barbaric behavior. Shots fired into the air had no effect. It almost appeared that death was a worthwhile gamble to get aboard the train. We were surprised that the military guards only protected the train officer's car, and then only firing into the air or ground. They permitted the climbing atop the cars, and the peasant displaced persons allowed them to enter their cars if there was room. It was easy to ascertain the cars housing the rebel ex-prisoners of war. Any attempt to enter their cars was greeted, as always, by "Throw your gear aboard, then we'll help you climb up."

We could hear ourselves screaming, "Don't, don't!" to no avail. We knew from past experiences the help afforded was a kick in the face that separated the man from his belongings. A return engagement to recover his belongings was usually rewarded by a shot into his open, protesting mouth.

Throughout this unbelievable scenario, a group of hospital train visitors arrived. It wasn't hard to locate the uninvited guest - he was the only one with his face covered with bandages. I wondered how much time we had to play out our game, and if we could in some way finger this bastard to a military guard.

"We have to try to keep this prick from boarding. What recourse would he have if we don't invite any of our audience to come aboard?" I asked.

"Timing is most important. If our visitors are escorted back as the train moves out, our friend will be left with his finger up his ass. He has to either go back with them, or break his cover by attempting to board our car. Now, the door is closed in his face," the Englishman laughingly related

It was about this time that our balloon of success began to deflate. The dealing officer from the hospital train was standing to the rear of our audience, displaying the OK sign, with a sneering smile that signaled an indisputable threat.

Amidst all the confusion, we were in no mood to entertain. Those who came within reach of us extended their hands in friendship. Our unwelcome guest eased his way to the doorway, in anticipation of being asked aboard as planned. When we didn't respond, his eyes blazed with hate, and he parted his jacket to expose a gun in his waist band. It was just at the moment of decision, do we or don't we, that the train whistle blew. The train responded with a hissing sound as the expelling air released the brakes from captivity. This action not only signaled the trains readiness for departure, it also activated the return of our guests to the hospital train by their escorting officers.

The train began to back out of the siding, leaving our guest standing alone, as the rest of the contingent made their way down the track. Desperation causes desperate acts, and our guest, with the aid of his officer friend, threw caution to the wind. Without any attempt to conceal their intent they ran up to the door of our car, which was moving slowly, and pulled their weapons in an attempt to coerce us into their bidding. The guest reached for the stirrup with his foot as his friend boosted him into the doorway. With the combination of climbing and boosting, their weapons were in no position to intimidate us.

Our guard placed a boot into the face of our boarding guest. The result was a duo of bodies locked in fond embrace defying gravity for a few moments, as they were separated from the train and mother earth.

"Now, we close the door in their faces," the Englishman repeated again, laughingly.

The train reached the end of the spur and backed onto the main track, braked to a squealing halt, and moved in a forward direction, until spinning wheels finally touched the tracks. We were on our way.

"I forgot to tell you, this express train to Odessa," the guard happily related.

"If you believe that, you'll believe anything," I said. "Express train? Like the Lexington express in New York City?" I kiddingly responded.

We hadn't moved fifty yards when we ground to a halt. We opened the door slightly, and realized we were only on the main track feeder line. We had to stop to allow a train going west to clear the spur we were about to enter.

"Here goes your express train, from express to local, in the first fifty yards," I chided.

"Give him the benefit of doubt. We're not really on the main track yet," volunteered the Navigator.

"You wouldn't know one track from the other. Remember," the Pilot added, "'somewhere in a cloud over Germany'? Now we're somewhere on a track in Poland."

The train stopping caused an unexpected surprise: from out of every conceivable hiding place arrived hundreds of people looking for transportation. Being on the perimeter of the marshalling yard, we had only the train commander's guards to quiet the ensuing riot. Those who were armed intimidated themselves into a place on the train. The Russian and American ex-prisoners of war were not intimidated more than once, and stopped any intrusion by shooting the first to venture into their domain. The train's whistle announced its departure, and prefaced the most deplorable confrontation one could imagine. The newly arriving displaced people challenged the first come first served cliche, and the flailing bodies were dislodging one another from the top of the trains. In the cold and the gathering speed of the train, the strongest survived, and the weakest were thrown to the roadbed. Their condition faded from view as the train sped on.

"Our major concern now is that that fucking murderer may have had an opportunity to get aboard the train," I pointed out.

"You have a point. We had better plan accordingly," instructed the Englishman

"We'll have to be especially vigilant if we come to a stop. He'll have a tough time reaching our car while in motion, unless he's atop our car now," I calculated.

With the train gradually gathering speed, we felt a sort of partial security. The guard being sober, and my weapon available in my shoulder holster, at the ready, also made for a more relaxing atmosphere. The wealth of food at our disposal almost, I say almost, had us thanking the bastard for our goodies.

"And to think we still have two chickens left. Let's not waste any time. If this train is an express, as our guard says, we won't have time to enjoy and make up for all the meals we missed," I suggested.

The Englishman carefully selected ingredients from our food stores, to enhance the chicken and greens concoction. The canned foods he selected posed an opening problem, until the guard produced a knife similar to our American Bowie knife. The Del Monte peas, carrots and stringbeans added a home cooked touch. The rationing was eliminated our food supply was in such abundance. We made hogs of ourselves. I thanked God for our blessings, and said Grace. All joined in with a grateful, "Amen."

As the train sped on at a steady rate of speed, the guard's statement that this was an express was vindicated. Our contentment bordered on stupidity, as we enjoyed our after dinner drink and Lucky Strike cigarettes. The pot belly stove's heat and the humidity produced by the simmering pot warranted the door being opened for cooling air. Without warning a body appeared in the doorway by swinging from the top of the car.

He was in civilian clothes, and appeared unarmed. Our guard quickly grabbed his burp-gun, and the intruder raised his hands above his head.

"Nyet," we understood, but the Russian he practically screamed in addition bordered on frantic, frightened behavior.

"Do not shoot," the guard instructed, "he is all right."

I thought to myself, how easy it was to kill someone if you felt threatened. I thanked God for my reluctant reaction.

The guard explained that he was with a group of people atop the adjacent car. The smell of the cooking food reached the car to our rear as it was wafted by the slipstream. He explained how the cold, biting wind hindered any opportunity to get at any food they had stored in their gear. The crowded condition of people clinging together to keep from falling from their precarious perch was only rewarded by the thought of reaching home. The guard continued that the word had reached them that Americans were in the car without roof top occupation. They decided to chance a confrontation of good will, and possibly obtain some food.

"Good God," I said, "now is our chance to do some good for these unfortunate people. We have plenty to spare."

"Let's make sure what we give them is not grabbed up by those leeching cocksuckers," the Navigator suggested.

"Their car is back of train, far from here," the guard went on to explain. "They not make move in open, they know the train officer has personal guards keeping close watch."

"Give them some of the hot soup concoction. Have him climb back to above the door, and we'll pass it up in one of the pots," the Pilot suggested.

"It will be a tricky balancing act to accomplish the passing, and what will they use to eat off of?" I asked.

The guard posed that question to him, and his response said it was no problem, all had mess kits of sorts, easily reached.

It was heart warming. We had a real sense of achievement after all the dehumanizing acts we had seen, with no opportunity to intercede on their behalf.

After supplying them with what we felt we could spare, we settled back and enjoyed the musical clicking sound of the wheels which sounded like, home, home, home, as they passed over the butted tracks. The guard explained that the recipients of our generosity were very thankful, and our reaction to their plight dispelled the Russians' degrading attitude toward American participation. The guard added that he had spoken to the man who had entered our car, who appeared to be a leader. He explained the situation we were in concerning the fugitive officer.

"I tell him, we not sure he is aboard train, but could have boarded when train made stop." He then added, "I ask him to watch for anyone who looks like he is heading for our car, if so, warn us. He promised to do so."

Again I felt, and made it known to the others, that at the rate of speed we were going and with the crowded conditions atop the cars, it was almost impossible for him to reach our car without being spotted. Especially now that we had a friendly lookout.

Every click of the wheels without interruption lulled us into a sense of false security. The relaxed feeling struck our guard into unconsciousness, as he had had more than his share of the whisky gift. We laid him to rest in the usual corner, and placed his weapon within reach. Mine I placed under my blanket.

"All kidding aside," the Navigator volunteered, "we should be out of Poland, within the hour, and on into Russia."

We weren't sure if he knew what he was talking about, but as long as it was a positive utterance, we accepted it as Gospel. The Pilot never let him forget "somewhere in a cloud over Germany." When you look back at that scene, who was thinking of anything other than save their ass?

Suddenly, without warning, the train began to slow down, and come to an abrupt stop. The wheels screeched to a halt, and shook our guard into a semblance of attentiveness.

"What is happening?" he asked.

"Your fucking express is now the expressless express," I chided.

He dragged himself to his feet. His recovery amazed us.

"That whisky must have been watered down, or he didn't consume as much as we thought," someone suggested.

He went to the door, stepped over the bench, and dropped to the ground into the darkness. He returned in a few minutes, and climbed aboard with the reason for our stop.

"We near bridge. Will wait few minutes for permission to cross Vistula River, into Russia," was his explanation.

The metallic sound of the wheels as we rolled along had permeated the dark stillness. The train grinding to a halt stilled the night into a mysterious quiet.

Unintelligible voices suddenly grew into a loud, almost frenetic crescendo, which was punctuated by identifiable, authoritative commands, enforced by gun shots. Large search lights illuminated a large military contingent, backed by tanks and armed weapons carriers, definitely Russian. After all the atrocious, murderous, inhuman acts we had seen, this was the most degenerate act perpetrated on innocent people. Those atop the cars were forced to the ground. Those who did not respond quickly enough, or uttered what sounded like a question, were fired on. They were removed in such haste, that their belongings were thrown to the ground indiscriminately. This caused violent reactions, and a near-riot, as people fought over ownership.

Our guard, although he didn't approve, defended his compatriots' actions by explaining we could not cross the bridge with people riding on top. Unless they lay absolutely flat, they would be swept off by the bridge's super-structure. Not to show favorites, all must get off. They may walk across the bridge, after we cross, and wait for another train, on the other side.

Although outwardly his explanation made some sense, I ventured to ask him, "Why use such deadly force?"

His answer revived the words of Novak: "They are so brain washed, there is no in between. Either obey or die."

Some were helped into cars where there was some room. Others fought for hand or foot holds on the roof ladders or between the cars atop the couplings. These positions were precarious at best, even at a stop. The cold and the encumbrance of their possessions posed an immediate danger of falling once the train moved out.

We couldn't see the bridge; we were about a half a mile away, and it was concealed by a total blackout.

The guard explained that the bridge had a long gradual approach, crossed the Vistula river, now frozen, and a long descending decline to the main track into Russia proper.

"Once we hit main track, we are on way to Odessa. No more stops," he said.

I would have sworn the statement was made with tongue in cheek. Even so I prayed he spoke the truth.

The train's engine hissed into motion, its wheels moving in short bursts of spinning and rolling. The whistle announced intended departure, and the spinning became a constant rolling action. We were on the move. The speed of the move was hindered by the incline of the bridge's approach. It was then the unexpected happened: jogging alongside our car a person in civilian garb appeared. Without warning, he fired two shots in the direction of the guard. The guard wasn't hit, but the suddenness of the action caused us all to duck for cover, giving this intruder the opportunity to board our car. His initial command was easily understood: we raised our hands. He retrieved the guard's weapon and belted his own. He next spoke to the guard in Russian; the interpretation ordered us all to sit against the rear bulkhead. I moved up to my bunk where my weapon was hidden under my blanket. I was happy that I had removed my gun from my person when we had felt secure as we were under way.

He spoke to us through the guard, explaining he meant us no harm, and just wanted the opportunity to get to Odessa, where he had friends to spirit him out of Russia. He felt his sharing the food was no imposition, since his friend had supplied it. Things seemed acceptable for the present, but we knew somewhere along the route, we could get involved in a unacceptable crossfire.

He obtained his fill from the simmering pot, and locked himself into the whisky, causing his demeanor to change radically. He began to slobber, and his tone and gestures towards us became a personal affront, substantiated by the guard. He had us empty our pockets. He noticed my wedding band, and a pinky ring I wore.

"He wants your rings," the guard directed to me.

"He can go fuck himself," I retorted.

It was like he understood my response, but his response never was culminated. The train, I believe with God's blessing, began its descent, with its speed increasing rapidly. He had turned to place his food tray upon the bench across the doorway. The sudden movement by the train caused him to stumble against the bench. The food tray exited through the open door, and our friend, with the help of a boot up his ass, followed the tray. The train's wheels clicked louder, but failed to blot out the fading cries of an air-born prick.

CHAPTER 42 — MURDEROUS DESPERATION

The train continued the long decline exiting the bridge. The speed was noticeably increasing, but then just as noticeably, suddenly slowed to a grinding halt.

"What the hell is going on now?" someone asked.

The guard opened the door a crack. The reason for stopping was immediately visible. The whole area was filled with a multitude of people, larger than the group left behind on the other side of the bridge. They were herded in a line parallel to the track by armed Russian soldiers who were backed up by tanks and armed troop carriers. I couldn't fathom the reason for such a show of military force. The guard explained that these were people removed from a previous train. They walked across the bridge with the hope of catching a ride on the next available train. He explained how the delay gave the Russians the opportunity to screen them thoroughly. The screening process must be working, as the guard pointed out a barbed wire enclosure housing a group of civilians and military. The enclosure was surrounded by heavily armed Russian soldiers.

"Look closely. Our two prick friends may be among them," I wished aloud.

"No such luck," the Pilot responded. "They're somewhere on this train."

The train had stopped on a curve in the track, affording a clear view of the whole train from the front to the rear. When the train came to a complete stop, the order was apparently given to board the train. They were released in small groups which prevented the usual mad dash to death we had witnessed on other occasions. The most unusual happening was the occupants of the rebel cars welcoming the newcomers to board their cars without interference, and actually assisting them.

"Will you look at that. Can we believe what we see?" I asked.

The guard surveyed the scene, and quickly diagnosed the intent of the rebel bastards.

"They know search and seizure will come, they want to use good people for cover," he explained.

"To think there are Americans included. God should strike them dead! They deserve no pity," I added. It's a strange thought to believe in human dignity as a way of life, then realizing that this is war, and war is dehumanizing.

There were few confrontations, even when the people who rode across the bridge, barely clinging in precarious modes, clambered for more secure positions. There was some semblance of fair play when the guards allowed those aboard the train to change their positions. It took quite a while to reload the train, and the procedure used by the Russians was questionable. They suddenly began to search each car after it was loaded.

"Why the hell didn't they check the cars before they allowed those already screened to mix with those already aboard?" I wondered aloud.

It was as if my mind was read. They must have realized their error. They started to empty each car, one at a time. We knew the first cars to be emptied were adjacent to the last car, the caboose, housing the train escort guards. The next was a car loaded with rebels. As they lined up the car's occupants, I strained to identify the two rebels from Lodtz. The mass confusion in obeying the order to disembark surely disrupted the orderly behavior expected by the Russians. The already checked people blinded the guards when they pressed towards them in great numbers, waving their newly acquired passes in their faces. It was in the midst of this wave of screaming, disorderly humanity, that we witnessed the stealthy disengagement by a group of the rebel horde. Without one act of prevention, we watched their unhindered escape into the adjacent woods.

The next car was inspected without benefit of mass confusion. The Russians posted guards around the car, called down the outside riders, lined them up and checked their papers. Armed guards were stationed atop the car, for complete coverage of the surrounding area. This action must have caused serious concern to the rebels, which was soon apparent. As they were requested to exit the car, about six civilian-garbed men came out shooting. Their indiscriminate fusillade decimated a number of poor civilians. Their sudden outburst surprised the Russians, giving them time to crawl under the car and make for the wooded area. The guards atop the car, and those to the rear, opened fire on the fleeing men. We opened our rear door just in time to see two of the men hit, and left abandoned, as they crawled desperately to reach the woods. We had no way of knowing if they were American or Russian military rebels. With the way they were beaten, kicked, and rifle-butted, they would have welcomed death, if they had a choice. A group of guards disappeared into the woods after the fleeing men. We heard gun fire, but we had no way of knowing the fate of the participants in the ensuing fire fight.

When the pursuing guards returned, they had no prisoners. I didn't have to be a mathematical genius to know who won the encounter. The obvious answer was the instant demise of the two wounded escapees.

The regimentation tightened; everyone was treated with scorn, and a belligerent mood permeated the entire scenario. A ranking officer spoke to our guard, which caused him to close both doors, without one word of explanation.

"I wish we could get the hell out of here. There's going to be hell to pay. Those sons of bitches must have killed some of those pursuing guards," I suggested.

The words were scarcely out of my mouth, when staccato gunfire broke the stillness of our internal thinking. There were shouts of pain, deadly dying pain, punctuated with utterances of foreign tongues joined with American voices.

After an hour or so, our door was opened by a Russian officer. His tone to our guard was without question one of official insistence. Our guard nodded as he saluted in military reverence.

"There was mass escape, many Russian soldiers were killed, and wounded. The rebels were heavily armed, many killed, no wounded," he said with a broken toothed smile. "Many got away, that is problem. The Russians will probably make for interior, Americans have only one chance for escape, Odessa," he concluded.

It was an obvious conclusion. They had to clear Russian and American authorities to board the ship waiting for us. I wondered if the loot they had acquired was worth the tortuous, deadly future that was genuinely assured them.

"They can't just wander around a strange country side. They have to get aboard this train somehow," I explained. The guard agreed.

"I believe if those two pricks from Lodtz are still alive, they still have you airmen in mind. You are their best bet to circumvent any search when we reach Odessa," the Englishman volunteered. "If I were in their shoes, I would think the same thing."

"It seems almost impossible for any of them to get aboard this train, now that they have openly declared themselves," I hopefully stated.

"They are now in a murderous, desperate attitude; nothing they do should be unexpected or surprising," warned the Englishman.

It took hours to reload the train. Kidding the guard about his expressless express wore thin, so we let it drop. We felt thankful that we had plenty of food, whisky, and decent smokes. The good riddance of our murderous interloper also dismissed half of our immediate personal involvement. We felt if if we could stay clear of any direct confrontation with the two Lodtz renegades until we reached Odessa, we could seek protection from those in authority.

Every time the train slowed or stopped for whatever reason, we reached for our weapons. We felt every such action was an opportunity for them to board. It became a paranoiac response from all of us, and the situation bordered on the hilarious. We slept in shifts: two remained awake at all times, and we changed every two hours.

"No one will drink any whisky four hours before his turn for guard duty," the Pilot ordered. "We can't afford a sleepy or drunk guard."

"Maybe they will be picked up before we have to face them down," I hopefully suggested.

"I don't know why, but I have a feeling we'll never see them again," the Navigator said.

"You're living in a bloody dream world. If they aren't dead, they will turn up, believe me," the Englishman promised.

I wondered how far we as a group would go if a showdown developed. Would I have the balls to turn in Americans to the Russians, if they were the only authority in Odessa? I knew for sure some of our crew would play the three monkey scenario: "No see, no hear, no speak." I knew the Englishman and the Sergeant didn't wish to be involved, for fear of being detained as witnesses. Their incarceration, in my mind, made them deserving of their choice. I, in my heart, wanted to get home as soon as possible, but also in my heart, I could not forget the atrocities I had witnessed. My mind was made up: no matter the consequences, I had a story to tell, to whomever would listen.

The train moved on, with a steady melodic symphony from its clicking wheels. I made myself read the notes as "home, home," but somehow "danger, danger," seemed more appropriate. We opened the doors, and watched the snow covered countryside pass us by. There were caravans of people moving along the adjacent roadways. Most were walking, carrying their meager belongings, sliding and slipping on the icy terrain. The few lucky ones who were blessed with a horse drawn cart were only better off because their belongings were in the cart. They had to walk also, because the horses were as tired and beat as the poor souls leading them. You had to feel that their misery, witnessed by us had a more sorrowful effect, looking in from the outside. Realistically, being on the way home, no matter what trials and tribulations they encountered at this period of their lives, they must feel survival at any cost was God's blessing.

It was when the train slowed or stopped that our troubles multiplied. The roving multitude of displaced persons grew into larger numbers. Most times they outnumbered the train guards, and were armed. They would barricade the tracks, forcing the train to either stop, or slow down. If they placed a formidable barrier on the track, it would usually necessitate a fire fight, causing wholesale slaughter to break out. If the barrier was weak, or a human barrier as many times was the case, they would pick up speed and plow right through, firing with indiscriminate abandon. The dead and injured became the victims of the surviving horde of pillaging animals. White snow stained red with blood had the same effect as graffiti painted objects, seeming common place.

If the interference to the train's progress was eliminated, and a steady rate of speed was maintained, a half a days travel would put us in Odessa," the Navigator stated.

"From what I can see, between the right of way conditions of displaced persons, and military trains going to the front, we're in for a long haul," the guard retorted.

"Frankly," I replied, "I'm not concerned with the time frame, as long as we are heading in the right direction, and we are not forced into a direct confrontation with any of the renegades."

"I feel the same way," the Englishman agreed. "I have no bloody qualms about doing away with any of the other bastards. You'll have to handle your American compatriots, if need be."

We bantered about with this type of meaningful conversation, but actually, I didn't believe anyone really felt a serious condition existed. It was just a current topic to be discussed, as a matter of course.

It appeared the train was never moving at a decent rate of speed. You got the feeling that the train was always about to stop, and usually did. The stuttering action of the stopping train usually caught someone off guard, which resulted in bodies tossed about like ten pins. It was during one of these sudden unexpected stops that we faced two uninvited guests. Their appearance was aided by two uniformed officers, one Russian, the other an English-speaking Lithuanian.

"Here are two American ex-prisoners of the Germans. They were wandering the countryside. They wish to accompany you to Odessa, and return with you to England. They have no papers, but claim to be Eighth Air Force flyers, shot down early in the war. Being airmen, like yourselves, we felt it best for them to travel with you," the Lithuanian explained.

Before we could position ourselves to protest, they were aboard. The officers left with a wave of their hands, which to me was a wave-off of responsibility. The gun that was produced gave warning that we were expected to adhere to their commands. It was only a few seconds after the officers left, when from under our car appeared two other, definitely unwelcome guests: the two pricks from Lodtz.

They also produced weapons, with a warning: "One, two, or as many as is required killings, doesn't matter as long as we are cleared through to Odessa."

These were desperate men, and their intent to frighten us made their mark. Without asking, they made for our food supply. Locating the whisky cache seemed to relax their demeanor.

"There is no reason for us not to be friends. You're not involved in any of our escapades; it's just that fact that makes you so valuable to us. You are our only chance of returning to freedom," one of them almost pleadingly explained.

They frisked us for weapons, but missed mine under my bed roll. They seized the guard's burp gun as he stupidly attempted to retrieve it, taking a gun butt to the side of his head for his troubles.

"We want this to be a peaceful adventure. Any more foolish attempts like his will only force us to tie you up for our protection." The nastiest one of the four, the more insidious prick from Lodtz, made his presence known.

I had no way of knowing what the rest of our group were thinking, but the gleam of hatred in the eyes of the Englishman was revealing.

"You, you bloody Limey, you're real army, not one of us, but you know loyalty. Don't depend on our loyalty, one misgiving act on your part and you're dead," was stated with conviction.

We settled into a semblance of compliance. My mind was a maze of utter confusion, attempting to unravel its anxieties strategically.

Four armed killers, and knowing their murderous acts in the past, posed a real problem. We had no way of communicating with each other. I prayed that when the opportunity arrived, we would act as one. It appeared we had one idea in common: play it cool, play it by ear. As the time passed and the train was in motion, a relaxing atmosphere prevailed. We shared our cooked meals prepared by the Englishman, making them feel welcome. After a few whiskeys, they talked about their escapades in almost a confessional air. They appeared to be attempting to paint a picture of accountable reasons for their murderous acts. They spoke of the terrible conditions of depravity they had to endure while incarcerated by the Germans. They added, almost with the same deep imbedded hate we felt towards the Russian, that when the Russians released them from the Stalags, they stole every bit of personal belongings the Germans had let them retain.

"They actually looked down on us, because we let ourselves be captured. They turned us loose with, 'You are on your own.'"

It was then that most of them felt whatever they could obtain was spoils of war, including feminine flesh. They made themselves believe it was deserved retribution.

I sided up to my bedroll, and casually felt for my weapon; it was still there. I continued planning some way to eliminate our dilemma without bloodshed. The alternatives were vivid: a direct confrontation within the car, or a direct approach to the authorities in Odessa. I knew without question the Englishman, and the infantry sergeant, would follow any lead of mine without question. It suddenly occurred to me that our best and safest action would be to declare the situation to the authorities in Odessa. What could they do to us then? We would just deny any association with these murderous pricks, and let the chips fall where they may.

Questioning looks among us went unanswered. Somehow I had to let them know what I thought was best, under the existing circumstances.

"By the way," I directed to the apparent spokesman, "how do we connect you with our group, when we are questioned in Odessa?"

I apparently caught him by surprise. Before he could muster some answer, I threw a quick, "We're under Russian escort. Our identity is established. Where do you fit in?"

"You will vouch for us as American ex-prisoners, given permission in Lodtz to travel with you, with your consent. Your Pilot, being the ranking officer, will concur," he responded.

I was hoping this exchange of words would be received by my friends in the spirit intended. Their reliance on our establishing their identity was our ace in the hole.

CHAPTER 43 — VINDICTIVE JUSTICE

We made the best of a volatile situation. Having these creeps share our food and drink was at best acceptable; we had enough to share. It was when they confiscated all our Lucky Strike cigarettes and left us with the usual crappy do-it-yourself tobacco, that they issued the ultimate insult. They should have realized they were jeopardizing any effort on our part to assist them, if we considered it even the most remote possibility.

Their actions were always threatening. Their efforts to minimize their hostility were a facade which was easily penetrated. It was obvious to them we would not comply without threats, and we out numbered them. They kept a constant watch on our Russian guard and the Englishman. As a matter of fact, they kept us separated. The Englishman was allowed to cook, but the guard had to stand at his side during the process. As long as the train was moving they appeared more relaxed. It was when the train slowed or stopped, that they feared either a roving band of other renegades or Russian search forces boarding our car. A direct confrontation with either could afford us the opportunity to either expose them or evade them during the confusion. It must have been obvious that such an opportunity was uppermost in our minds; their threatening attitude was obviously a deterrent to such a situation.

The train suddenly slowed, and the squealing, grinding, screeching of its wheels meant a move through a switching area. The door was opened slightly to view the situation, it was as suspected, we were being sidetracked. The two wanted men crawled to the rear of the shelf-type bunks. Food, gear, and whatever could be used as a barricade to shield them was placed in front of them. The two so-called Air Force men knowingly placed with us would confront any searching party. With all of us under armed threat, it would be impossible to refute any statement they made. I wondered if the hidden bastards were in a position to aid these two pricks. The reasons we didn't use the bunks except for storage became an advantage. They couldn't possibly turn around, which in my mind meant they were trapped.

"For what reason are you two getting involved with those two?" I asked.

They didn't answer immediately, then one responded, "We are Americans, we should stick together."

"Bullshit, they must have promised to share some of their ill gotten loot," I guessed.

I must have struck a nerve. His response was just short of killing me. He jabbed his gun into my belly, hard. I doubled over, as the air was forced out by the impact. In a sort of hazy observation, I saw the Englishman make a move to my aid, as did all the others.

"Don't take another step," I heard, as I crumpled to the floor.

The next thing I clearly observed was the arrival of the two Lithuanian officers who wished these two bastards on us. The next observation was my location. Crumpled, and more or less no threat in my apparent condition, they left me unnoticed. Here within my reach, was my bed roll with my hidden gun. With my eyes slitted enough to observe any awareness of my intent, I moaned as if still semi-conscious. Neither of the two glanced my way, as they conversed with the two officers. I made immediate use of their lack of observation, retrieved my weapon, and secluded it in my waistband under my jacket. The conversation had an air of congeniality, punctuated by hearty laughter. One of our uninvited guests jumped from the car. He walked away with the Lithuanian officers.

"Don't get any ideas," the remaining one ordered, as he raised the guard's burp gun in our direction. He added, "All of you, back against the rear door," while waving the gun in that direction.

His next words were directed to the hidden men: "Stay put, the officers may return with my buddy. As soon as we move out, we'll clear the crap in front of you."

There was a muffled response of agreement, barely audible. Things were shaping up in our favor, and the darting glances between each of us confirmed a meeting of the minds. It was apparent our threatening friend was ill at ease with the situation that confronted him.

The voices that approached our car were recognizable, and their approach stiffened the back of our adversary.

"Move back," he ordered, with a wave of the confiscated burp gun.

I thought, this is not the time to combat the situation. The ensuing incidents confirmed the validity of that decision.

The returning American was being escorted by one of the Lithuanians, who was prodding two resisting persons with the a baton of sorts. It was hard to identify their gender, since they were bundled up against the cold. When they arrived outside our car, their voices speaking Russian dialogue, were easily identified as feminine, and pleading.

They were literally thrown up into our car. "Have a good time," the departing officer shouted over his shoulder.

Any thought of helping these two unfortunates was cut short by the menacing gun of the other American. The first mistake by these two bastards had a selfish motive, as they closed the door and informed the other two pricks, "You'll have to wait awhile, before we can let you out."

The muffled response was one of vile curses and threatening overtures.

"Keep your shirts on, the officer may return before we leave. They have no idea of your existence. Let's leave it at that, I don't want to chance any confrontation," he explained.

You could sense the disappointment of the two trapped cohorts, as they responded with a very shallow, "OK."

This setup resulted from the desire of the Lodtz pricks to isolate the women for their own intentions, but in my mind, it couldn't have presented a better opportunity for reprisal.

The two women were huddled next to the stove, and their glances in our direction, through eyes that were the only part of their faces uncovered, were terrified. They must have realized that the threatening weapon we faced placed us in the same captive situation as they. The one without the gun started to strip the clothing from one of the women. The other, using the threat of his weapon, made it clear what they wanted. One of the women, disrobed to her bare skin, tried to shield the other with her naked body. It was obvious she would submit, if the other would be spared.

She was grabbed by her arm and spun across the car to the gun wielder. He held her around the waist, and placed his weapon against her head to thwart any heroics on our part. His threat caused a momentary stop in the action. Her naked body became a focal point. She was feminine only because God made her that way. She had the body of a working Russian, reminding me of the Russian seamen back in the Bethlehem shipyards on Staten Island and the Russian tank commanders we encountered at the bathhouse in Warsaw. I didn't think even our nympholeptic Navigator was excited by the sight of her naked body.

The squeal of resistance by the other definitely was the outcry of a very frightened child. The unceremonious tearing of her garments, and the vile language directed at her, made us readily tense.

"You little cunt, if you have a cherry, I'm about to take it!" he screamed as he completely disrobed her.

She couldn't have been more than nine or ten years old. Her breasts were buttons, and her pubic hairs were scattered like misplaced afterthoughts. One didn't have to understand the language of the other woman. Her pleading was stilled by a gun butt to the side of her head. In her semi-conscious state, her concern was towards the little girl, and she attempted to reach her.

In the midst of all this, the weapon carrying prick never relaxed his threatening attitude. In an almost jovial air, the one hovering over the child, pinning her arms down, complained he couldn't penetrate her. With his hardened penis held in his hand, he slid up the child's body.

"Open your mouth," he said as he knelt on her shoulders, and squeezed her neck with his free hand.

The other woman reacted with such a frenzy she tore herself away from her captor, and threw herself at the child molester. The sudden action caused a burst of fire from the burp gun. Voices could be heard emitting from the entrapped duo.

"What the hell is going on out there?" We could hear them attempt to extricate themselves.

The suddenness of the woman's action unbalanced the gun-toting bastard. I found myself at this juncture to be to his rear. I unlimbered my .45 and lunged at him from his blind side, wrapped my left arm around his neck in a strangle hold, placed my weapon with no regard to his safety under his chin against his Adam's apple.

"Drop your weapon, or I'll blow your fucking brains all over the ceiling. You, you fucking degenerate, get off that kid, or I'll blow your prick into eternity," I added.

Of course all the others helped to disarm the two, and tended to the two females. We ignored the pleas of the two, as the Englishman and our guard played football with their heads.

The two trapped were unusually quiet, which caused some concern. We knew they were armed. We had to plan a way to get them out, without them knowing the situation. The Englishman didn't even ask our permission, as he grabbed one of our captives by the throat.

"Listen, you bloody bastard, you do as we ask or I'll squeeze the bloody life right out of you," as he squeezed the prick's neck until his face turned purple, and his eyes bulged outward.

"You will tell them all is clear, convincingly, and clear away the barricade," he directed.

"We will pretend you still have us under control. You will be up front as they come out. Your lives and theirs are in your hands. One false move, and so help me, you are all dead," he warned. Our guard punctuated the request by bolting a round into his burp gun.

The woman and child quickly clothed themselves, and we placed them in the furthest area of the car for safety. "Now you two, start to remove the barricade, and inform your two buddies that it is safe to come out," ordered the Englishman, who added, "Your tone of voice had better be convincing."

"Have a heart! We have no control over their actions, they could come out shooting!" one pleaded.

"If they do, you'll be our shield, and we'll get to them right through you fucking degenerates," I warned.

"You'd shoot us in the back?" they questioned as one.

"In your back, up your ass, what difference would it make to animals like you? What do you want, the Congressional Medal of Honor for dying with your boots on?" the Englishman replied, more as a directive than a question.

When the barricade was removed, they could be observed coming out feet first. This was to our advantage: sliding on their backs, they were using their hands to propel themselves forward. Quickly realizing our luck, we yanked the two welcoming committee pricks aside, pinning them down out of reach. The guard with his reclaimed burp gun stood to one side; I with my forty five cocked and ready stood to the other side of the two exiting renegades. The surprised looks on their faces, was accentuated by their crossed eyes pivoted on the gun barrels between their eyes.

"Slide out slowly," was directed to one. "You stay put," was directed to the other.

When he was completely out, we pinned him to the floor, frisked him thoroughly, removed his weapon, and placed under guard with his friends. The other suffered the same fate, but wasn't as docile as his compatriot. This was the mean one of the two, and proceeded to emphasize his nationality and rank.

"I'm an American, and a Major, I order you to release me at once!" he screamed.

"You're talking in the past, you fucking degenerate murderer, your ass belongs to the Russians," I retorted.

"We may, I say may, give you the chance to turn yourselves in to the first American contingent, but without our help," the Pilot added.

"How the hell do we do that?" he queried.

"Easy, when the train commences to move, out you go on your own," the Pilot said, and added, "The easy way or the hard way, it's up to you."

The guard spoke to the women, then explained that they were taken from a car up the track.

"There is young boy there, the woman's son. Her husband was killed early in the war. They thank you, know you are Americans," the guard concluded.

"Get them out of here before we start to move. Give them some food. We don't want to be obligated to protect them if a problem arises," the Pilot stated.

We checked outside. People were milling about. It was simple to ease the women out of the car into the shielding confines of the milling people.

Now the problem of dispatching these four unwanted guests faced us. We realized that two of them were not wanted for any crimes by the Russians, but we were witnesses to their disgusting actions against the woman and especially the child. We discussed which avenues to pursue, and finally arrived at a feasible conclusion.

"You two pigs are getting the best of the situation. We will let you go now. You will tell the officers who brought you here our car is too crowded. This choice will separate you from these two wanted pricks. The choice is yours. Stay here with them and you become attached to their heinous crimes," the Pilot related our decision.

It didn't take long to make a decision: almost instantly they chose their immediate freedom. They didn't even say thank you as they fell over themselves exiting the car. It was almost comical as they parted the milling people into all directions as they bolted through them.

The guard had bound the hands of the two remaining men as we discussed their fate.

"We could turn them over to the Russians now. Their fate would be no mystery," the Englishman stated. Then added, "Being Americans, it will have to be your decision."

"They're not Americans as far as I'm concerned, they're barbaric animals who deserve no mercy," I replied.

We decided to take a vote; only we Americans participated. The majority chose to dump them at the first isolated stop we made, and leave them to their own resources. When we informed them of our decision, the loud-mouthed one became incensed.

"You can't do this to us. At least let us ride into Odessa with you. We'll take our chances with the American authority," he pleaded.

His request stirred some compassion from a few of us, and it caused us to place a final decision on the back burner.

"If we ride in with these two bastards, and turn them in, we'll have to testify to what we know about their heinous deeds," I professed, then asked, "Are you all willing to do so? We had better think it out some more."

The train's sudden movement helped us make the decision. We decided to take our first choice and dump them out the first opportunity, ridding ourselves of them once and for all. Our decision brought a tirade of foul language and threats bordering on the maniacal from the loud mouthed one.

"Who the fuck do think you are, judge and jury?" he raved.

"I wish the hell we were, you son of a bitch, you'd be dead already," I retorted.

He continued to rant on continuously, so much so we decided to gag him. The other, as always, appeared to be a follower, and humbly volunteered to do as we asked. We suggested to the gagged one a mutual truce, if he remained quiet. He nodded in the affirmative; we ungagged him. What the guard did surprised us: he proceeded to tie them together, back back to back. He immediately explained his actions.

"This way can not run very far, still able to use hands, we no need to feed them. They can even wipe own asses," he explained.

We joined in the frivolity of the situation. The loud mouthed one gritted his teeth in obvious anger. The other curled his lips in a half hearted smirk, resembling the usual response to a gas pain.

The train made the main track with no problems. The whereabouts of the other two were unknown to us. When we decided to sleep, we made sure the two renegades were isolated in one of the shelf-type bunks. There they could be watched by one man who remained on guard. We shared our food generously with them, but offered them no smokes or whiskey. The guard felt we should have very few stops before Odessa, since most trains were heading to Odessa and few would be coming from Odessa to the front. As always he was wrong. As we slowed at a water tower, the shit hit the fan. The water tower was under the control of a band of armed renegade military and civilian forces. It was apparent their aim was to commandeer the train by physical force. We were aware the military guards aboard the train were outnumbered, and our safety was in jeopardy.

It suddenly dawned on me: if these bastards take over the train and these two have an opportunity to talk to them, we're dead.

"I'll make a promise right now," I directed my voice at the two pricks, "if it comes to you or us, I will personally blow your fucking brains out."

Even I knew my threats were from rage, fear, and indecision.

As quick as the situation appeared, it just as quickly disappeared. Before any confrontation between the train military and the attacking band commenced, a group of armored vehicles appeared out of nowhere, followed by platoons of foot soldiers. They cleared the area with their first volley of gunfire. The renegade forces scattered, completely disorganized, leaving their dead and wounded, staining the virgin snow with blood. We watered our engines and moved out, hopefully a step closer to home.

CHAPTER 44 — DIDN'T SEE, DIDN'T HEAR, DON'T TELL

We discussed the options facing us concerning the fate we planned for the two without any guise of secrecy. This resulted in the usual expected tirades from the big mouthed one; these were stifled by the threat of regagging. We had to decide seriously how to rid ourselves of these two interlopers. We had no idea what we would find in Odessa upon our arrival. Who would be in command was a wild guess. We had been told that a Scottish ship would carry us our first leg home. So many unexpected things had happened, we decided to play it by ear.

"We'll just dump them out in Odessa, and wash our hands of them once and for all," the Pilot suggested.

"Just like that? Forget their threats, their murderous acts? You must be kidding," I responded. I then added, "We have them by the balls! If they ride in with us, we go the full route, fuck them where they breathe."

"OK, we'll dump them outside of Odessa. They will be on their own. That way we can report our information as witnesses, without personally having to confront these two pricks," the Pilot added.

"Let's not forget the treatment we received from our Russian allies," the Navigator volunteered.

"It's none of my bloody concern," the Englishman offered, "but I'd wait until I was in complete American authority before I would complain about anything relating to the Russians, or anyone. Your life wouldn't be worth a tupence if word got out that you were tattling."

We all agreed that we were and would be in hostile territory, and vengeance or retribution would have to wait.

The train moved at an aggravating pace, never completely at a free roll. Just when it appeared to be making some headway, the squeal of brakes and accompanying stop-and-go jerks rattled your teeth. We didn't realize it at the time, but this action was caused by occasional barricades placed on the right of way by roving bands of displaced persons. From the very beginning of our travels up to the present, it was apparent no organized program was put into effect to handle the multitude of persons left to their own destinies. Although these delays were painful to us, we never realized they became an ally to our two guests. I always felt, as did the others, their main goal was to use us as a cover when we reached Odessa. The must have weighed their options: go in with us, and we could blow the whistle on them, if we so chose. They chose to evade our hospitality, when on a rare occasion we untied them to defecate. The train had slowed to clear the track, and off they went, lost in the confusion of milling desperate people. At that instant we had two feelings: one of good riddance, the other as an accomplice to murder, we let the bastards get away.

The barren snow-covered wastelands we traversed, cluttered with scars of war, became a topic of interest. The conversation amongst us was sporadic, and I could sense the feeling of apprehension. We looked upon the passing signs of chaos as you would view a movie on a large screen. Your mind moved in and out of fantasy and reality, but you retained only what you felt may affect you personally.

"If only these roving renegades appreciated the blessings of the war's ending, and cooperated-" I never finished my thoughts.

"We have arrived," said the guard. "This is Odessa."

We were entering a marshaling yard, and the crowds of people, both civilian and military, slowed the train to a crawl. The speed of the train didn't matter at this point, especially when we saw the silhouette of a large ocean liner, framed by a body of water, the Black Sea.

The train rolled into a siding, and came to its usual squeaking, clattering stop. The mass exodus from the train became a nightmare of charging multitudes, to where was anyone's guess. The cordon of armed soldiers corralled as many as possible, but many made off in all directions. The only ones having a reason for taking off had to be the renegades who survived the train search. We stayed put as our guard exited to find the authority for our orders for travel. He was gone quite a long period, and returned with a small truck.

"We will go to a billet for processing, before boarding ship," the guard instructed, then added, "You should not have problem, they expect you, and I will vouch for you."

The problems he said we wouldn't encounter came to the fore when we arrived at this so-called billet. He was right; the problems weren't ours, but the problems surely were deadly for those who were caught in the search process, and resisted.

What the guard referred to as a billet, was nothing but a large warehouse. There were thousands of people segregated into groups of displaced civilians, and military personnel. I strained my eyes looking for our two phony civilian-dressed skunks among the civilian horde; no luck. They certainly had to declare themselves as ex POW's for any chance to get aboard the rescue ship. Although we had no more fear of them personally, I hoped their fate was just what they deserved, know it would salve my conscience for letting them get away. We were led by our guard and a Russian officer to a room adjacent to the main hall.

"Here is where you will remain, until boat is ready to receive you," the guard explained.

The Russian officer exchanged salutes with our guard, and departed. The door was locked behind him.

"Here we go again, locked up as prisoners," I said.

"It is for your protection," the guard replied.

"Well, I guess we can put up with this shit, since we're close to getting the fuck out of here," I agreed.

There were bunks for all of us, and to our amazement a complete bathroom, with showers. A closer inspection revealed a kitchen of sorts, with American canned food, English cigarettes, and candy. We made the best of the goodies, especially the shower. The Englishman cooked up some English concoction, combining the American rations with the English wooley beef. It wasn't bad.

We had to admit the disposition of the Russians appeared to have improved. This attitude was compounded when a Russian officer appeared, and asked if we were satisfied,

"If there anything you want or need, ask through your guard," he offered through our guard.

"There's something fishy with this change," I suggested.

"Come on," everyone said simultaneously.

"I don't know why, but I have a feeling there is a reason for this sudden turnabout," I reiterated my beliefs.

This controversial conversation was ended when our loving Navigator suggested we take the Russian officer's offer. "Maybe a few lovable females to pass the time away can be supplied, and ease your doubts."

My theory of misrepresentation was substantiated when to our surprise an English officer appeared. He bid us welcome, and identified himself and the function he commanded.

"I'm the commanding officer here. My job is to afford all allied ex-prisoners of war and other repatriated personnel a avenue of return to your commands," he explained.

"You will take orders from no one except me, or my subordinates, whom I will identify to you," he added.

"What about the Russians?" the Pilot asked.

"Here we go again," I remarked. "Fuck the Russians, can't you understand they're not our friends? We're being used, just as we were told by Helena and Novak."

"Now, I must warn you, be careful of what you say about the Russians," he said in the tone of an order.

"But we have so much to report! They're getting away with murder," I replied.

"You didn't see, you didn't hear, so don't tell," was as emphatic as one could state it.

"We want to get you out of here as quickly as possible. We do not wish to get involved in any direct confrontation with the Russians. We accept all actions, devious or otherwise as the product of a painful war. Thank your God for your safe return home," he instructed.

It all sounded like a prepared speech. We looked at each other questioningly.

"What about the American renegades, who raped and killed like so many animals?" I asked. Then added, "Stole, pillaged, even robbed the dead."

"Spoils of war, on most occasions," was his reply.

What a cop out. We figured this was not the authority to report our complaints to.

We could hear, but not see what was going on in the main hall. There was constant shouting, sometimes punctuated by gunfire. We asked the guard, locked in with us, to find out what was going on. He knocked on the door as he spoke in Russian. The door was opened in response to his knock, and apparently to his Russian dialogue. The conversation was in Russian, and its duration was very short. The guard explained that the main hall was being overrun by hordes of renegade ex-prisoners of war, both military and civilian. They refused to turn over their ill gotten spoils. They are accusing the permanent party of Russians of confiscating their property for their own use. The arguments become violent, and actually lead to a gun fight. The rebels were sleeping with one eye open and a loaded gun in hand.

"They will rot here before the are able to board ship, must have clearance pass," the guard explained.

We were thankful that we had been separated from the others, and enjoyed the luxuries presented to us. What made it more pleasing was that we didn't have to change our opinion about the Russians.

The next day provided a treat we would never expect under the prevailing conditions. An English sergeant offered us the opportunity to attend an honest to goodness Russian ballet. It may sound trite, but I, even with my usual callused behavior, had a fetish for opera and ballet. Only the Navigator, Co-Pilot, and I accepted. We were supplied with civilian clothes, and more or less secreted out of the building to a waiting Dodge auto, and driven to a theater in the center of Odessa. Once inside the theater, the lights were dimmed, and all evidence of the existing war was obliterated by the music and the graceful gyrations of a ballerina story unfolding before our eyes. The joy of feeling like a civilian, even for a short period of time, lessened the dread of returning to reality, which was imminent.

On our return we conveyed the beauty of the ballet, and the feeling of being free from the confinement of this room.

"Being confined has it's rewards," the Pilot explained. "There have been wholesale killings, between the renegades and the Russian military. It got so hot out there, that the English officer and his subordinates came here for safety.

"The word has reached us that the ship is going to set sail days ahead of schedule, most likely tomorrow. We will board tonight, if the disorders outside subside," he added.

A feeling of frustration, and a deep resentment towards the Russians, was obvious throughout the room. Their utter lack of cooperation was surely evident, but their lack of respect was even more obvious. To even imagine that at this stage of the war, with victory in sight, we had to use subversive behavior to effect our survival. Russian arrogance, especially throughout the high command when word of victory in Europe arrived, caused not only jubilation, but violent overreaction to any breach of orders. It appeared that at this point in time they could afford to be independent. "Who the fuck needs the Americans" was easy to understand even in a foreign tongue.

That evening we were secreted out of the billet, and were walked to the ship via an winding route. It was almost funny to be able to see the ship, and at times seem to be walking away from our destination. It was when we observed drunken Russian military patrols that our crazy course made sense. They would without reason discharge their weapons in any and all directions with reckless abandon.

"We do not wish to give these bloody bastards any reason to force a confrontation. Be patient," stated the English officer, leading our walk to freedom.

"What shit, escaping from our ally," I retorted.

"Let's get the hell aboard the ship! Forget our personal feelings, our chance will come!" the Pilot responded.

"It may sound trite, but I can't dismiss the treatment we received from our so called allies, and the murderous treatment of the civilian population. Never one word of gratitude, except from the Poles and the Lithuanians. Shit, we're not professional soldiers, our lives have been altered in their behalf. Just say thanks, just once, even if they don't mean it," I recited with a venomous intent.

Suddenly there was the ship before us. Its gangway appeared as a gateway to heaven. The gateway to heaven was blocked by a bevy of Russian military. They were certainly there to prevent desertions of Russian military or defecting civilians. The taste of western living, even as a internee under the Germans, was a far cry from the totalitarian Russian government. Defections have become a problem since there was no preparedness to control the mass exodus caused by the sudden end to the war. Of course, I thought to myself, we Americans didn't have such a problem, except the ones who chose to use their new found freedom to repay themselves with the lives and loot of whom they referred to as their enemies.

The English soldiers guarding the gangway were warned about our arrival, and the prearranged plan went into effect. The bow of the ship became the focal point. It was the farthest point since we were approaching from the stern. The English guards ran towards the bow, shouting, "Halt, halt," then emphasized their actions by firing their weapons into the air. There was an object clinging to the bow line. This object and the actions from the English guards motivated the Russian guards to follow suit. The only difference was the Russians, fired point blank at the clinging object. Their burp guns shattered the object as we made our way to the gateway to freedom. We were aboard.

The voices were Russian, but the language they used was as understandable as if the same words were used under the same circumstances and spoken in English. As a matter of fact the intensity of the Russian displeasure was lessened by the guffaws of the English guards, when the clinging object was nothing but a sack of laundry.

We were dispatched with great haste to a stateroom occupied by a group of high ranking English officers, and civilian-dressed men. We were offered seats before a large conference type desk. The apparent officer in command vocally identified himself, and bid us welcome. He went on to explain that the purpose for the intended interrogation was to identify our rank, arm of service, and to establish the route necessary to return us to our respective commands.

"We have separated you from the other military and civilian personnel because you have been under supervised detention and have no misgivings to hide," the officer related.

"We may not have any personnel misgivings to hide, but we sure as hell have misgivings that we witnessed perpetrated by both the Russians and some ex-POW's, including murder," I volunteered.

My outburst caused a flurry of glances between the men present, and a look of disdain from the Pilot.

"I would at this juncture advise all of you, you didn't see, you didn't hear, don't tell, we are not interested," was instructed by the Officer in command.

Apparently we still hadn't arrived at the proper place, or found the proper people interested in our tale of woe.

CHAPTER 45 — CRUISE

The interrogation ended abruptly. "Sergeant, escort these men to their respective quarters."

This was the first time we were actually separated from each other. We never got together again until we reached Italy. The officers were given staterooms; the non-coms were assigned to hammocks lashed just below the main deck.

It was a fair test of skill just to get into one, and the closeness to the deck above you was not an antidote for claustrophobia. After many attempts only three of us conquered the hammock problem. The rest chose to recline on the deck.

The engines vibrated into life, and an uneasy feeling of joy was audibly expressed by a rousing cheer. A blast of its horns and an increase of vibration signalled the ship's departure. We all made our way to the port holes, and watched as the ship without tug boat assistance eased its way into the Black Sea. It struck me that the only ship of any consequence that I had sailed on was the Queen Elizabeth that carried me to England. Being confined to quarters, and never on deck, dispelled any semblance of an ocean voyage. The heavy seas, and the regurgitating results negated any pleasurable experience connected to an ocean cruise. The only other sailing I had done was on the ferry trips from Staten Island, to Brooklyn or Manhattan.

It was when the ship began to pitch and yaw, under clear sailing, that the condition of one's equilibrium brought up the best or worst in some. I never suffered either from sea or air sickness, but the hammock and the ceiling lights swaying in opposite directions made an upper deck tenant of me.

Daylight brought into focus a serene picture of rolling swells, penetrated by the ship's knife-like bow. An effervescent glow seemed to permeate the spray as it joined the wake formed by the plowing ship. As the day progressed the serenity that prevailed was embellished further by nature. There alongside the ship's hull on both sides appeared a number of porpoises. They seemed to playfully engage in riding the bow's wake, while gently scratching their bodies against the hull. Their graceful motions seemed to me as a welcoming committee leading us to home.

We were suddenly land locked, and it was obvious we were entering the Dardanelles. The white alabaster vision on the starboard side was obviously Greece; the port side was Turkey. The porpoises continued to lead us, and almost in a show of deference they crisscrossed in front of the bow, appearing to bid us bon voyage, dove and disappeared.

I had worked on some ships at the Bethlehem shipyards, but they were either in a drydock or tied up to a pier. Being aboard an ocean-going liner gracefully knifing its way through rolling swells, landlocked between countries of historical origin, prompted me to imagine a return sojourn, under more pleasant conditions.

The Dardanelles suddenly opened into a large expanse of water. "We're in the Mediterranean Sea!" someone shouted.

The rolling swells soon became white capped waves, accentuated by an aquamarine and emerald hue. Although I knew from my geography learnings that this body of water was landlocked, the disappearance of the mouth of the Dardanelles soon placed us in a vast void of ever-increasing, raging water.

Its only benefit was the act of keeping the ship afloat, and leading to a port of call and home.

This happy feeling was forgotten when the railside observers of the aforementioned beauty became railside pukers. It was the same condition aboard this ship as it was aboard the Queen Elizabeth. The long chow lines were diminished by the absentee pukers, so the non-pukers had free reign to chow. As matter of fact, you were encouraged to chow down as much as you wanted, and retire to your bunking area with a doggie bag.

The next landfall was Sicily, just off the boot of Italy. We passed through the Strait of Messina, which separated Sicily from the mainland of Italy. Someone mentioned that the port of Messina was the location of one of the bloodiest battles of the invasion of Italy by the Allies.

The next place of consequence was the port of Naples. A port is a port, and one expects a docking area with piers, wharf buildings with docking facilities. As we edged into the pier area, it was obvious we could never reach the pier. There lying on its side adjacent to the pier was a large ocean liner. The keel was submerged, and the tip of one of its screws barely broke the surface. The entire exposed super structure and hull were the supporting members for a bridge, erected from the docking ships to the pier proper. This was certainly a scar of the war, and a closer observation of the surrounding area emphasized the utter futility of global conflict.

Our group was the first to disembark. We were shunted to an office type room. Here we were joined by the officers of our crew, but the Englishman and the infantry sergeant were missing.

When we inquired of their absence, we were informed that ground force personnel, and other than American military, were assigned to authority of their own command.

"Damn, after being together and sharing the trials and tribulations, we can't even say good bye," I complained.

The American officer who heard my statement answered, and not too politely, "This is no social club. You repatriates and ex-POW's are problem enough. We haven't the time to socialize you."

I'll be a son of a bitch, this prick probably just arrived from stateside, a damn conscientious objector, I thought to myself. It was futile to even think of reporting our feelings or the atrocities we witnessed. Maybe, when we were assigned to an all American command. We could only hope.

We were escorted to a truck, loaded, and moved out. The road led out into the countryside, and the local population displayed reverence and acceptance, waving American flags as we passed by. The driver of the truck snickered as we waved in response.

"These people would slit your throat a few months back. Now they want to be friends," he explained.

"I understand that there were many Italians who hated Mussolini, and helped us through the underground with our invasion," the Navigator stated.

"I was told through a relative, a New York City Magistrate, that he and a Deputy Commissioner of the New York City Police Department parachuted into Sicily. With the aid of the Italian underground forces, they helped prepare for the invasion of Italy," I related with conviction.

"By the way, big mouth," the Pilot added, "What battles did you fight in?"

Hell, it was a known fact that there were sympathetic Germans, who aided shot down American and English airmen before and even after we occupied Europe.

"Hell, can't you allow a people set free from a dictator to vent their true feelings? Look at those women on the hillside raising their arms with the V for victory sign."

We had to join the driver in a hearty laugh when he explained, "That's not a V sign,. They are telling you that you can get fucked for two dollars."

A true fact or not, it was apropos at the time, and ended a political confrontation.

The road became a winding one, and we appeared to be climbing a mountain. The driver slowed, then came to a stop. Before he could explain his actions, the scene that presented itself answered any questions we might've had.

High up a mountain side could be seen the battered remains of a fortress type building. "Those are the remains of one of the most heavily defended German entrenchments. Every one of our infantry assaults to take that fort resulted in defeat, and hundreds of lives lost. It became a matter of pride, because that fucking mountain meant nothing to us. They were cut off. Our Air Force bombed them incessantly to no avail. We eventually just waited them out. German attempts to air drop them supplies were easily prevented, and they, too, realized the futility of holding a position of no consequence to the outcome of the war. This battle of Concerta will long be remembered as one of our follies. It was a costly and shallow accomplishment, not a victory, when they surrendered."

We were assigned to a tent city, and briefed by a Sergeant with a wait and see attitude. There were many military personnel of all ranks and assignments, awaiting transportation to their respective commands. No one could give us a reasonable answer as to our future.

"We have been asking and waiting for weeks; just sit tight. The food is good, there's plenty of sports activities, movies from the states. Just stay cool," was the standard response of all you asked.

I suppose the reason for not fraternizing with the enemy was proper and understandable, but it still didn't always make sense. When we chowed down for the first time, I pointed to the sign that read,"DO NOT FRATERNIZE WITH THE ENEMY." The enemy were little emaciated children outside the fenced-in mess area. The edict of nonfraternization became, to me, an unnecessary war horror. There were actually MP's stationed there to prevent the rule being violated. A second sign read, "THROWING FOOD OVER THE FENCE IS A COURT MARTIAL OFFENSE. YOUR MEALS WILL BE SERVED IN A STOCKADE." This order was at the disposal cans where we dumped our leftovers.

To scrape good food into a garbage can was a travesty of human dignity. The feelings about the unjust treatment we received from our Russian allies were compounded by the treatment we saw imposed on other humans by our own people. By whom and where would our tales of inhumanity be received and acted upon with any authority?

My unbelieving mind was jolted the next day when we went to chow. I had a few slices of real white bread on my tray at the disposal area. I looked around to observe the MP's location. Feeling safe, I sailed a slice of bread over the fence. The mad dash to retrieve it by about ten kids attracted the MP nearest the location. He eased his way to my side, and whispered, "If you don't throw that other piece of bread over the fence, I'll lock you up for smuggling food out of the mess hall."

Now I knew why those kids were back every day.

We fell into a routine. There was no reveille at a Godforsaken hour, no retreat parades, and best of all, no KP. After all the time spent in the frozen north, the complete change in the weather was a pleasant adjustment. As matter of fact it was baseball weather, perfect for my favorite past time. The war had stymied my baseball career professionally, but not my love of the game. While most of my crew ventured to the movies, I located the baseball diamond. The non-com club posted the upcoming schedule, which indicated the present games were for the Italian area championship. Most of this camp's team was comprised of permanent party members, with a few transients. The transients posed a problem when they were ordered to move out. Such a problem gave me the opportunity to enliven my stay.

I visited the field one day when practice was in order. A surprised blast over the loud speaker system jolted me: "We are looking for an outfielder with some experience. Transients are accepted."

It took a little time to locate the source of the announcement, but to me it seemed an eternity. I wanted to be first to locate the source of the announcement.

I located the Sergeant in charge, who was talking to two other men whom I suspected to be other candidates. They looked my way as I said, "I'd like a shot at that position."

The Sergeant introduced himself, and removed my thoughts of competition. One of the two was the outfielder needing replacement: he was being moved out. The other was a friend: they were just bidding the Sergeant good-bye. I introduced myself, with a brief description of my baseball background.

"The hardest part of building a competitive team, is that most of the real good players are transients. We are about three games away from the Italian area championship, and we are losing one of our best players," the Sergeant explained. Then he added, "That is why so few transients apply. You get used to the good life, then bam, you're on your way."

"Hell, Sergeant, I don't care if it's only until I get my traveling papers, I don't like being bored. If I can help, I'd appreciate the chance," I responded.

Not only did I make the team, but I got to see parts of Italy I never would have seen. I only played three games, one in Foggia, and two at our home field. I helped, winning two of the three games, which left us with one more win to be champs. In the interim, I had the opportunity to visit the Island of Capri, with the team when we won the semi-final game, as a reward. The rest of my crew had the opportunity to visit the opera in Naples, and I was included. We went two times, and the reaction to my being included was, "Why are you included in the Opera trips, when we aren't included in your baseball escapades?"

What compounded their jealous behavior was my invitation to visit the Vatican, in Rome, the day before we shipped out. No matter what your religious denomination, the Vatican is a must to visit.

The Sergeant knew a few of the ballplayers I had played with back in the States, and we spent many hours reminiscing. I felt maybe he could, if I intruded on our friendship, help me reach someone who would listen to our tales. I briefed him on my intentions, and his response was one of indifference.

"I like it here. I don't want to get involved in a political confrontation, and I can assure you, no one else stationed here would jeopardize his soft assignment. Forget it," he warned.

I didn't tell the rest of my crew, and they never even suggested approaching anyone to divulge our almost forgotten escapades. The old cliche, "Time heals all wounds," was certainly in evidence here. We boarded a plane the next day to Paris. Maybe we'd have some luck there. I still had hope, but decided to keep it to myself.

We reached Paris, and again the officers were separated from the non-coms. Our hope, that in numbers there would be strength, was diminished. The crew itself seemed to drift part; we divided into "special interest" groups. We became tourists of sorts. Being in Paris was a rare treat, even under the prevailing conditions. Our loving Navigator soon found his long abstinence repaired when he located Pigalle, the street of love. The Eiffel Tower was focal point of interest, if only because it was a geographical identification of France. To me it was an abomination of erector set construction.

It was obvious the French had preserved their monumental heritage, by surrendering before it was devastated by the invading Germans. I couldn't help but compare the ruins of England to the country we were now fighting and shedding our blood for. All this to save the Eiffel Tower. Some shit.

There seemed to be no real authority to effect repatriation. It happened piecemeal, and it was piecemeal that we were dispatched back to England. At no time were we addressed in an interrogative manner; no one gave a damn. Get rid of these men as quickly as possible was the mandate. Maybe in England someone, somewhere, would be interested.

CHAPTER 46 — ENEMY VICTORY

The officers left by plane a day or two before the non-coms. The officers were flown directly to our home base. We were flown to another group's field. It took us days to convince anyone in authority that we were not where we belonged. We all had good reasons to get where we could notify our families personally of our location. We had no way of knowing if they had ever been notified, other than we were missing in action.

There appeared to be a breakdown in military decorum, not that Air Force decorum was ever really West Point level after washing out of Pilot training. Each crew commander established his own decorum among his crew. There was an air of forthcoming victory, and all combat missions had been canceled. The word of Patton's march into Berlin being stopped to allow our Russian ally to enter first was like a shot into my heart. I went to our commander's quarters, and requested an interview. When I was identified as a returning evadee out of Germany, through Russia, he sent word that as soon as he was able, he intended to interview us personally.

Word spread that the Germans were beaten, and ready to surrender officially. General Patton's outspoken edict, "Let's rearm the Germans and turn them around towards Russia, our true enemy," was the profound feeling of our group, from the top commander down. When we finally received our interview with our group Commander, he personally reiterated verbatim Patton's words. He had opened the door; his feelings were in the vein of retribution, and now was the time to reveal our treatment by the Russians. I waited to see if there was to be any cooperation from my cohorts; there was none.

"Christ! Excuse me, sir, but we are able, as a group, to substantiate Patton's belief that our enemy is Russia, now and in the future," I volunteered.

Speak for yourself, was etched in the faces of my crew, although not a word was spoken. I awaited a response from our commander; none was evident.

"I want to congratulate you all on your daring escapades, and will recommend an additional Air Medal to each of you." He added, "To your Radio Operator, a Distinguished Flying Cross, recommended by your Pilot, should satisfy your efforts, with the God-given blessing that you all survived."

Not one word about what had happened in Russia to make us so hostile. The interview ended on an unhappy note to me, but appeared to satisfy the others.

I kept thinking to myself, how can you, a mere Radio Operator/Gunner, involve yourself in a situation of such international magnitude? Not easily, as I recalled the words of Helena & Novak, and the merciless killings I witnessed, by both the Russians and our own people. The next day a thought entered my mind: I'll write to the *Stars and Stripes*. They would like a hot item such as ours. I had another guess coming: their answer was completely gutless. "One derogatory remark about the Russians, at the time we are negotiating compatibility, would bring court martial proceedings for me as well as you." It was signed by the Editor. I wouldn't make myself believe that everyone's attitude was one of condescendence. I suddenly awoke to the magnitude of the revelations entrusted to us when General Patton's untimely death reestablished my impotent position. Where did I ever find the balls to think I could prevent what appeared to be a political sell out?

We were asked to volunteer to retrieve what was described as humans from the concentration camps in Germany. Just the Pilot, Co-Pilot, Navigator, and Radio Operator made up the crew. A B-17's bomb bay was fitted with a plywood deck, to carry the living remains of walking zombies. They were loaded almost as cords of wood into the bomb bay and the waist position. The officers were isolated from the horror perpetrated on these poor creatures. I was the only one in the position to check on their condition while in flight. The stench was unbearable. Even though we flew at an altitude where oxygen wasn't necessary, I donned my oxygen mask to prevent puking. I made two such trips, which in my mind forgave any misgivings I may have harbored for the deaths committed by me, directly or indirectly. The delousing after each such mission, did nothing to remove the stench that lingered when absorbed by the hairs in your nose.

The war in Europe ended, and as an evadee I would qualify for discharge. It was just a matter of getting stateside to a discharge area. Unexpectedly we were assigned a new B-17 to fly home. We were given heavy fur lined parkas, which confirmed the Pilot's guess, "We are flying the Northern route. I think I'll volunteer for a boat ride home."

Everyone but me agreed, they had enough of this flying shit. Get me home, get me out, was the mutual feelings of most of the surviving airmen.

Two days later, loaded with our regular crew and a few ground personnel, a course to Iceland was plotted by the Navigator. Map wise it appeared a long, out of the way route, and its choice was never explained. Our destination was Reykjavik, whose location was a test of flying as demanding and trying as formation flying on a bomb run. Only one approach was available into Reykjavik: up a narrow fjord, which afforded very few feet of clearance on both wing tips. Miscalculations were visibly evident, if you had the inclination and the fortitude to glance downward at the base of the mountains on both sides. The runway was covered with snow. We cleared the fjord, bringing a well-jockeyed aircraft to a skidding landing. It was an odd day-light, or was it an odd light of night? Experienced heads soon cleared the mystery: it was the long day part of the equinox.

We were led to a parking area by a Jeep with a sign that blinked, "FOLLOW ME." We did. After securing our aircraft, we were led to a large Quonset hut, no different than our home away from home in England. There we were briefed by an American Major, whose orders were concise, and to the point.

"You are our guest here. You have no rank or jurisdiction. Where you have been or what you have done, has no bearing. Your behavior will govern our report on you. Most of all, don't get mixed up with the permanent party here. Keep to your own, for your own good," he related.

Our response was an inquiring look at each other. I for one couldn't believe what we were hearing. One would think that the red carpet for welcoming heroes would great us. Even our classification as "guests" had a degrading connotation. The only words out of his mouth that breathed friendliness was his order to a Sergeant, to lead us to our quarters and the Post Exchange.

"By the way," he concluded, "your plane will be serviced as quickly as possible. You should be on your way in two days." He laughingly added, "Forty eight hours, not two of the equinox days."

Our quarters were neat and warm. There was another crew also bedded down. We introduced ourselves, and exchanged the same feelings of disbelief towards the attitude of the command here. They were from another Bomb Group, and happily reported that they would be on their way come morning.

"Morning?" I asked. "How do you tell when it's morning?"

"It's a standing joke here: when you have a piss hard on, it's morning."

"If you just have a hard on, you have a choice. An Army WAC, or a Red Cross worker, they're in constant competition for your flying pay," another man volunteered.

Of course this kind of rhetoric perked the ears of our ever-loving Navigator. "Where is this competition taking place?"

"Don't fret, you don't have to find them, they will find you," was the answer to his question.

We were pointed towards the Post Exchange. The Navigator led the way; only the Engineer and myself followed. The Post Exchange was a semblance of both a small grocery store and a luncheonette. The grocery store appeared well stocked, both in edible items and souvenirs. What was most attractive was the soda fountain, missing in all our worldly travels. The booths along the walls were replicas of my Drug Store hang out at home. There was one empty. We made for it, but not without a problem.

"Just a minute," a voice bellowed, "this booth is reserved for permanent personnel."

Looking around, I noticed all the other booths were occupied, but their status wasn't clear. I looked for any posted signs relating such jurisdiction. Chancing a challenge, I posed a question to the interloper, "By whose authority?"

"By squatters' rights. You're just passing through," he responded.

I'll never understand why, but every time there is any kind of belligerent attitude offered, it is always by a small, insignificant asshole. We just ignored his presence, and entered the booth. He stood there looking over his shoulder at his two buddies. For some support, I guessed.

"Why don't you check on your reservation time? I think you are about an hour or so early," I suggested.

His face reddened, more so when his buddies turned away. He started to say something. I cut him short. "Fuck off, creep, before you're pounded into the floor."

He left, not only from our location, but from the building, with embarrassing laughter trailing his every step, until it was deafened by the door closing behind him.

Looking up at the menu brought surprising items, that relived the past. Hot Nestle's chocolate caught my eye, with whipped cream, I hoped. Not only with whipped cream, but little sugar wafers too.

"I guess we can put up with a little chicken shit, for these little pleasures," I said.

"Here comes my idea of pleasure," came from the Navigator.

The door had opened, and entering was a beautiful woman, dressed in a Red Cross uniform. The statement, "They will find you," had come to pass. Her approach was strictly business, and belied her apparent beauty.

"New arrivals, from England," was her introduction.

Her next statement boarded on the vulgar, an intrusion of one's personal privacy.

"Had enough of English meat? Want some American cooking?"

Of course we knew she wasn't referring to animal flesh. I thought, was this an American Red Cross giveaway, part of their service to service men? My fantasy was short lived when she, without one iota of the discomfort I knew I felt, spelled out the tariff necessary to partake of some American meat.

"Three girls, a quicky, will cost each of you twenty five American dollars," she quoted.

"American dollars, what else would we have?" the Navigator asked.

"You would be surprised what we are offered. German marks, Italian lire, even English pounds," she explained.

"What the fuck, we could get laid in England for a chocolate bar, or a pack of gum.

Shit, if you had to pay, it was usually a real prostitute, and sometimes they offered you all the pop corn you could eat," the Navigator added.

"Well, you're not in England. A full night with one of your choice, will cost you one hundred dollars." She concluded with, "Make up your minds, and by the way, a full night is from midnight to eight o'clock in the morning, in our dorm."

As she departed, we wondered if she or any one of her was considered permanent party. The Navigator was the only interested party, but we had been paid only partial pay since we returned from Russia. No one had a hundred bucks. While we were contemplating a revenue collection from our whole crew, to satisfy our nympholeptic buddy, a competing attraction appeared: an Army WAC. Her sad sack Army uniform did nothing to enhance her cosmetic appearance, in comparison to her Red Cross counterpart. She wore Master Sergeant stripes, and her approach verbally typecast her as such.

"Don't waste your money on those prim bitches. Servicing you guys is just a business to them. We WAC's are at your service to make you appreciate your Army's gratitude for your contribution when duty called. We have WAC officers for your officers, but you may share, so that discrimination isn't a must." She concluded with, "A voluntary contribution is acceptable, but nothing less than twenty five dollars for a complete ejaculation, no responsive orgasm is guaranteed."

We attempted to draw her into elongated conversation; her manner and descriptive vocabulary were entertaining. She left with the suggestion that reservations were in order before bed call.

"You have to be in the bed of your choice. Don't let this long day fool you, night time and bed time are by the Army clock," she explained.

We had our feed, and left to return to our quarters, anxious to convey our findings to the rest of the crew. On the way we encountered a group of transient flyers playing softball on a snow covered clearing.

"What time is it?" I asked aloud.

"It's about eight thirty PM," someone answered.

"This would be a twilight game, back in the States," I added.

After reaching our quarters, and relating our encounters with the flesh traders, the next hour was determining who was anxious to trade. It was soon obvious that money would curtail the number of traders able to trade. Suggesting that we pool our monies, wasn't acceptable to all. The chosen one was of course the Navigator. Although we agreed he should test the waters, most had reasons for not contributing to his sexual desires. Although we would be fed at the mess hall, most felt having some spare change for the luxuries at the Post Exchange offset the luxury of sex, that only one would share. That closed the book on the flesh traders. We never even decided whom we would patronize, if we were able.

The part of the crew that remained behind gave us a brief on the food served at the mess hall.

"Would you believe that there is a special mess hall for the transients? Like in Poland and Russia, our food didn't compare to theirs," the Pilot remarked.

"Screw them, they deserve what they get. When we're gone they will still be here in this God forsaken hole," I answered.

"Hell, our complaints fade in the distance. We would make asses of ourselves, if we tried to register a complaint here," someone suggested.

"Or anywhere else," was added by a subtle voice.

I realized that the closer we got to home, the less of a chance of support from my crew, if and when the opportunity to register a complaint arrived. I just couldn't wipe from my mind the atrocities we witnessed committed by our own people. I compared them to the atrocities perpetrated by the Germans against the Jewish people, which we so vehemently protested, as did our allies.

The next morning (by the clock, not the nature of the light of day) that other crew and plane took off. Not a hint of a farewell gesture was made. As a matter of observation, there was a "good riddance" atmosphere on the base. We sweated out the service of our plane and found the recreation barrack. Killed some time between mess hall meals, and visited the Post Exchange. We played some pool and ping pong. The only obvious change was the absence of solicitation from our Red Cross and WAC flesh peddlers. As a matter of record, they shied away from us like we were the enemy. I wondered to myself if feeling like a survivor rather than a hero would lessen my feelings of non-appreciation.

We were informed that our plane was ready, and we could depart to the States in the morning. The only semblance of the past experience of preflight preparation was encountered in the morning. We entered a briefing room similar to the ones in England. We were briefed on the weather, navigational headings, radio frequencies, and procedures. The only information not presented was enemy fighter and flak locations. We were driven to our plane, and the WAC who was driving left us with a note of endearment, which surprised the shit out of us.

"Good luck," she said. "Thank you for your efforts. If you had agreed, I would have thanked you physically, free of charge."

All we heard the whole trip home from takeoff to landing from the Navigator, was, "What a sack partner I missed, because of you cheap bastards."

The trip home was uneventful. The weather was perfect, and landfall was a blessing. I thanked God as we hit the black skid marks of the preceding planes, and followed a jeep to our parking area. Just to touch mother earth was always a thrill, but to touch mother earth in the United States, after being so close to death, was uppermost in our minds.

"Don't anyone leave this aircraft until given permission, and I mean nobody," was bellowed in a most hostile tone.

The Pilot and Co-Pilot had dropped from the nose hatch. They were ordered to re-enter the same way. We wondered if we had by mistake landed in Japan, as the war was still in progress there. This guy isn't Japanese - what gives? I wondered.

"Now, one at a time approach the waist door. Throw your gear to the ground. Everything except what you are wearing, including your parachute. Let's go," he ordered.

We complied with reluctance, and dismounted. All the gear was in a pile adjacent to the plane. After we were all clear, the plane was restarted and immediately taxied off. A group of non-coms sorted out our gear, and laughingly picked the items of their choice. Since we had very little except the sun tan uniforms, with no rank or insignia, the only items of consequence were the outer garments such as the hooded parkas, which everyone cherished. They were flying personnel issue, and were coveted by the ground personnel and were confiscated without redress.

"Why in hell don't you officers complain?" I asked.

Their answer was, "Who the hell needs that shit anyway? Let's get the hell out of here."

Sure, they all had their nice officer's uniforms.

They returned what they didn't steal, and directed us to the registration and check-in office. It was about meal time, and we were ordered to feed up and return afterwards. This mess hall was for returning flying personnel only, and there were hundreds of returning flying personal awaiting reassignment. The line to the chow was a winding one, starting about a hundred feet outside the mess hall. Some of the returning flyers hadn't seen combat, and the large sign that greeted us upon entering the mess hall proper had no impact on them. To those as we and others who faced death, and witnessed others dying at the hands of the Germans, made us want to puke. "IF YOU DON"T LIKE THE HELP HERE, EAT SOMEPLACE ELSE." The help were German prisoners of war.

"Don't tell me I can't have more potatoes," could be heard in a loud challenging voice, "you fucking Heinie," as the crash of a tray against the head of the German server brought the MP's with batons swinging at the enraged flyer. We found out later that the attacker was the only flying Master Sergeant, a Medal of Honor winner who flew fifty missions and had a brother killed by the Germans.

Based on our receptions since heading home, and the lack of respect shown toward fighting men, it appeared our complaints would fall on deaf ears. I was convinced the enemy on both sides were the victors.

CHAPTER 47 — REWARD WITHOUT RECOGNITION

The next morning we were greeted with a bit of good news. The Sergeant, arrested for misconduct in the mess hall because of his attack on the German prisoner of war, was only verbally chastised, confined to quarters, and scheduled to ship out at the first opportunity, with no loss in rank. The better part of the news that day was the order for all to report to the commanding officer.

We were directed to what appeared to be a conference room. Therein were seated five officers ranked from a two star to a silver-birded Colonel. The two star was seated at the head of the conference table. The others were seated to his right side. We were offered seats to the left of the two star, whose bemedaled chest emphasized his authority.

I'll never understand why, but commanding officers of high rank are always blessed with voices that reek with belittlement. They always, and in all ways, look down at you. If you happen to be taller in height, they will sit you down and stand above you.

"You gentleman seem to have a tale to tell. Your attempts to gain a listener have followed you from every stop on your way home to here," he stated, in a contemptuous tone.

"But, sir-" the Pilot started, but was cut off.

"But nothing," the two star interrupted. "We don't want to hear your tales of woe. Thank your lucky stars you survived whatever you encountered. We are only here to classify you, and set you up by points to be discharged."

These words, primarily "discharge," brought a resounding cheer from my crew. I thought they would be put down for their outburst, but instead broad smiles appeared on the officer's faces. The two star noticed my reluctance to join in the revelry, and questioned my abstaining.

"What gives, soldier? From the information we have on this group, not only do you possess the necessary points for discharge, but the fact that you are evadees can effect an immediate discharge. Not only immediate, but from any base of your choosing," he stated, causing another outburst of obvious happiness.

"Your next assignment will be Atlantic City, New Jersey, for a rest you deserve. You will be officially classified there while enjoying freedoms of your choice, with little or no regimentation. You will be able to choose your area of discharge, unless you wish to remain in the Air Force," he added with a laugh..

The next half hour was a question and answer period, with no opportunity to open an avenue to relate the stories I wanted to inject. It was obvious that the rewards offered at the outset were an attempt to brainwash us into forgetting our tales of woe. It was also obvious that the attempt was successful, as far as my crewmates were concerned. We were dismissed with a handshake by each of the officers, and wished "good luck."

"By the way, anyone living within distance of a weekend pass can visit home, if you desire," the two star threw over his shoulder in a matter of fact manner.

Who did he think he was kidding? I was the only one close enough to make use of his offer. It was another attempt to prevent me from telling my story. The others picked up on his meaning, and let it be known that they felt the same way.

Two days later we were aboard a train, headed to Atlantic City. This train ride had far better accommodations than the train rides I had when traveling interstate, before going overseas. We were assigned pullman compartments, traveling with civilians. I tried not to compare this train with the train ride through Poland and Russia, for fear of reviving and reliving the atrocious acts of depredation that were focal points of horror, forever imbedded in my mind.

Atlantic City was the first time we felt welcome. We were assigned to one of the larger hotels, two to a room, spacious and civilized. There were no items to link the hotel to the military, even though the hotel was completely occupied by returning vets of all services. Of course the apparel worn by occupants was military, but the decorum was definitely non-military. We were served in the civilian dining room by civilian waiters and waitresses. We ordered from a menu, and the choices were numerous and attractively palatable. I thought to myself that this may be the place to get someone to listen to the story I had to tell. I made no mention of my intentions to my cohorts; their minds led in one direction, home.

Daytime was spent calling home, as we weren't permitted visitors. I planned to accept the chance to go home the coming weekend, and my wife and family were ecstatic. My brother, on leave, volunteered to pick me up. Knowing this, I invited any two of my crew to join me. They chose to draw straws, and would decide by the weekend.

The evenings were spent walking the boardwalk. Amusements were available; even the famous Steel Pier was in full swing, girlie shows included.

All the interesting items were put to rest when the wheelchair paraplegics and the amputees performed entertainments that were pathetic, but self serving. The cliche, "Misery loves company," was emphasized ten times over. The wheelchair paraplegics had races up and down the boardwalk, to the cheering of crowds of vacationing visitors. The amputees would remove their artificial limbs, place them in the trash cans with the feet exposed, thus giving the appearance of someone being head first in the can. The sight of these performances at first shocked the civilian passersby, but they laughed when the amputee would remove them and wave them on high. I couldn't help but feel this sort of behavior could only be a coverup of one's true feelings over a lifetime's loss of being a complete human being.

On returning to the hotel one evening we noted very few windows were lighted, but hundreds of glowing cigarettes appeared as blinking stars in the darkened windows. Across the street was a hotel solely inhabited by vacationing civilians, and a few Army WAC's. Every now and then a voice could be heard from one of the darkened windows, encouraging the continuation of some sexual act.

"What the hell is going on?" I wondered aloud.

When we entered the building and got to our rooms, we found we were located on the opposite side of the building. Interested in the mystery of what was so great an attraction, we went to the darkened side of the building. The largest attendance was located in what was set up as a day room, with plenty of windows. Chairs were set up in grand stand fashion, and they were completely filled.

"What's the attraction tonight?" I asked.

"You guys must be newcomers. It's a little early for the main attraction, the star was still strutting the boardwalk a few minutes ago," someone volunteered.

"The star of what?" I questioned.

"It's a WAC sergeant, been here all week. Loves to dress and undress in front of an open window, with the lights on during darkness. She plays with herself, using a vibrator, we think. You can hear her sighs of pleasure when she has an orgasm. She knows we're watching, and usually bumps and grinds in our direction. She then throws a kiss in our direction, then douses the lights."

"Why doesn't-" The question was never completed.

"All the new comers ask the same question - has anyone approached her when she was out of her room? The answer is yes, and her answers are cordial, pleasant, with an apparent concern for your well being, always inquiring about your health."

I wondered why she would continue her exhibition with the attitude she had when approached directly.

"Maybe she feels a compulsion to ease our stay here, knowing only combat veterans are housed here," I suggested.

"Whatever the reason, it is enjoyable, and while we're awaiting her arrival, there are many other attractions framed in the windows of the other rooms. It kills time, which we have plenty of," the spokesman concluded.

We joked about the degrading aspect of the situation, and were about to leave, when someone near the window shouted-

"Here she comes!"

The scramble to obtain a spot near a window was instantaneous, and not one soldier missed the chance to see a free exhibition of this nature, including myself.

It was unbelievable. Binoculars appeared out of nowhere. Most everyone had some. I had noticed one or two equipped with binoculars when we arrived, and a few with spy glasses. Knowing either are not usual military issue, I asked, "Where the hell do you acquire field glasses?"

"You have to reserve them at the Post Exchange, and for only one day at a time. If you don't return in the morning, an MP will greet you at breakfast. If they miss you, your stay here is negated immediately, and all privileges are canceled," were the rules laid down.

"You must be kidding. Who would enforce such a rule, especially if they know how the glasses are used?" I inquired.

"There have been no registered complaints, and believe it or not, the doctors believe these sightings have a beneficial, therapeutic effect on the viewers, like in group therapy,"

The spokesman sort of eased us into a corner, out of earshot of the rest.

"Come on fellows, I'm in charge of this contingent, permanent party here. Most of these guys are deranged mental cases. The others are like yourselves, inquisitive, casual viewers, whose presence assists, by intelligent conversation, in offsetting the babbling of an injured mind. You would be amazed how many of these war shattered brains have responded to the association with fellows like yourselves, by sharing the same thoughts and reactions."

I didn't know what effect the viewing would have on the mental patients. I was concerned of the effects on our sex sick Navigator.

The act she performed was seductive, but not vulgar, if bumping her vagina in your direction can be performed without vulgarity. Maybe it was the smile, and the manipulation of her breast in a slow rotating manner, that belied the true intent of her actions. The known fact of her refusal to accommodate anyone who approached her sort of removed the pornographic aspect.

"Maybe she was a stripper in civilian life," I suggested.

"Where I come from, she would be called a cock teaser," someone volunteered.

This brought a rebuff from the man in charge. I guess he didn't want the mental cases to become disillusioned. When she finally blew her kiss and doused the lights, the chorus of "one more time" from other rooms in the hotel was most embarrassing to me. I found out immediately that it was expected, and accepted by her. The room would light up, and there in the window would be our star, with her back to the window. She would bend over and spread her cheeks in a "kiss my ass" manner. Cheers would fill the air. I found myself cheering with them.

I found out later on future visits word would arrive that some honeymooners or cheaters were in rooms facing our vantage point. The ones who failed to douse their lights or pull blinds were in for suggestive encouragement at the most inconvenient times.

We checked the day's activity program the next morning. They certainly had many types of diversionary activities, to offset waiting for darkness and the star's performance. Looking at the board I realized that although I enjoyed many sports, golf was never a favorite. There was a golf invitation for that morning, and all interested personnel were welcome. Golf didn't interest me, but the name of the Officer who was to be in charge did. He was a baseball player from my home town, and although older than me, I had played many a game with him and against him. He was an avid golfer, but most of all he was an Air Force Major. I prayed he would help rid me of the burdensome nightmares forever imbedded in my mind. I filed for the Golf tour. I talked our tail-gunner into joining me; he too had never played Golf, but agreed to give it a go. We boarded the bus assigned to transport us to the Golf course; I was disappointed when my Major friend wasn't present. I hadn't told my companion about the Major or my intentions. I didn't want to spoil his day, although he was the only one who felt as I did, but was brainwashed by the others to remain mute.

We arrived at the golf course, which was a beautifully laid out. The scenery matched the beautiful day. Adding to the positive first impression was the presence of my Major friend. He walked towards me with an air of recognition, and extended his hand.

"I saw your name on the roster, and wondered if there could be two of you," he said with a smile.

"How are you, sir?" I answered, and introduced my tail-gunner to him.

"I heard from my father that you were missing in action. I checked all the reports to find out if your status was changed. When I received word of your return, and your sojourn in Russia, I knew you would be sent here for a rest period," he explained.

Geez, I thought to myself, he knows of our travels in Russia. He's certainly going to ask some questions, not as an officer, but as a inquisitive friend.

We were first taken to a driving range and given a few lessons by the Major, and a couple of other golf pros introduced to us. After the driving range we were taken to a practice putting green. A combined three hours were spent between both activities, with not one opportunity to talk with the Major one on one. We broke for lunch, with the instructions to report to the first tee afterwards. We retired to the club house, and my thoughts of having lunch with the Major were shattered when the non-coms and the officers ate at different tables. The only compensation was that we all ordered off the same menu. The only communication between the Major and me was his nod of acknowledgement in my direction, of my presence

We were broken into six man groups, with one instructor.

"The proper count normally is four, designated a foursome," the Major explained. "We haven't enough instructors, so we will have a sixsome," he laughingly added.

To my disbelief, the Major was not my instructor. I approached him and posed the question, "Why can't I be in your group?"

He answered me in a tone that surprised me, and reflected the same attitude we have received everywhere on our return home.

"You can see, there are only officers in my group," was his terse response.

It was beyond my comprehension why his attitude became so distant. He seemed genuinely pleased to see me, and the concern for my well being during my missing in action period magnified his present behavior. I tried not to ruin my day by attending to the teachings of the instructor, who certainly knew his golf. We were told we would play nine holes, and by the sixth hole, I really got into it. I made up my mind at that time that I would take up golf seriously, when I got out of the service. As a matter of fact, I was sorry when we finished. My tail-gunner wasn't very athletic, and he admitted he would probably never even touch a golf club again. After the third hole he quit completely, and became my caddie the rest of the way.

When we returned to the club house to return our equipment, I chanced to corner the Major in the locker room. I didn't attempt to question his attitude, for I felt I may be interpreting it selfishly.

"I would like to talk with you in private," I blurted out, almost hysterically.

Without even batting an eye, or answering affirmatively or negatively, he answered, "If you are going to tell me your tales of woe, forget it. As a friend, don't embarrass me or yourself by having me refuse you."

"Damn, haven't we got anyone with balls in this man's Army?" I almost screamed.

My reaction drew the attention of the other people in the locker room, including my tail-gunner.

He came up to me and said, "For God's sake, you'll have us all blackballed. We're here for a good time, get off that fucking bullshit, it's all over, forget it."

I was totally devastated, as both the Major and my crewmate walked away. The rest appeared to look at each other, and shrugged their shoulders in utter bewilderment.

The next morning at breakfast, the rest of my crew questioned my actions at the golf outing. I looked at my golfing partner with a questioning stare. He responded with a palms up gesture, and a shrug of his shoulders, indicating a "don't blame me" attitude.

"Wait until we're out of here, and maybe it would be best if you waited until we are separated, as to not include us," the Pilot instructed.

"Your yellow streak is still showing," I retorted.

Breakfast was spent in a non-congenial atmosphere. I cut mine short to remove myself from an uneasy position. As I was leaving the dining room, an MP approached me.

"You will please accompany me to the commandant's office, Sergeant," he ordered

The word "please" did not lessen the authority of his request. I didn't even ask why; I would soon find out.

I was greeted surprisingly cordially, and offered a seat before a three star general. He extended his hand across his desk, and with a friendly, firm grip, congratulated me on my heroic service.

"You and your crew are unique. Your escapades were tremendously interesting, and one day will make a tremendous impact, but not at the present," he informed me.

His voice was temperate in tone, but his meaning was readily understood.

"I want to commend you for your volunteering to go into B-29 training, especially when each of you can request a discharge because of your evadee status."

I had forgotten that I had volunteered for continued service in the Air Force, and I didn't know now under the existing circumstances if I was being B.S'ed. The next words of endearment clarified the meaning of this whole scenario.

"You will, with an accompanying officer, fly into Washington, DC, tomorrow. There you will be interrogated by Air Force intelligence. You have been selected because of your wish to remain in service, and because you are the only one interested in telling your story," I was told.

The next morning after breakfast, we were winging our way to the nation's capital.

CHAPTER 48 — NATIONAL SECURITY

I had visited Washington, DC, only once before, and its magnificence enthralled me. Of course the reason for its existence solidified my reason for my being in this man's army. To find myself in the bowels of the famous yet mysterious Pentagon caused an involuntary weakness in my knees.

"What the hell am I doing here?" I asked my escort.

He didn't respond, but eased me towards an open door with a gentle pressure on my elbow. Now my heart beat caught up with the weakness of my knees, and combined they gave me a feeling of utter dismay. Only in the movies had I ever witnessed such a scene, complete with people of authority, both military and civilian. I blinked my eyes in disbelief as I went around the large table from person to person, almost expecting to see the president of the United States chairing this conference. "God, what have I gotten myself into?" I wondered.

At the head of this impressive table sat a civilian. To his right were a number of military officers, from a four star General down. To his left were a contingent of civilian gentlemen. My guess was that they were connected with the intelligence community.

I was offered a seat, to my amazement at the opposite end of the table. I didn't know if I should be honored, or shit my pants.

"Welcome, Sergeant. Be at ease, you are among friends. You are here for multiple purposes, which will be explained to you in due time," was the opening statement from the civilian at the head of the table.

Although not another intelligible word was spoken from any of the others, their collective mumblings sounded in the affirmative.

I was thinking, "Why me?" and I actually heard myself repeat it aloud, "Why me?"

I could have bit my tongue, but the involuntary question opened the door. I was to be the focal point of all in the room, and it was an uneasy sick feeling.

The first to address me was a uniformed officer, a two star. His face looked familiar. The wings of a Command Pilot said "Air Force."

"I am in command of a B-29 training group in Sioux Falls, South Dakota. You volunteered for continued service in the Air Force, and B-29 training is only for those with security clearance," he stated. "There are certain criteria for physical and mental behavior that must be maintained," he added.

Again like robots, all others smiled and nodded in agreement. Hell, I wasn't worried about that score, but I felt there had to be more than just security concerning B-29's. From New Jersey to Washington DC, who was kidding who?

"You are the only one of your crew not wishing a discharge. Your remaining in the service poses a problem," the statement came from a civilian, also familiar, a statesman of prominence.

At this stage, I felt I had to exercise some semblance of manhood. After what I had gone through, what did I have to lose? I wasn't being court martialed, I wasn't looking for any favors, and besides, I wasn't even asking out.

"What is it that poses a problem with my assignment to B-29 training?" I asked as a general question, not directed to anyone in particular.

"It's not your possible assignment to B-29's that worries us, it's your insistence to tell the world of your exploits in the hands of our ally Russia. The rest of your crew are only interested in being discharged. They profess to want no involvement in substantiating any wild claims by testifying in any prolonged investigation, and hearings that would necessitate their remaining in service. Since you are remaining, you will be among service men whose thinking could be challenged by your stories, and cause disruptions in the political process during negotiations with our allies."

I thought to myself, I could understand a man like General Patton causing a controversy with derogatory remarks about the Russians, but me, I wouldn't believe it. The next piece of conversation brought this meeting to an abrupt end, and it was I who initiated it, to the mass surprise of all in the room.

"Gentlemen," I started, "why don't you all come down to earth, and stop this fencing. What is it you want of me?"

"It is a simple request: keep your tales to yourself, for the present time. The war with Japan is still in progress. We don't want our fighting men to become disillusioned with our allies. Our feelings for the Russians are at best shaky. Some day, some how, you will be able to tell your story, when it won't reflect on the outcome of world tensions and negotiations."

Realizing where these requests were originating, I suddenly understood it wasn't the importance of the man's status that counted, but the information the man possessed. It became apparent that a statement from a man of prominence, such as General Patton, could indicate a political motivation, and not have the impact of a unimportant non-professional Airman speaking the truth, with no personal gain in mind.

I made no commitment, either one way or the other. The last question was simply put to me, "Do you want to continue in the Air Force in B-29 training?"

It was as simple as intended, shit or get off the pot. They never in any manner made it appear that I was offered a choice under threat. My accepting would relieve the posed threat of my remaining in the service. Yes, I wanted to continue service.

My first reward for relieving their collective minds was an offer to fly me into New York that weekend, to visit with my family. Naturally I accepted, and the revelry of the weekend made it easier to forget the things I really didn't want to forget. My visit to Washington, DC, ended, Atlantic City was my next stop.

I briefed my crew with very few revelations of the actual context of my visit to the Pentagon. I made it sound that my possible assignment to B-29 training, and the security clearance necessary, necessitated a close scrutiny by those involved in the training program. They accepted my explanation with a grain of doubt, knowing my attitude towards the Russians, and all those other misfits of humanity. They chose to let dead dogs lay, since they were no longer involved.

Nothing had changed since I left for Washington, DC. The main entertainment was still the boardwalk activities by the crippled veterans, and the nighttime performances of the occupants in the adjoining hotel. The performing WAC had departed, but only after a final performance with another WAC.

"She was a fucking lesbian," I was told by my crew members. They explained how the whole hotel went wild when they performed. Every possible foul insinuation, with no holds barred, was shouted across the roadway, with the suggestions being accepted and performed in reply.

"I'm telling you, you missed one sucking good performance!" the Navigator injected.

A completely new twist for daytime peeping Toms came to fore: watching women changing into their bathing suits for a sojourn to the beach. Since it was daytime, usually lights weren't used, therefore the rooms were dark and visibility was limited. Approaching the hotel one day, I was amazed to see flashes of sun light reflecting off mirrors in the windows. I asked my crew members if they knew what was going on. They laughingly explained that the morning sun faced our building. It was discovered by some inventive individual that the sun's rays could be directed by mirror to the rooms across the street. They were powerful enough to light the interior of the room selected.

"Geez, doesn't the person in the room see the light bouncing around?" I asked.

"That was the most interesting aspect of this new found pleasure," the man in charge explained. "If they realized what was going on, and didn't draw the blinds, we had a possible target, and a few scored when they encountered them on the beach and asked for a date."

"I guess these women feel a patriotic duty to offer their pleasures to we returning veterans." the Navigator, offered.

We let it go at that, with, "I suppose you would like to return the favor. It's no more than right to reciprocate."

Between the visit to Washington DC, and our stay in Atlantic City, it added up to three weeks. Although the timing was unexpected, the order to move out was expected. Arrangements were made for me to fly to Sioux Falls, South Dakota. I barely had time to say good bye to the rest of my crew, let alone notify my wife. Sioux Falls had a soft spot in my heart: it was where I was married, while attending Radio School. Renewing friendships with the people who were so hospitable to my wife, mother, and sister, added to the expectations of my new assignment.

On arriving, the obvious changes were visible. The radio school was now an encampment of eager retreads, still gung-ho to fly combat against the Japanese. It was amazing: almost to a man, each professed a greater hatred of the Japanese. They all felt the war in Europe was politically motivated, and our entry was calculated, by almost inviting the Japanese attack on Pearl Harbor. The effrontery of the Japs in attacking us directly, and a sneak attack at that, was the greatest inspiration to patriotic response. It was this kind of response that brought me, and the others, here to see the war to a victorious end.

All the preempting and preparation was accepted, but the day we went to the flight line was the moment of truth. To actually board a B-29 made all the anxieties worthwhile. This bird made the B-17 appear a toy. The modern application of engineering technology made the national security horse shit make sense. There were many aspects of air training and operations that were completely vulnerable to security leaks, especially the types of payload this aircraft was able to deploy upon the enemy.

The first weekend pass I received gave me the opportunity to visit the hospitable friends who housed my family during their stay here. I promised to visit them at every opportunity, but my promise was never fulfilled. We were confined to camp, with no explanation. The days were very boring, and even training classes were curtailed. The only change of consequence was a visit from Sioux Falls's flying ace, Major Foss. He was tabbed the town's bad boy, and proved that bad boys beat on bad boys.

Why the sudden curtailment of our training? The hedge hopping of retaking the islands occupied by the Japs was costly, and air bombing by the B-29's was certainly a necessary weapon in achieving our goals. As always in the service, the cliche "it is not ours to reason why, but only ours to do or die," was apropos at this time.

The notice appeared on each barrack bulletin board: "PREPARE TO MOVE OUT."

Of course all wondered when, as we packed our belongings. That question was answered at breakfast the next morning.

"There will be transportation at each barrack that will take each of you to a specific mode of transportation, air, bus, or train. Your orders will be handed you at that time. Your new assignments will be therein. Don't ask questions," was directed by a Master Sergeant.

Why the sudden evacuation? became a moot question that remained unanswered, even as I sat in a railroad Pullman car with my traveling orders unopened, as directed.

"Do not open your orders until the train is underway."

I asked the train conductor, our destination. "We make many stops along the way, they will be announced in plenty of time for you to prepare to detrain," he answered.

The train had progressed to a steady speed, and although I was inquisitive to know my assignment, I also felt there was no great haste, since I had no means of changing it short of going AWOL.

The time had arrived. I teased myself by tearing the envelope open slowly, slipping the enclosed paper out of its captivity, exposing its contents a little at a time. I laughed to myself; how I detested that procedure when they did just that at briefing before a mission when they slowly exposed the map with the colored ribbons designating the targets for the day.

The contents were fully exposed: my assignment was the West Point Military Academy.

I had never envisioned myself any kind of military person, but the precision marching of the West Point cadets and the Naval Academy always enthralled me. Now finding myself assigned to this historical training place of our nation's leaders, both military, and political, tugged at the strings of my patriotic heart. "What service could I render there?" I asked myself.

The first stop was in Minneapolis for a fifteen minute lay over. I left the train, entered the station, and was greeted by shouting, screaming civilians and military people. Everyone appeared to be waving a newspaper, exposing the headlines, which read, "ATOM BOMB DROPPED ON HIROSHIMA." I purchased a newspaper, and boarded the train, thinking, "What the hell is an Atom Bomb?"

The description of the damage caused, and the lives lost, sent chills up my spine. I actually felt for the Japanese. There was a schematic drawing depicting the theory of splitting the atom, and the end explosive result so devastating it boggled one's mind.

The sudden freeze on our B-29 training was immediately explained: the war with Japan was about over.

I was greeted by a Cadet Officer, who "Sir'd" me at every opportunity. I explained that I was a lowly Tech Sergeant, and calling me "Sir" was not necessary. He explained that I was to teach Radio Communication and Radio Mechanics, therefore as an instructor I was to be addressed as "Sir."

I let it go at that, and accepted his welcome as he led me to my room, the comfort and size of which surprised me. I found out later that the Officers of the academy, assigned as instructors, were assigned the same rooms. I wondered if all this a part of a blanket to curtail any breach of security on my part.

I was instructed by the cadet as to the what's, wheres, and whens, of the academy layout, which were clearly defined in a book of procedures he gave me. I was instructed to spend the rest of the day acclimating myself to the academy grounds, and by all means to report to the academy commander at 0900 the next morning.

My meeting with the commanding officer was initiated a lot sooner, that same day. I ventured out on the grounds, and was associating landmarks with the various buildings necessary to my personal needs. Of course I located the Officer's mess, which was exactly where the procedure book designated, as were all the other locations I required. Apparently, my interest in the mess hall was too intense.

"Who are you? What are you doing here? What kind of uniform is that?" The sharp voice snapped the questions, with no hesitation between the demands.

I hadn't realized that an A2 flying jacket, with bombs painted on the back, depicting number of missions flown, and a man dangling from a parachute, topped by a Garrison hat with a thousand hour crunch, would not be recognized as acceptable uniform dress. It was typical Air Force, at least when associated with the gunner's wings and the 8th Air Force patch.

Surprised, I stuttered on answer, not really knowing how to respond with clarity. "This is, this is, an 8th Air Force, you know, a combat outfit from overseas." I paused only a moment. "Hell, how could you know, when you ask such an asinine question?" I answered.

"I don't accept your answer, and whatever that outfit is, it is not acceptable here at the Point," he challenged. Then he added, "What are you doing here in the first place?"

"I'm assigned here as a Communication instructor, my first day here," I replied.

"We'll check into your story. I can't see how a uniform bearing a clown and four aces, painted bombs, a dangling parachutist, could be acceptable as a regulation uniform," he again challenged.

I attempted to calm him by explaining the allowance of such a uniform was the reward for combat flying, and a proud symbol of duties performed. It made no impression on him, and his rank of Warrant Officer, was one grade above mine, a non-com.

"Follow me," he directed. About this time, a group of cadets had appeared at the scene of our debate. One was the Cadet who met me on my arrival. He looked on questionably, but made no attempt to interfere, just smiled, as if to tell me not to worry.

"I would like to see the Commanding Officer," the doubting man asked of the receptionist. The Sergeant opened the door behind him, which bore a sign, "COMMANDING OFFICER," entered, and closed it behind him.

He returned to advise the Warrant Officer, "The General will see you."

We entered, and both of us snapped to rigid attention, with an accompanying salute.

"At ease men, take a seat," he cordially stated. "What seems to be the problem?" he added.

Before the Warrant Officer could answer, the General rose from his chair, and extended his hand in my direction. "I didn't realize who you were, Sergeant. I knew you had arrived, and scheduled a meeting with you at 0900 tomorrow. What brings you here ahead of schedule?"

I could feel the embarrassment of the Warrant Officer, so I chose for him to explain our visit. He sheepishly explained his doubt of my uniform being acceptable at the Point. The General's answer was a diplomatic one, realizing the Warrant Officer's uneasy situation.

"You are right, Officer, his uniform would not be acceptable at the Point. First because it is not the uniform issued to our Cadets. Secondly it would not be worn by any of our Cadets, or you yourself, because you, they, and even I, have not earned the right to wear it."

He concluded by dismissing the Warrant Officer, asking me to remain. I was certain the Warrant Officer heard the General say, before the door closed behind him, "What do you expect from a mess officer? Welcome aboard, Sergeant."

We chattered with an air of comradeship. His rank never created a wall of separation; he made me feel at ease. He made it sound that I, being assigned to the Point, was a reward to him. I was surprised at his congeniality, and accepted it as a truthful, exuberant behavior. He explained my duties, wished me luck, and suggested I contact him personally for any problems that may arise. His last words as he led me to the door, his arm around my shoulders, burst the bubble of contentment.

"Your record of achievement is worthy, but you are here to teach Radio Procedure and Technology. Your air missions will be of interest to the young Cadets, but please don't discuss any personal grievances," he concluded with a pat on my back.

His subtle request, by saying please, only strengthened the warnings from whence they came.

Revelry at six in the morning could not possibly mean me. This hope faded when a knock sounded on my door, and my response, "Come in," revealed my welcoming Cadet.

"We have thirty minutes to wash up, dress, fall in for morning roll call, then to breakfast. I have been assigned to you for this morning only, to get you started. You can, after this morning, set your own time to prepare for your days activities. Only in regard to your classroom time must be punctual," he explained.

"The head Communications Officer will meet you at your first class, to lay out your course of instructions." he concluded as he fell in with his platoon.

It was a fascinating sight to see the hustle and bustle of these eager Cadets as they fell in and marched with such precision to the chow hall. I made my way to the Officer's mess, indulged in a fine breakfast. I was greeted in a sort of a quizzical manner by those unfamiliar with my assignment. One could sense the questions: "What, and who, are you?"

My mysterious existence and presence were clarified by an Officer, a Major, who stood up and raised his cup of coffee. "Gentlemen, let us welcome into our midst a bonafide flying hero, who will impart to you all his knowledge of personal application of war time communications."

I had no way of knowing if I was being put on, but the cheers that greeted his introduction certainly seemed genuine.

After breakfast I was intercepted by the Communications Officer, and led to my classroom. There was no one there, and I was told they were in their barracks, preparing for morning inspection. He apprised me of the itinerary I was to follow, but informed me that my presentation was as I saw fit. He left me, wished me luck, and then added almost as an afterthought, "By the way, don't use your platform for any personal grievances."

I had about an half an hour before class. I hung up my A2 jacket and thousand hour crush hat, and made my way down the hall to a sitting room to have a smoke. When I returned to the class room, it was occupied with about fifty cadets. Their interest was focused on my jacket and hat on the clothes tree.

"Please be seated," I requested, and they obeyed with military obedience. I introduced myself, and my connection with their studies. I continued by laying out the importance of precision of continuity, and the value of a prearranged format. I went on that the basic book rules will get you the essential grades to pass this course, but during my tenure, I would also teach them the area of improvisation, sometimes necessary to survive, when the book does not apply. This not only applied to communication procedures, but all the situations they might encounter during their military career.

My introduction brought a raise of hands; my first encounter had a meaningful effect. The rest of the session was spent in an impromptu question and answer session, including personal questions about the missions I had been on, the results, and their importance. The dangling parachutist, painted on the back of my A2 jacket, naturally was an item of interest, which placed me in a precarious position. How do I answer their questions without lying? Everyone connected with that infamous raid knew it's true intent, it was an "arms, legs, and asshole" target. Those Dresden dolls sure as hell were Germany's deadliest weapons. The end of this session arrived to my relief, and the applause by the cadets before departing gave me a chilling reward.

The next morning, my welcoming cadet awakened me with a directive to report to the commanding Officer, at 0900. I completed my morning chores, had breakfast, and was there at 0900 as directed. I was greeted in an indifferent, yet cordial manner. He put me at ease, before I completed my attentive position and salute.

"Sergeant, I have good news, and bad news. The good news will protect you from the possible results of the bad news," he stated. "I'll explain what I mean, and I believe you will be happy with the final result," he added.

I wasn't about to question his prediction; I remained mute.

"You were skating on thin ice in your first class, and your tenure here was in jeopardy, as you drifted into areas you were asked to avoid," he explained.

I felt no need to defend myself. I continued to remain mute.

"That is the bad news, but now the good: you can request a discharge immediately. We have dropped another Atom Bomb on Nagasaki, Japan. The Japanese have surrendered - the war is over," he concluded, as he shook my hand, and wished me luck.

I requested Mitchell Field, Long Island as my discharge base, a stones throw from Staten Island, my home.

CHAPTER 49 — THE END - A NEW BEGINNING

Being home, the reappearance of a card bearing what was intended to be good news when dispatched caused the reopening of scars of war that had never really healed. My arriving safely at home was the end of my story and the beginning of a new life. I returned to my old job as a welder, in the Bethlehem Shipyard on Staten Island. The Government had guaranteed one year's employment for returning veterans who had previously worked in a defense plant. After about six months, it was decided by Congress that shipyards were not defense plants. Having never being a union member didn't help my situation, as seniority carried a lot of weight. The plant supervisor asked me to stay on as an administrative snapper therefore negating the necessity of being a union member. I had no intention of accepting; there were many men of longer employment who would resent my sudden rise.

"It wouldn't be for long, since you are awaiting a call from the New York City Police Department," he offered. My wife had informed me of the blessed good news she was pregnant; this was no time to be unemployed.

"If it won't cause you any grief, I'll accept your offer until I'm called for appointment to the Police Department, or our positions become untenable," I suggested.

Life soon became routine. Like they say, "Once you return, it's like you have never been gone." I had hoped this philosophy would apply to me, but lingering visions of atrocities and acts of depredation often blinded me to the rewards of my wife's beauty and presence. It wasn't long before the return of a combat veteran became common place and glory was a thing of the past. The parades, even the public announcements in the local tabloids became obscure. Military organizations, such as the American Legion or the Veterans of Foreign Wars, lost their fraternal intent. They became platforms for political aspirations, or individual conscience cleansing. It seemed that most who used these formats were the ones who never left the security of the United States, let alone saw combat. Their desire to play soldier created a void for respect towards their patriotic frivolity.

The war itself became a political football, with the lowliest countries asking for a voice in major decisions. War crimes became a tremendous issue. We always appeared conciliatory to the actions of our political adversaries, especially the Russians. To read of the perpetual endeavor to locate and bring to trial the animals who made lamp shades out of human flesh, and used humans as guinea pigs without one instant of remorse, inflamed my mind to complete indifference. It was obvious that the atrocities perpetrated by the Japanese, although as infamous, didn't carry the same degree of public scorn, or demand for retribution. Of course, the acts of our ally, the Russians, or the acts of our own military, during occupation or conquering sorties were never an issue of political or media interest. The holocaust perpetrated against the Jewish people became the focal point of Germany's war against the world. It appeared the only reward for ending the war would be the annihilation of all the Germans. The thousands of Poles slaughtered in Warsaw were mere casualties. The Filipinos' dying defense of their islands and the infamous death marches of Americans became movies depicting their lot as the acts of heroism.

Every once in awhile a mention of a local figure participating in some sporting event would include his military background. Since I was such a local sports figure, I received on a few occasions such notoriety. When I was awarded the New York State Governor's Conspicuous Service Cross, I felt an interview was in order. Now I would be able to expose the acts of inhuman behavior not reserved just to the Germans. No interview ever materialized, not even a telephone call to document name, address, rank, and arm of service. I made up my mind that the story I had to tell would never be told, the war to end all wars was over. The emblem of a veterans discharge, the "Golden Eagle," became the "Ruptured Duck," and it disappeared from the veteran's lapel as if it were a badge of scorn.

Most of my friends, as returning veterans, felt a need for rest.

"Damn, they owe us something," was the common denominator, along with the cry for a war bonus.

I wasn't in the position to play soldier. My wife was expecting a child, which meant responsibilities, and a steady income was paramount. Those who chose to continue with the attitude, "The world owes me a living," jumped at the "fifty-two twenty club," where they received twenty dollars for fifty-two weeks. It was afforded to only those who were unemployed.

Just when it appeared that the scars of war were diminishing a march on Washington took place. There were those in our country who grasped the opportunity to use the neglect of our veterans as a stepping stone to prominence. With all the turmoil within our own boundaries, the give-away of Eastern Europe to the Russians was the hardest blow of all. Splitting Germany and giving control of all the Slavic countries to Russia was never explained to lessen the disbelief. Here we fought and died on foreign soil, and the only reward was the "Marshall Plan," where the conqueror was the conquered.

About six months of the pregnancy had passed, and the expectation of fatherhood began to sink in. We began to guess at the gender of the blessed child, and names, some wild, were suggested in sincerity, and sometimes in jest. To me the reward of surviving was crowned with God's blessing of life to replace the death of a dear friend. We would, if it was a boy, name him "Kevin," in memory of that friend.

The mailman could always be heard walking across the front porch to the mailbox, where he would deposit the mail and press the doorbell button. This time as when I first arrived home, he hit the bell, and knocked on the door. I went to the door, and he smiled when he said, "There is a letter from Poland. Do you save stamps?"

His question was amusing, but irrelevant. The letter, not the stamp, was my concern.

"No, I don't save stamps. Give me the letter," I admonished him, as I snatched the mail from his hand.

He retreated a step in a defensive manner. His smile became a picture of surprise. I practically threw the mail to the floor, separating the one from Poland. Realizing my rudeness, I apologized to the mailman, and qualified it with, "Stick around, I'll give you the stamp."

The letter was stamped with a Warsaw cancellation, and Lodtz was the return address, with no name. What was most significant was the fact the letter was addressed to my wife. I called to my wife who was in the kitchen, and my exuberance must have been conveyed in the tone of my voice, as she responded in like manner.

"What have you received that excites you so?" she asked.

"It's a letter addressed to you, please open it," I pleaded, handing her the letter.

Everything happened so fast I suddenly realized the mailman was still present. I also realized it was he who brought the postcard, that fostered the reliving of a part of my life, that although rewarding as a part of history, will always be a scar of inhuman behavior.

It was a two page letter. She turned to the last page.

"It's from Helena, one of your interpreters," she exclaimed.

"Why would she write to me personally?" my wife asked.

It was funny: the mailman and I simultaneously said, "Read the letter." The only difference in our request was I said "damn letter."

"Dear friend," it started,"I pray this letter finds you and my heaven boy well."

"What's this heaven boy bit?" my wife injected.

"I can only recall she always referred to me as her boy who came from heaven, you know, out of the sky," I answered.

We both looked at the mailman with surprise when he said, "Either finish reading the letter, or give me the stamp. I have to complete my route."

"Here's your stamp," as I tore it from the envelope, and handed it to him.

He thanked me, with a parting request. "Please, if you can without revealing anything personal, fill me in when I see you again. I sort of feel a part of this scenario."

His request was heard, but not heard; at this juncture the remainder of the letter was the focal point.

"I would appreciate, if you can do so," my wife read, "please send me from your wonderful country things that I can use. Under clothing, nylon stockings, handkerchiefs, and all the wonderful makeup cosmetics, to make me beautiful."

My wife sort of mumbled the next part of the letter to herself, shaking her head in a bewildered manner.

"Why the hell did you stop reading aloud? What's so secretive?" I inquired.

"Now I know why she addressed this letter to me. What nerve, but I can understand why," she answered.

She went on with the reading, "My heaven boy was such a gentleman. He gave me respect that I had not seen since the beginning of the war. For this I have fallen in love with him, and make this request of you. If I come to America, would you not divorce my heaven boy, so I may marry him?"

We looked at each other, each having the same feeling: bewildering pity. Helena certainly was serious in her request, but we couldn't possibly believe she expected an affirmative answer. She closed the letter with a reminder of the good things she did for us. I didn't believe she intended the reminder as a "you owe me," but in my heart, I felt I personally did owe her. A address where to send the package was on the last page, a location in Warsaw.

"I'll tend to her request for material things, and answer her request for her 'heaven boy' in a gentle, unembarrassing way," she laughingly volunteered, as she hugged and kissed me.

It was few weeks later that my wife informed me that she had acquired the items requested by Helena. Nylon was still a commodity in short supply, but she had enough to make up an appreciable package, including the cosmetic items.

I was wrapping the package for mailing, when my wife asked me to hold off until she completed a letter she wanted to put in the package. She appeared to be completing the letter with a wry smile, followed by a hearty laugh.

"What's so funny?" I asked, as she handed me the letter.

"Dear Helena," she started. "Your heaven boy without reservations, has told me of your kindnesses, and the danger you faced in helping him and his friends. He told me of the hardships you and your friend Novak faced to provide them with the necessities to survive. He also told me of your final request the night before you parted. I believed him when he told me he refused your request to leave you with a baby. Your requests in your letter for material things, with no mention of you mothering his child, surely solidified my trust in my 'heaven boy.' Besides there is no possible way I could honor your request of divorcing my husband, because at this very moment, I am with child."

She closed with a prayer for her welfare, and God's blessings in the years to come.

"Jerk her off a little, tell her she would be welcome, if she ever arrived in the states," I kidded.

"Don't even joke about her coming here. I can thank her for what she did for you, and that's it. From what you told me about how she survived under the German and Russian occupations, and even her advances to you, she's an opportunistic, calculating whore in my book. The goodies we're sending her is the last contact I want to have with her. That's it, and I mean it," she retorted with a tone of finality.

I didn't even attempt to explain that I was only kidding. I let it end right there, as I continued to wrap the package, and left for the Post Office.

About seven months or so passed, and my position at the shipyard was in doubt. The union head had made a protest about my status, and wanted me removed. The pleading of the yard supervisor, emphasizing my war record, made no impression on the union prick. Knowing this son of a bitch used his classification to remain out of service only continued to substantiate that we veterans were back in the worldly jungle, and the flag waving days were over.

All the personal hurt and disappointments were forgotten the day when I was called to the super's office. "I received a call from the Staten Island Hospital. Your wife was brought there in labor," he informed me.

"God, she's not due for at least a month and a half," I challenged.

"Go to her, I'll punch you out," the super suggested.

The hospital was about fifteen minutes away, but it seemed like ages before I pulled into the Emergency parking lot. She had been taken to the delivery room, I was told.

"There must be a mistake, she's not due yet," I insisted.

The Doctor corrected the mistake when he arrived in the waiting room.

"Sir," he said, "You are a very lucky man. Your son was a breech delivery, and had to be removed prematurely. He only weighs four and one half pounds, and will have to remain in an incubator until he gains some weight," he explained.

"Please, how is my wife? May I see her?" I asked.

"She is fine. Yes, the nurse will take you to her," he responded as he gestured to the nurse to accede to my request.

She was not out of it all together, and acknowledged my presence with a weak smile, and an extended hand. I gently grasped her hand, kissed her on her forehead. She mumbled something, like she was sorry to have had a girl.

"Honey," I corrected her, "you had a boy."

"I don't believe you, bring my baby to me," she screamed.

The nurse calmed her by telling her the baby will be brought in a few minutes to be breast fed.

"I hope I'm wrong, I know you wanted a son," she tearfully stated.

"Whatever it is, it is ours, and after surviving the agonies of war, no greater reward than the good Lord's blessed event could make living any greater," I whispered to her, in an attempt to make a personal choice immaterial.

A few minutes passed. The baby had not arrived, and in those few minutes my wife had slipped into a deep sleep.

"Let her sleep. It is not yet time for the baby's feeding. Come with me to the nursery, I'll show you your son," the nurse instructed.

She stationed me at the viewing window, and proceeded to enter the nursery. As I waited for her to appear, I attempted to pick out my son from about twenty new born babies. I then realized that I was told my son was in an incubator. They were to the rear of the room, and it was impossible to see the babies from my vantage point. I saw the nurse enter the room, and speak to the nurse who seemed to be in charge. She finally walked to an incubator, and gently rolled it in my direction. When she reached that portion of the viewing window, she pulled back the blanket, exposing the little infant's head. The baby's head was cocked to one side. I couldn't really get a full view. I motioned to her through the window to straighten his head, by using my head, in my hands in a turning gesture. She seemed reluctant to heed my wishes, but after my insistence by motion and in a loud enough voice, which I was sure penetrated the barrier between us, she complied.

I could understand her reluctance. The poor child was a physical mess. His head was misshapen, and his left eye was completely closed and blackened. With one ear appearing as a fighter's cauliflower ear, this kid looked like he'd been in some battle. The nurse raised her hand, gesturing for me to wait, as she removed my son to the rear of the room. She appeared shortly, and her explanation to relieve my anxiety was forthright and direct.

"You were told by the Doctor your son was a breech delivery. In layman's terms it was an instrument delivery. There is no way to turn a fetus into the right position for delivery without some superficial damage. The procedure must be done as quickly as possible, for the baby could be strangled by the umbilical cord," she explained.

"My wife will die, if she sees him as he is," I responded.

"He will be shielded from her view as she feeds him," she promised, and concluded with, "By the time he is ready to go home, he will be as handsome as you," she said, as she pinched my cheek.

The baby's arrival at home cushioned the bad news of my losing my position at the local shipyard. The yard super made a call to Todd's Shipyard in Brooklyn, and I was without employment for only one week. Life now became a reality, with responsibilities. I wondered if the security of becoming a policeman would afford enough income to offset the loss of income as a welder. We decided a steady payday, and the future pension would in the long term provide more security than a welder's potential. When I was called for appointment, and went through the Police Academy to graduation, my achievement was gratifying to me and my whole family.

I now found myself in a quasi-military organization, with rules of discipline and authority. Most of the new officers appointed were war veterans, and each had a story to tell. Their stories never had any element of depredation, and were always in the vein of personal conquest, mostly feminine. I never felt my tales of woe would ever be accepted. I lived with them eating away my heart and soul. I tried to be a good policeman, and use the new life to wipe from my mind what I found so hard to forget. There were times when obvious bigotry motivated some officers to act with the same inhuman treatment that rekindled the fury within me. Survival again played an important part of my daily life.

The biggest part of our lives was our first born, and although he blessed our home with love, his presence was a living reminder of that part of my life I deplored. Each and every anniversary of his birth was the moment, almost to the minute, of the infamous day of the bombing of Dresden, and my becoming the guest of an ally.

ABOUT THE AUTHOR

Anthony J. Leone was born in White Plains, New York, on July 20, 1920. Volunteered for the Army Air Force on July 13, 1942, he flew in the European Theater with the 8th Air Force, 390th Bomb Group, (H), 570th Squadron.

Among the missions he flew was one over Dresden, during which he was shot down. This book is about the experiences he had as a result of that.

After being discharged from the military, he spent 21 years as a New York City police officer, followed by plastics manufacturing in Florida. He has two sons, Kevin and Raymond, with Gertrude, his wife of fifty years. This is his first book.

The hat he is wearing in the above photograph was presented to him at Yankee Stadium in 1935 for being Most Valuable Player in the American Legion League. It had belonged to Joe DiMaggio, but unfortunately went down with the plane on the Dresden raid.